SAYERET
MATKAL

SAYERET MATKAL

The Greatest Operations of
Israel's Elite Commandos

AVNER SHUR
AND
AVIRAM HALEVI

Translated from Hebrew by Eylon Levy

Skyhorse Publishing

Skyhorse Publishing books may be purchased in bulk at special discounts for sales promotion, corporate gifts, fund-raising, or educational purposes. Special editions can also be created to specifications. For details, contact the Special Sales Department, Skyhorse Publishing, 307 West 36th Street, 11th Floor, New York, NY 10018 or info@skyhorsepublishing.com.

Skyhorse® and Skyhorse Publishing® are registered trademarks of Skyhorse Publishing, Inc.®, a Delaware corporation.

Visit our website at www.skyhorsepublishing.com.

10 9 8 7 6 5 4 3 2 1

Library of Congress Cataloging-in-Publication Data is available on file.

Cover design by David Ter-Avanesyan
Cover image by Wikimedia Commons

Print ISBN: 978-1-5107-7193-2
Ebook ISBN: 978-1-5107-7320-2

Printed in the United States of America

CONTENTS

INTRODUCTION

This book was written by two people who served in Sayeret Matkal, Israel's most elite commando force, for many years: as conscript soldiers, as full-time officers, and in reserves. So this story is told through the crosshairs of those who have almost seen it all. It's a story from the heart, a heart still pumping fast with fear. It's a story that smells of the kind of gunpowder that burns your nostrils, set to the sound of rattling machine guns. And it's punctuated with the stopped breaths and the cries of men who forged their brotherhood-in-arms through blood, tears, and sweat. And no, that's not an empty slogan dreamed up by politicians or their speechwriters, but the real-life experience of those who fight so hard together that the sweat trickling down their faces really brings on tears. And yes, there is also real blood there—lots of it.

We personally know many of the participants in the operations described in this book and must offer this disclaimer: we love them and feel strongly attached to them, in a way that will probably never fade. But there's no reason this should impinge on the accuracy of the factual accounts of these operations and of the details, large and small.

These accounts, colorful and dramatic as they may be, are based on rigorous and precise investigative research and interviews, and our affection for the protagonists has had no impact on our step-by-step narration of these daring missions. At most, it might make us withhold criticism, to the extent we have any, out of consideration and understanding, but no more.

We must emphasize: this is not a military book, and despite its whirlwind tour of the most audacious missions pulled off by a legendary commando unit, this is ultimately a book about people. The story of Sayeret Matkal is an intensely human story, and we have tried to give expression to this human dimension throughout the book.

Sayeret Matkal engages in two kinds of missions, which are practically opposites, or at least in completely different in nature.

On the one hand, Sayeret Matkal is a reconnaissance unit, whose intelligence operations will remain top-secret forever; it is an exemplar of rigor and long-term, meticulous planning, down to the millimeter, or even the micron, for every sort of possible or impossible scenario, which makes complicated mathematical calculations of the number of breaths each commando will take on the way to his target, and which ensures endless backup for each soldier, for each limb of each soldier, for each piece of equipment, and even for moonlight and starlight. In order to disguise the unit's affiliation with the IDF Intelligence Directorate, its soldiers wear paratroopers' uniforms with red berets and boots, which certainly gives them an extra flair.

On the other hand, as this book describes, Sayeret Matkal is also sent to free hostages and engage in other high-stakes military activity all around the globe. In hostage rescue missions, timing is everything and preparations must be conducted as quickly as possible, leaving no time for the lengthy and meticulous planning on which the unit was founded.

Every Sayeret Matkal commando is therefore two soldiers in one: one is drilled from the day he enlists to undertake practically endless preparations for each mission; the other must learn to get ready to spring into action in a matter of minutes—and then to respond at lightning speed, down to the millisecond, like an expert gunman, to a quick succession of often totally unpredictable developments.

In other words, in the first kind of mission—encountering the enemy, any enemy, is a kind of failure. In the second kind of mission, a clash with enemy forces is necessary and inevitable, because this is the only way in which Sayeret Matkal can do its job and achieve its goals.

But there is one element that is common to both kinds of mission: creative, out-of-the-box thinking. There is no doubt that the operational pressures that have forced Sayeret Matkal to constantly reinvent itself over the years, time after time, is also the source of much of the fuel and energy for creative planning behind operations of both kinds. Without this creativity and wild, unconventional way of thinking, it's doubtful whether such legendary operations as Sabena, Spring of Youth, Entebbe, the assassination of Abu Jihad, and more could have happened.

* * *

This book presents a rundown of Sayeret Matkal's most sensational operations over the space of some thirty-five years and profiles the key protagonists. Many of them, mostly modest and unassuming characters, took part over and over again in audacious rescue missions where the chances of coming out alive were slim but still the need to save innocent hostages—including women, children, and even babies (in the gruesome Misgav Am hostage crisis)—left no room for double-guessing or doubt.

If you've never been in these situations, you'll never understand the crippling fear and terror of entering a pitch-black room with three guns pointed at the door from the inside, unleashing gunfire on anyone who tries to break in. Nothing could be scarier, and nothing could be braver than knowing how to squash this paralyzing fear. Keep this in mind throughout this book. Yet despite the blood-soaked legacy of many of these hostage rescue missions, Sayeret Matkal's commandos still stand in line, and often run around it, in order to participate in these missions, in total contradiction of human nature and the natural will to live.

Some of Sayeret Matkal's officers, thrust into such missions time and again over many years of service, were injured in one mission but refused under any circumstances to be benched in the next mission or the one after that. You would think that injuries make soldiers much more fearful of similar operations in the future, but in Sayeret Matkal's case, they serve as catalysts for further action. Paradoxically, instead of making soldiers more cautious, these wounds heal and form a more ferocious and audacious desire to succeed. Not always, of course. There were a few lone cases that worked out otherwise. But who can judge them?

Sayeret Matkal's commandos are not war machines. They are consummate professionals in their fields, but they are not "Rambos," as they might be described in other countries or contexts. They are young men thrust into unbearably hard situations, who put themselves forward, time and again, without asking questions, to endanger their own lives in order to save the lives of others. Even in the few missions, which can be counted on one hand, that might be called operational failures—such as the bungled hostage rescue mission in Ma'alot—it would be hard to accuse anyone of insufficient determination. And since the difference between success and failure ultimately depends on milliseconds or millimeters, it is obviously impossible to succeed 100 percent of the time.

You will almost never find Sayeret Matkal's soldiers jubilantly celebrating a success or victory. It just doesn't happen. When Israel sent forces thousands of miles away to Uganda to free hostages on a hijacked airliner, in perhaps the most stunning commando operation in world history, Sayeret Matkal grieved the loss of its commander, Lt. Col. Yoni Netanyahu. In the mission to free hostages aboard a hijacked Sabena flight, another success by any metric, a twenty-two-year-old hostage by the name of Marie Holzberg was injured and died ten days later. In the Bus 300 hijacking, an Israeli soldier called Irit Portuguez was killed. In the raid on Green Island, ranked by an American think tank as one of the nineteen most successful commando raids in human history, six soldiers were killed—three from Sayeret Matkal, and three from Shayetet 13, the Israeli Navy's commando unit.[1] These are just a few examples.

Nearly always, the joy of success is drowned out by cries of sorrow. In many but not all of Sayeret Matkal's missions, its men return to base

---

1   Samuel A. Southworth, ed., *Great Raids in History* (New York: Sarpedon, 1997).

dejected and despondent. Sometimes it's the strange feeling, after hours of nail-biting tensions, of knowing they were so close to death.

Some former Sayeret Matkal commandos, despite their personal heroism, refused to be named in this book. In their minds, they were just doing their jobs, and they have no interest in dropping the anonymity they have enjoyed for so long. The Israeli public associates Sayeret Matkal with the few veterans who have become politicians and senior officials, who out of a professional need to draw attention to themselves tend to transgress the bounds of modesty typical of the unit. The large majority of the unit's officers and soldiers prefer to stay in the shadows, during and after their service, not just to hermetically protect the unit's secrets but also because the value of modesty was drilled into them from day one. No success, however grand and intoxicating, has ever managed to tarnish the steely self-restraint that the unit's men have always shown. Sayeret Matkal's commandos never break into outpourings of joy like you might see at a soccer or basketball final, not even when returning from death-defying missions whose importance to Israel's national security cannot be exaggerated.

* * *

In and around Sayeret Matkal, there has been a long, intergenerational debate between those who are convinced that any public mention of the unit, whatever the context, will damage it, Israeli intelligence, and the whole IDF, and those who believe that responsible and selective revelations will help to build the historical tradition and infrastructure that will ultimately shape the State of Israel, its institutions, and its values.

We belong to the second school, the one that believes that whatever stories can be told—cautiously, responsibly, and without damaging national security—should be told. This is the way to motivate future generations to keep aiming to serve in elite special forces units.

That's why we think it's time to tell the parts of the story that we are allowed to tell, and to shine a powerful spotlight on the parts of the story that are already illuminated in the moonlight. This is the most detailed and diverse story that you will ever be able to read about the greatest operations of Sayeret Matkal, Israel's elite commando unit.

We dedicate this book in memory of the soldiers who embarked with us on the missions described in this book and never returned:

> **First Lieutenant Chaim Ben-Yona,** killed in an operation in the Suez Canal, May 13, 1969.
>
> **Maj. Ehud Ram, Staff-Sergeant Danny Vazza, and Private Yuval Meron,** killed in the raid on Green Island, July 20, 1969.
>
> **Staff-Sergeant Shai Shacham,** who froze to death on Mount Hermon, November 2, 1973.
>
> **Col. Uzi Yairi and Staff-Sergeant Itamar Ben-David**, killed in the rescue operation during the Savoy Hotel hostage crisis, March 6, 1975.
>
> **Lt. Col. Yoni Netanyahu**, the unit's commander, killed in the hostage rescue mission in Entebbe, July 4, 1976.
>
> **Captain Nir Poraz,** killed in the mission to free the abducted solider Nachshon Wachsman, October 14, 1994.

We shall remember them, and the other members of Sayeret Matkal who fell in the line of duty, forever.

Chapter 1

OPERATION SHOW OF FORCE— THE ASSASSINATION OF ABU JIHAD IN TUNIS, 1988

On his way to Abu Jihad's home, walking on the sidewalk with Yochai on his left dressed as a woman, Nahum Lev silently releases the safety catch of his Ruger gun, tucked inside the "gift box" under his right arm. Years of intense preparations, unprecedented intelligence campaigns, and rigorous planning have all been leading up to the first bullet, or the first hail of bullets—all silenced, of course—that Nahum will fire from his Ruger when he pulls the trigger with his sweaty finger. This bullet is supposed to hit, down to the millimeter, the middle of the heart or head of the security guard outside Abu Jihad's fortress-like house in Tunis.

The whole operation is like a giant inverse pyramid, and at its tip, carrying the weight of years of investment, stands Nahum Lev, alone, with his Ruger. He is supposed to set in motion a chain of events that will lead to Abu Jihad meeting his maker. Behind him is a long column of soldiers, and on a ship in the middle of the sea, off the Tunisian coast, await the high-ranking officers of the command center, holding their breath. But right now, it's all on Nahum's shoulders.

The guard is sitting in a dark vehicle. Nahum identifies him and pulls out a brochure of a local hotel. According to the plan, he is supposed to walk up to the guard and ask him how to get there. Yochai, standing to his right, clutches his pistol and releases the safety. There are two guns, ready to shoot, on which the whole mission will rise or fall.

Nahum decides not to approach the guard directly, but first to check that there are no other guards across the street or in the yard of the house. He can't see anyone else nearby, so he focuses his efforts and attention on the single guard sitting in the car. Glancing toward the car, Nahum identifies the gate to the yard and the path in the entrance. Everything outside is illuminated, allowing Nahum to visually sweep the area over and over again. The security booth at the entrance to the yard is empty and dark, and the gate is slightly ajar. Everything seems to match his prior intelligence, gathered over several months. Now, it's time to eliminate the guard. This will give the signal to Yuval Rachmilevitch and his men to approach the front door and lay down a hydraulic piston that will force the door open and allow the hit squad to burst in.

Nahum knows that the right way to kill the guard is to make him step out of the car. If he fires his Ruger through the window, despite using a silencer, the impact of the bullet on the glass and metal will cause needless noise and wake the inhabitants of the house, jeopardizing the whole operation. Thousands of miles away from his home in Israel, on a dark night in enemy territory, exercising icy restraint, Nahum performs a blitz of precise calculations about the options available to him, in order to pick the one that will maximize the mission's chances of success.

He approaches the window on the driver's side and taps it gently, putting on the most charming smile he can muster. "Excuse me, sir," he says to the guard through the window. The guard immediately opens the car door and steps out. He's doing his job. By opening the door, the guard switches on the light in the vehicle, revealing his face and body. The guard asks Nahum, in polished English, whether he speaks English. Nahum replies in the affirmative and calmly walks around the vehicle in order to stand next to his new friend. Having a common language slightly dissipates the atmosphere of suspicion, and Nahum asks the guard whether he knows where the hotel is, pointing at the brochure in his hand. The guard takes the brochure for a moment and reads it as Nahum raises the tiny red laser dot from his Ruger to the center of the guard's forehead and quickly ejects three bullets, which bring the man down, slumped by the car's tires, and signal the start of the operation.

Nahum looks around. Silence. Only in the corner of his eye does he see Yochai signaling with a thumbs-up to Moshe "Bogie" Ya'alon, the commander of Sayeret Matkal and of this operation, to advance on the house with his strike force. He places his Ruger on the ground for a quick moment, along with the "gift box" concealing it, his movements not betraying a hint of panic, and he whips out the Micro Uzi that will serve him till the end of the mission.

At the same time, Yuval breaches the front door of the house with ease and sends the strike force in, deep into the scene of the assassination.

When Nahum, who is responsible for securing the strike force from the outside after replacing the slain guard at the front, hears loud and rapid gunfire inside the house, he enters the yard and spots a man walking down the path on his left. The man briefly steps out of the darkness, into the floodlights. He's young, wearing a beige keffiyeh, a thick mustache covering his upper lip. Nahum lurches forward in a second, and the mustachioed man turns around to run away. A long hail of bullets, this time from the Uzi, and the man slumps down, never to awake again.

* * *

Nahum Lev is a one-of-a-kind, inspirational character, even for a unit full of so many extraordinary figures: the warriors who became Israeli national legends, and the commanders who broke new records of derring-do and imagination. He has always been different. The kind of person for whom the cliché "thinks out of the box" seems to have been coined. But this description doesn't capture the truth. Because as far as Nahum is concerned, there has never been a box he needs to think out of.

From the get-go, Nahum has stood out in the elite Sayeret Matkal commando unit as an original, determined, and extremely thorough fighter and commander. It is impossible not to sense his special aura, beyond his quiet and modest demeanor, which charms everyone around him. He is the kind of person who is destined to put little stock by order and discipline in his civilian life; but in times of trouble, he becomes one of Sayeret Matkal's most talented and highly-sought commanders, the sort who return to civilian life after every tour of duty in the unit and then keep getting called to command the sort of missions that require groundbreaking levels of daring and imagination.

* * *

Khalil al-Wazir, better known as Abu Jihad, has served for many years as Arafat's number two in the command of the Palestine Liberation Organization and as the head of its military arm. In this capacity, he has planned and spearheaded many of the PLO's most brutal terror attacks against Israeli civilians, including women and children.

It is Abu Jihad who leads the terror attack in Nahariya in 1974, which murders six civilians, including two children, and injures another six. It is also he who plans the attack at the Savoy Hotel in Tel Aviv, in which eight civilians are murdered and two soldiers are killed, including a former Sayeret Matkal commander, Col. Uzi Yairi. The same year, he also masterminds and leads the bombing in Zion Square in Jerusalem using a booby-trapped refrigerator, which claims the lives of fifteen civilians. In 1978, he dispatches the cell that perpetrates the Coastal Road Massacre, murdering thirty-five Israelis and injuring over seventy. This attack is the trigger for Operation Litani, in which Israeli forces invade southern Lebanon to drive back Palestinian terrorists. Abu Jihad's hands are therefore stained with the blood of dozens of Israelis.

In 1982, during the First Lebanon War, Abu Jihad is expelled from Lebanon and relocates to Jordan. In 1985, he plans a mega-attack for

Israeli Independence Day, but the IDF manages to thwart it.[1] In 1986, he is exiled from Jordan and settles in Tunis. From there, he spearheads Fatah's operations, including fomenting Palestinian public opinion in the West Bank, fueling the First Intifada in December 1987.

By late 1987, it is clear to the whole of Israel's political and security leadership that there was no way to stem Abu Jihad's blitz of murderous terror attacks other than by assassinating him. As if to drive the final nail in his own coffin, in March 1988 Abu Jihad adds one more lethal atrocity to his resumé: the "Mothers' Bus Attack" on the road to Dimona, in which three passengers on the bus are murdered.[2]

The assassination of Abu Jihad is formally entrusted to Sayeret Matkal, under the command of Moshe Ya'alon at the end of 1987. "Bogie," as he is known, joins the unit in 1979 as the commander of its training division. From the first moment he enters the unit's gates, it is clear that this tall and taciturn paratrooper will not fit in with the homogeneous clique of short officers, who naturally wish to repel any outside actors seeking a foothold and influence in their unit.

Bogie possesses a certain aura, having commanded the Paratroopers' special forces after Operation Litani and having led countless operations in Lebanon—but what place does his square demeanor, evident from his

---

1 According to the terrorists' plan, the Attaviros ship was supposed to drop three boats carrying around twenty terrorists, who would land on the beach in Bat Yam, hijack a bus, drive it to the Kirya defense compound in Tel Aviv, and seize one of the buildings, taking a large number of hostages, in the hope of getting them released in exchange for Palestinian security prisoners in Israeli jails. The Israeli Navy located the ship and after a long pursuit, sank it off the Egyptian coast.

2 On March 7, 1988, three armed terrorists hijacked a bus transporting workers to the Nuclear Research Center near the southern city of Dimona. The terrorists took hostage eleven passengers, who had not managed to escape, and executed one of them, a man by the name of Victor Ram. The YAMAM, the Israeli police counterterror unit, took control of the bus in a siege lasting forty seconds. During the takeover, the three hostage-takers were killed, but not before they managed to murder another two hostages: Miriam Ben-Yair and Rina Shiratzki. The commander of the YAMAM at the time of the operation was Alik Ron, a veteran of Sayeret Matkal.

tidy attire and ironclad military discipline, have in Sayeret Matkal's rambunctious atmosphere, which its men embraced as a badge of honor and practically the key to their success?

This is all just a prelude to the main obstacle to Bogie's promotion in Sayeret Matkal: he wears glasses. No one has ever seen a pair of glasses before in the officers' and soldiers' quarters.

But the apparent importance of Bogie's outside appearance fades over time, and what emerges is a man whose character is totally different from what his looks suggest. Moshe "Bogie" Ya'alon proves to be a professional like few the unit has ever seen. His many years of training in the Paratroopers' combat units, including his command of their special forces, and his formative experiences in the War of Attrition and the Yom Kippur War—undoubtedly the best bootcamp for warfare in difficult conditions—make Bogie a highly esteemed commander. They also mark him out as someone who, if he can only master the secrets of the unit's intelligence activities, might one day become its commander.

Bogie was a paragon of personal example, the sort of commander who does everything with his soldiers and thus, without much talk, made them all real partners in every exercise or operation. Because who can stand to the side when the commander takes part in every physical exercise, shooting practice, or morning workout? He also possesses a certain integrity and impartiality, long before politics roughen him up.

After ending his role as the commander of Sayeret Matkal's training division, Bogie is appointed Uzi Dayan's deputy at the helm of the whole unit and stays on as the commander of a force during the First Lebanon War. He then decides to retire for the first time from the military, because of what he calls the "inappropriate behavior" of the IDF top brass: IDF Chief of Staff Rafael "Raful" Eitan and Central Command head Amir Drori, who want to send a Sayeret Matkal team on a suicide mission in the vicinity of Beirut's airport.

In 1983, the Kahan Commission, the official inquiry that investigates the circumstances surrounding the Christian Phalangists' massacre of Palestinian civilians at the Sabra and Shatila refugee camps, publishes its findings. The report forces Defense Minister Ariel Sharon and the military intelligence chief to resign, and this change makes it easier for Bogie to decide to stay in the IDF after all. He accepts the command of the 890th Paratroopers' Battalion and later the deputy command of the Paratroopers' Brigade. And then, in mid-1986, Bogie is approached by military intelligence chief Amnon Lipkin-Shahak, who asks him to replace Omer Bar-Lev at the helm of Sayeret Matkal.[3]

Bogie has participated in countless Sayeret Matkal operations as a commander, including in the field, and he has studied the fine details of the unit's intelligence doctrines, but he is always careful to leave his subordinate commanders enough freedom of maneuver, since they are responsible for planning and executing the intricate technical and intelligence details of each operation. They are deeply aware that Bogie will always have their backs and inspire them: the two things that commanders must always do when conducting extremely risky missions.

When he is appointed the commander of Sayeret Matkal in 1987, Moshe "Bogie" Ya'alon is much older than anyone before or after him in the job. At the grand old age of thirty-seven, he is long past his predecessors' average age of thirty. [4] He also holds a higher rank than his predecessors: he is the first colonel to command Sayeret Matkal, thanks to his long military career, and he quickly becomes a respected and highly-regarded commander who succeeds, partly thanks to his age and experience, to stabilize the unit's command structure and to surround himself with an outstanding team, who help him to lead the unit into one of the most fruitful and successful periods in his history.

---

3 The Kahan Commission was headed by Supreme Court President Yitzhak Kahan, joined by Supreme Court Justice Aharon Barak and retired general Yona Efrat. Among the committee's recommendations were the termination of Ariel Sharon's tenure as defense minister and the sacking of the head of military intelligence, Maj. Gen. Yehoshua Sagi.

4 All of Ya'alon's predecessors were around thirty when they entered the job, except for Yoseph Castel, who was thirty-five years old when he replaced Avraham Arnan for a year as the unit's commander.

He taps Pinchas Buchris as his deputy. He also nabs Eyal Ragonis from the Paratroopers as his chief intelligence officer, and the rare symbiosis between the commander and his intelligence officer gives rise to one of the most productive relationships the unit has ever seen. They serve alongside such high-caliber squad commanders as Yuval Rachmilevitch and Nitzan Alon (two future commanders of the unit), and others. And Bogie, as we have already seen, is truly a maestro at giving his officers both free rein and a strong embrace. He gives them guidance and leeway, adding only a few wise remarks here and there, without dampening the unit's signature operational creativity. He is like a talented soccer or basketball coach, who gives the team a ball and says, "Give it your best shot." They give it their best shot, and boy, what a shot . . .

When a military commander has enough confidence in himself and his abilities, and when his age and experience help him put up with talented officers' caprices and quirks, the results are inevitably superb. Bogie is also generous with the credit for his officers' outstanding execution. He can live perfectly well with his subordinates' successes and never insists on hogging the glory. On the contrary: he insists that if citations are being awarded, the whole unit should get one. Indeed, under his command, Sayeret Matkal is awarded several collective citations.

One of Bogie's biggest achievements in Sayeret Matkal in general, and in the operation to assassinate Abu Jihad in particular, is the long campaign to rope Eyal Ragonis into the unit as its chief intelligence officer. Bogie knows him from their service together in the Paratroopers, when Bogie was a fighter and commander, and Ragonis was the brigade's talented chief intelligence officer. He stood out for his drive and ability to fight for every morsel of information ahead of operations, as if every snippet were the most important link in the chain of intelligence he had to prepare, a vital condition for giving each mission the green light.

Ragonis has already left the IDF and starts studying architecture, and as soon as he begins his master's degree in early 1987, Bogie becomes the commander of Sayeret Matkal and starts applying immoderate pressure on him to drop everything and join the unit as its chief intelligence officer. Bogie's decision to storm this particular target is far from obvious, since Ragonis did not grow up in Sayeret Matkal and is a stranger to its intelligence activities. Moreover, he is already practically a senior citizen at the age of thirty-two, immersed in his studies, a world apart the military and covert intelligence. But Bogie's desire and determination are much stronger than Ragonis's resistance, and he eventually relents and dons a uniform for a second time, to join Sayeret Matkal.

Obviously, when Ragonis shows up in the unit as a total outsider, he is greeted with intense suspicion, bordering on hostility. Just as with Bogie before him, it is as hard as hell to integrate into this tight-knit set of battle-hardened combat officers or intelligence officers who have climbed the ranks of Sayeret Matkal or the IDF Intelligence Directorate's own special operations unit. It takes both grit and talent to integrate successfully as an esteemed member of this system. Ragonis has them both: he was a strong character, with talent to boot. Looking back, it is hard to imagine how the operation to assassinate Abu Jihad could have succeeded without the exemplary footwork that Ragonis puts in with the help of dozens of Mossad, Shin Bet, and IDF intelligence officers.

When it is decided to task Sayeret Matkal with assassinating Abu Jihad, Prime Minister Yitzhak Shamir is the head of a national unity government, Yitzhak Rabin is the defense minister, Shimon Peres is the foreign minister, Dan Shomron is the IDF chief of staff, Ehud Barak is the deputy chief of staff, Amnon Lipkin-Shahak is the head of the IDF Intelligence Directorate, and Nahum Admoni is the director of Mossad. Unusually, in fact almost without precedent, there is broad agreement among all these officials that Israel must do everything—that means *everything*—to introduce Abu Jihad to the angel of death.

In fact, Sayeret Matkal's pursuit of Abu Jihad begins long before the outbreak of the First Intifada in 1987 and the "Mothers' Bus Attack" in 1988. Back in the early 1980s, under Omer Bar-Lev's command, the unit began training and preparing for a mission to eliminate the man with the blood-soaked hands. The goal is to reach his home and assassinate him there. The operation did not seem especially complicated, not least because he lived not far from Israel, in Jordan.

The problem was that Abu Jihad was careful never to sleep in the same house for more than a few nights in a row, without planning his next stop in advance. When it became clear that he wasn't planning to return to his own home in the near future, it was decided to postpone the operation till further notice, until it was eventually called off.

After the operation was scrapped, the efforts to assassinate Abu Jihad fell off Sayeret Matkal's agenda for a while, partly because it was so over-burdened with other intelligence missions. Abu Jihad's mugshot reappears on the tables of Sayeret Matkal's intelligence officers in late 1987, after he relocates from Jordan to Tunis and stops darting so frenetically around the Middle East—making it possible for Sayeret Matkal to start planning his assassination more methodically.

Abu Jihad's location in faraway Tunis naturally makes the planning much more complicated and requires the massive involvement of the IDF Intelligence Directorate, Mossad, the Shin Bet, the Navy, and the Air Force. Luckily for Sayeret Matkal, Mossad already has an intensive presence in Tunis, ever since the PLO's leadership moved there after the First Lebanon War, and it possesses a range of unusual reconnaissance abilities in a neighborhood popular with the PLO. When Nahum Lev is appointed the project director of Operation Show of Force, to assassinate Abu Jihad, it is clear to him and to his commanders that contact with Mossad, as an intelligence supplier, is key to the operation's success.

Nahum Lev immediately recruits Ragonis as his chief intelligence officer, and their solid relationship gives the project an extraordinary tail-wind, which is essential to its success. Like many of his comrades, Nahum is extremely suspicious of Ragonis when he joins the unit, but their joint work on a covert intelligence mission that Nahum commands in the late fall of 1987, which serves as Ragonis's induction to Sayeret Matkal, fosters extraordinary mutual respect between the two officers, which becomes a profound friendship ahead of Operation Show of Force.

In the first stage, the bulk of the planning is on the operational side: to collect heaps of accurate information about the target's house and surroundings, his movements in and beyond Tunis, and his security detail. Sayeret Matkal knows that getting final approval for such a mission, especially from Yitzhak Rabin, Israel's most eagle-eyed and rigorous defense minister to date, will require giving compelling answers to seemingly banal questions, such as what to do if the first gun jams and hundreds of other scenarios and reactions that they have to consider before turning up at Rabin's office at the Defense Ministry HQ in Tel Aviv.

Ragonis and Nahum, two unimpeachably rigorous officers, as good and as dedicated as they come, are by far the most suitable candidates for the Sisyphean task of gathering and sifting through the intelligence. They build a remarkably accurate model of Abu Jihad's house, with an exact internal division of the rooms and floors, including the basement, the front yard, the perimeter wall, the garden, and the guards' sleeping quarters. They add information from Mossad patrols around the area, during which agents photograph the house and the neighborhood, map out the approach the house, and locate landing beaches for the Navy, hiding places where the commandos can change clothes after storming the beach, and other minute details without which such a complex mission could never have been launched.

Nahum, for example, recalls examining "perhaps a thousand" ships during the preparations, in order to understand exactly what the voyage from Haifa to Tunis would look like. Usually, the choice of ship is totally up to the Navy. Not on Nahum's watch. He has to be involved in every detail of the mission, going far beyond his job description.

* * *

Nahum is in charge of planning and commanding the mission from the moment of its inception, but as Operation Show of Force begins to take shape, it's clear to everyone that Bogie, as Sayeret Matkal's commander, has no intention of running this operation from a distance, and that he is going to personally participate as the supreme field commander. Bogie's decision, however reasonable, causes several high-ranking noses in the IDF General Staff to wrinkle, but nobody, not even the IDF chief of staff, can stop a unit commander who decides to join such a complex mission thousands of miles away from Israel. And thus, three Sayeret Matkal senior officers—Commander Bogie and two deputies, Nahum Lev and Pinhas Buchris—are scheduled to take part in the operation.

Nahum is taking a small demotion, to the role of deputy commander, but he has the special responsibility of leading the first pair of operatives to arrive on the scene, who will eliminate the guards at the entrance to the house and open the front gate for the strike force.

The last stage of preparations ahead of an operation raises everyone's spirits, giving them all a supreme sense of virtue ahead of a mission that is singularly complicated but also justified and unavoidable.

For the operation, Sayeret Matkal puts together an elite team, crossing squads and divisions. It includes not just Bogie and his deputies Lev and Buchris, but also two future Sayeret Matkal commanders, Yuval Rachmilevitch and Oded Raor; two division commanders, Shai and Avi; two squad commanders, Yoram Y. and H.; the unit's medic, Dr. Ofer; and another eleven men, the most battle-hardened and experienced fighters in the unit.

The target city, where Abu Jihad's house is located, is Tunis, which sits above the ruins of ancient Carthage, the sworn enemy of ancient Rome. The distance between the Carthaginian coast, where Sayeret Matkal's forces will land, and Abu Jihad's home is around three miles, so the training exercises ahead of the operation take place in a villa in Ramat Hasharon exactly five miles from Tel Baruch beach. The house standing in for Abu Jihad's is a Sayeret Matkal officer's family home.

In Nahum Lev's plan, Yochai, his partner (in more than one sense) at the start of the mission, is supposed to be disguised as a tall and exotic woman, while Nahum himself, with his Nordic appearance, will pose as a tourist, leading the couple through the streets of Tunis. Nahum, of course, will not even consider beginning an operation like this without a rigorous examination of its feasibility. He asks Yochai, therefore, to don his full costume and go for a long stroll around a new mall outside Tel Aviv. Yochai's gander around the mall ends with an impressive operational success: not only does nobody suspect that this elegant lady is actually a bloke, but he also leaves behind a trail of drooling men.

Finally, Nahum, Ragonis, Bogie, and the other officers in Sayeret Matkal, the IDF Intelligence Directorate, and Mossad are satisfied with the results of the drills, although doubts inevitably linger in such a mission, with so many unknowns. And then, in early 1988, they receive the news that always haunts Sayeret Matkal's operations, like an eagle circling its prey: the government decides to postpone the operation.

As bitter fate would have it, Abu Jihad decides to risk his own fortunes: in March 1988, he sends one of his murderous cells to commit the atrocity known as the Mothers' Bus Attack. This time, after three Israelis are murdered, nobody, either in the defense establishment or the government, can stand by and fail to approve this mission.

In the meeting the next day in Prime Minister Yitzhak Shamir's office, there is a rare agreement that it's time to immediately reactivate Operation Show of Force, which has been gathering dust in Sayeret Matkal's archives. Everyone present, at the vocal behest of IDF Deputy Chief of Staff Ehud Barak, who has already been everywhere the unit has visited, and who has an almost intimate acquaintance with nearly all the participants, supports an immediate operation to eliminate Abu Jihad.

* * *

Once the green light is given, the weapons are pulled out of the silos and the costumes from the wardrobe, and Sayeret Matkal's best officers and soldiers, long dispersed to their routine duties, are regrouped and placed in accelerated battle mode, ahead of the mission scheduled for mid-April.

Mossad agents land in Tunis again under false identities in order to make the final preparations, this time for the last time, for Sayeret Matkal's mission, which will include vast back-up from IDF military intelligence, the Israeli Navy and Air Force, and the Medical Corps.

Mossad hires two minivans from different rental agencies in Tunis. These vehicles will transport Sayeret Matkal's soldiers from the landing site on the beach to Abu Jihad's house. The cars will obviously be paid for in cash, in Tunisian dinars, as the agents know too well, in order not to leave any digital trace that might reveal the source of the money. Meanwhile, the Mossad agents keep revisiting the transport routes from the beach to the house, including potential escape routes in case of any surprises or an unexpected car chase.

And thus, on the night of April 13, 1988, twenty-one officers and soldiers from Sayeret Matkal board an Israeli Navy missile boat in Haifa, en route to Tunis. The naval force of four missile boats and a submarine begins its voyage toward its target in one of the most complex operations ever carried out by the IDF. One of the boats will function as a control room, under the command of Deputy Chief of Staff Ehud Barak, joined by military intelligence chief Amnon Lipkin-Shahak and Navy commander Alex Tal and his deputy Ami Ayalon, a former commander of Shayetet 13, Israel's answer to the U.S. Navy SEALS, who will command the naval force in this mission. Two Boeing 707 planes escort the flotilla from above, conducting various intelligence and reconnaissance activities relevant to the operation. One of the missile boats sets sail with a large Shayetet 13 force, led by the unit's commander, Yoav Galant. Shayetet 13 is supposed to escort Sayeret Matkal's squad on its Zodiac commando boats from the missile boat to a drop-off point in the sea near the beach in Tunis—but not before two sailors disembark and reach the shore in underwater Maiale manned torpedoes, in order to check that there are no unwanted passersby or worse, hostile operatives lying in wait for the Israeli forces.

The long voyage, which lasts nearly two days, is quiet and tense. In such a complicated operation so far from home, an almost infinite number of things can go wrong. Even the most experienced Sayeret Matkal fighters know that they can easily end such a mission in an Arab prison, or worse. And no ocean view, however quiet and calm, can expel these nagging thoughts.

Even the soldiers' typically cynical banter takes a backseat as the missile boats plough through the waves, far beyond Israel's territorial waters. The night of April 15 is bright and hot, and when the missile boat approaches the spot where it will drop anchor and the hit team will transfer to the Zodiac boats, it turns out that landing site might change at the recommendation of the Mossad agents who have lain the operational foundations in Tunis. It makes little difference to the Sayeret Matkal fighters descending from the boats into the gentle waves, not far from the beach, the Tunisian waters reaching up to their shoulders and giving them, finally, a first taste of the operation, which begins to unfold rapidly.

Still in the water, they spot the two Transporter cars waiting on the beach, their engines on. There's no time or desire for backslapping greetings in this "family reunion" with the Arabic-named Mossad agents waiting quietly inside the vehicles. Sayeret Matkal's fighters pull out their battle fatigues and their fighting gear, kept dry in their backpacks. The final preparation and equipment stages before entering the cars last around twenty minutes, but the final order to advance on the target comes only another twenty minutes later, when it becomes clear that the "object" is not yet home. Twenty minutes in which all the fighters feel their stomachs churning. The tense anticipation in an enemy land before the start of an operation will always violently pluck the nerves of any warrior, even the steeliest and bravest among them.

* * *

The advance toward the target begins at 02:00, Tunisia time. According to the latest reports streaming in from Mossad agents in Tunis to Barak's command room on the missile boat, which are then encrypted, scrambled, and sent back to Bogie on the mainland, Abu Jihad is finally at home, but he might leave again at 03:00. Bogie orders the drivers to step harder on the gas. There's no time for unexpected snags or last-minute adjustments.

The streets of Tunis are much more jammed than expected, despite the late hour. The only noise heard during the advance toward the target is Bogie's voice, muttering strange code words into his walkie-talkie, which are picked up on the huge transceiver on the missile boat, in front of a sweaty and tense Barak, Lipkin-Shahak, and other members of the command room. As Bogie whispers quietly into the tiny microphone attached to his neck, he misses the picturesque route by the ruins of Carthage, rising up to the Sidi Bou Said neighborhood, where, on a hill overlooking the sea, they will find Abu Jihad's house. The neighborhood looks much like parts of north Tel Aviv or Herzliya, with single-story buildings, painted white and surrounded by white stone fences. Abu Jihad's neighbors, besides many foreign diplomats, include future Palestinian Authority Chairman Mahmoud Abbas (Abu Mazen) and PLO intelligence chief Abu Hul and other senior Palestinian figures.

* * *

After Nahum Lev eliminates the guard sitting at the entrance, and successfully takes out another guard who pops up outside the house, the second squad arrives, headed by Yuval. He is an experienced squad commander, and with the three soldiers under his command, he is responsible for breaking into the house and then for operations on the ground floor and in the basement. When Yochai, Nahum Lev's "girlfriend," signals to Bogie with a thumbs-up that their mission is complete and that the first guard has collapsed onto the floor before even giving Nahum directions to the hotel, Bogie immediately sends Yuval and his team to the front door. Yuval Rachmilevitch approaches the door with another operative named Yuval, nicknamed "Zulu," and they put in place a special piston designed to blow open especially stubborn doors. The door opens with a faint noise, bidding the uninvited guests inside.

The living room is dark and empty, with not a soul around, and the squad starts to follow "Zulu" down to the basement. At the bottom of the stairs down the basement, a guard is asleep. Two gunshots, and his sleep becomes an eternal rest. They re-emerge in the living room, grab a bundle of documents from the dark office in the living room, and dart outside.

Quick on the heels of Yuval's squad is another team of six soldiers, headed by a Sayeret Matkal officer. He was in command of the second car en route to the target, and his job is to take control of the second floor of the house, the living quarters, and to fire the single bullet for which this whole operation was planned and executed. Just two gunshots will be critically important for the success of the mission. The first bullet, fired from Nahum's Ruger, takes out the first guard and thus gives the signal for the operation to proceed. The second bullet, from another officer's sub-machine gun, is supposed to end Abu Jihad's life and thus save the lives of the dozens if not hundreds of Israelis who would otherwise become the victims of his murderous schemes—and they are none the wiser. Abu Jihad's drawing board has been filling up with plans for lethal yet highly creative and inspired atrocities, which will unleash rivers of blood and fire in Israel if they ever see the light of day.

* * *

H. charges forward at the head of his squad, on the heels of Yuval and his men. They are not running too quickly, in order not to lose each other in Tunisian darkness. Six men in total climb up to the second floor, taking brisk steps. As they rush up the stairs, illuminated with the spotlight trainers attached to their weapons, they hear the unmistakable sound of a gun cocking upstairs, which accelerates both the soldiers' pace and of course their heart rate. H. turns to the corridor on the right, while Oded turns with his men to the corridor on the left. As soon as they turn right, even before a basic visual sweep of the corridor, H. spots the "object": Abu Jihad himself, standing a dozen feet in front of him, a pistol in his right hand and his wife by his side, clutching his arm and watching in horror as eight bullets whizz through the corridor, pierce her husband's chest one by one, and bring him down slowly to the floor, right outside their bedroom.

Just as Abu Jihad's life finally drains out of his body, Bogie, the commander of the operation, arrives on scene, understands the situation at once, and sends H. to scan the room from which Abu Jihad and his wife just emerged. Natan, the third fighter in H.'s squad, arrives from the other side of the corridor, grabs the "object's" eight-year-old daughter by the hand, her eyes open wide as the inevitable tears still resist streaming down her cheeks. Bogie declares that it's time to evacuate, and while H. and his men gallop down the stairs, he and Yuval quickly gather some documents from Abu Jihad's room before darting to the front door, and from there to the vehicles waiting with their engines on.

The whole operation, from the moment Nahum plants the first bullet in the guard's forehead until the whole team is back in the vehicles, ready to move, lasts exactly five minutes, a mere 300 seconds, far under the twenty minutes they had planned for, in case they had to treat the wounded and hunt down the arch-terrorist if he was hiding. None of this happened, making the operation a quick and accurate blitz of successes.

* * *

Now, Bogie orders an accurate count of the men sitting in the two Transporters, and when they hit twenty-one, exactly the number of fighters who set out on the mission, the cars set out on their way. Despite using silencers, the heavy gunfire in Abu Jihad's house seems to have woken up some of the dozens of PLO guards living nearby. A Mossad agent calls the local police, introduces himself as a local resident, and reports seeing the attackers' cars driving in the direction of the city center. This ruse leaves the route to the beach clear and quiet.

In any case, the fighters are ready to return fire through the car windows if they get into trouble. When they reach the beach, they get out of the vehicles, unload their weapons in the direction of the sea, and then spend a considerable amount of time thoroughly cleaning out the cars, in order not to leave any clues that might point in their direction.

They don their "buoyancy compensator" diving equipment and wade through the water to the naval commando boats waiting for them a few hundred feet from the beach. Their deep sighs of relief on the short voyage to the missile boats can be heard as far as Israel.

The Tunisian police and military, launching a hysterical manhunt for the hit team that assassinated Abu Jihad, discover only two abandoned cars on the beach at Carthage, scrubbed clean of any clues.

* * *

The following morning, April 16, 1988, Israel's fortieth Independence Day, the whole country is in a state of euphoria, which does not reach the same heights as after Operation Entebbe or Spring of Youth but still makes the national chest swell with pride. The State of Israel officially but limply denies any connection to the incident, and when Prime Minister Shamir is asked by reporters about Israel's involvement, he replies that he too first heard about it on the radio.[5]

It is this news item on the radio, which the prime minister and others hear, that brings Defense Minister Rabin, Chief of Staff Shomron, and military intelligence chief Lipkin-Shahak to award citations to three men who participated in the operation: Nahum Lev, who receives the Chief of General Staff's Citation, and H. and Yuval, who receive a citation from the chief of the IDF Intelligence Directorate.

And as the whole of Israel sings the soldiers' praises and briefly comes together in a kind of collective Hora dance to salute the courage and resourcefulness of just twenty-one operatives, these men, carrying all this glory on their lean shoulders, walk around with their eyes downcast and lips sealed, praying that their secret will not slip. That's another tough yet inevitable consequence of Sayeret Matkal's operations.

---

5   Only in 2012, twenty-four years after Abu Jihad's assassination, did the military censor allow publication of the fact that this was an Israeli operation.

And maybe, just maybe, it is Abu Jihad's demonic spirit that wanders the earth and causes three of the men who participated in this operation to meet their maker far too young, cut down in their prime.

Nahum Lev, who planned the operation and commanded it on the ground, is killed in a car crash on the Arava Highway in August 2000, when a car veering in the opposite direction crosses the solid white line to overtake the traffic and smashes headfirst into Nahum on his motorbike.

Eyal Ragonis, Sayeret Matkal's chief intelligence officer, including in this operation, an architect in his civilian life, meets his death aged just thirty-seven as a result of a blood clot.

And Col. Oded Raor, one of the participants in this mission, who later commands Sayeret Matkal during the Second Lebanon War, passes away in 2014 from a cardiac arrest in his sleep.

Chapter 2

AN ELITE FORCE IS BORN

Sayeret Matkal, or "The Unit" to use its cryptic nickname, is founded by an Israeli officer called Avraham Arnan in 1957 as the fifth company of a secretive IDF intelligence unit known only as Unit 154. Only more than a year later, in August 1958, is it declared its own independent unit with its own unit number: 269. In time, this unit will grow to genuinely mythological proportions, even after receiving a new number.

When Arnan founds Sayeret Matkal, he imagines an elite reconnaissance unit, hence its name: in Hebrew, a *sayeret* is a special reconnaissance unit, and *matkal* signifies its affiliation with the IDF General Staff. He sees the "commando" side of its job as relatively marginal, but he still harbors operational aspirations and imagines the unit raiding airfields during wartime, much like the British SAS did in Egypt's Western Desert during the Second World War. His fine intuitions, based on many years of military service, especially in intelligence, tell him that this new unit will need to have a single, crystal-clear, rock-solid mission if it wants to stand the test of time and gain institutional recognition in Israel's defense apparatus.

Other units around the world founded under the impressive-sounding, glory-grabbing umbrella of "commando" operations but with undefined combat goals have spent years walking around in circles, looking for their often-elusive special calling—and eventually disappear or find that special calling after a fateful delay of many years.

The mission statement that will propel Sayeret Matkal forward or send it crashing is built wisely and carefully, but David Ben-Gurion, Israel's prime minister and defense minister in these early years, was never a fan of sending Israeli soldiers over the border into neighboring Arab states. At this point, he was still licking his wounds from the Uri Ilan affair in late 1954, when five Israeli soldiers who embarked on a reconnaissance mission in Syria were taken captive and thrown into the Mezzeh Prison in Damascus. Uri Ilan, a soldier in the Golani brigade's special forces unit, feared that he wouldn't be able to withstand the pressure—and committed suicide. When his body was repatriated that same day, over the Daughters of Jacob Bridge near the Golan Heights, it was received by IDF Chief of Staff Moshe Dayan. Suddenly, small scraps of paper dropped out from between the dead man's toes, with Hebrew words punched into the notes with a toothpick: "I didn't commit treason, I took my life," read one of the notes.

This resounding military failure, and perhaps the fact that it was the son of a member of Knesset who committed suicide in a Syrian jail in order not to reveal secrets to the enemy, has a major influence on Israel's military and political decision-makers. Over the next few years, especially after the 1956 Suez War, they reject countless requests from the military to infiltrate neighboring states for reconnaissance missions. Some are approved, but only a handful. As if Ben-Gurion is personally standing guard on the borders to ensure that no Israeli soldier, however well trained and armed, cross over into enemy territory.

Many of the missions beyond Israel's borders, including retribution operations carried out by Unit 101 and the Paratroopers, unfold in the years before the Suez War, in October 1956. Things are totally different in the years afterwards. That's when Ben-Gurion takes fright at anything that might disrupt the fragile status quo after the withdrawal of Israeli forces from the Sinai Desert in early 1957. In the late 1950s, certain IDF units perform several forays into neighboring countries, especially to keep their soldiers fit or for training purposes, with Ben-Gurion's consent, but that consent is given only sparingly.

But Ben-Gurion, as short in stature as he is great in spirit, is opposed by another diminutive man with a titanic will to push this new unit to success, who sees it as the pinnacle of his military career, if not his life. Without Sayeret Matkal, Arnan is convinced, there will be no future for the IDF Intelligence Corps.

Two events, almost two years apart, play into Arnan's hands and deftly overturn Ben-Gurion's earlier decision. The first event is the Rotem Crisis in February–March 1960, when nearly the entire Egyptian army, headed by the 4th Armored Division and two almost complete infantry divisions—some 550 tanks and six or seven infantry brigades—roll into the Sinai Desert without Israeli intelligence having the faintest clue. The massive Egyptian advance into the supposedly demilitarized peninsula, which could genuinely imperil the State of Israel, leaves an in indelible mark on the top brass of the IDF and its intelligence directorate. The seeds of Israel's insatiable need to receive solid intelligence from within the armies encircling it are sown by this incident and begin to sprout roots. And Arnan goes knocking on every door at the Kirya, Israel's defense headquarters, at every hour, and at every opportunity, in order to water these seeds and turn his vision into a reality.

And the second event, less dramatic but just as important is the appointment of Meir Amit as the IDF intelligence chief in 1962. Sometimes one person really can change the world. Amit is a strong and authoritative character, highly opinionated, and an expert at grabbing the bull by its horns. And in this case, the bull is the immediate need for up-to-date and detailed information in order to create an accurate and complete intelligence picture. Just so nothing like the Rotem Crisis ever happens again.

This combination, between the concrete need for fresh intelligence about developments inside Arab armies and the new military intelligence chief's understanding of the situation and ability to turn this urgent need into a work plan, fits Arnan like a glove. And thus, despite Ben-Gurion's principled desire to keep the number of Israeli soldiers making incursions over the border to an absolute minimum, Sayeret Matkal and its commander finally receive the green light to launch.

Arnan, who saw action in the 1948 War of Independence as a solider in the pre-state Palmach paramilitary, has never seen himself as an heir to Bar Kokhba, the legendary Jewish general who launched an ultimately disastrous rebellion against the Romans in antiquity. No way. He is an intelligence agent, a man hungry for information, and he wants to build the unit in his image, but not exactly as clones of himself. He understands that Sayeret Matkal's soldiers, even if exemplary intelligence agents, will have to be first and foremost professional warriors *par excellence,* who know all the secrets of soldiering, from the most basic skills to the ability to jump into action in any possible terrain.

To Arnan's credit, he has never had any trouble attracting the finest fighters from the wider IDF to the unit, who might overshadow him as soldiers and even leaders—but as long as they can teach and train the unit's young men and build a lean fighting force with them, over which he can overlay the unit's reconnaissance work, that's all that matters.

Everyone comes to help put Sayeret Matkal's men through bootcamp, but also to lend Arnan's new unit a much more professional and combative profile than it really has. Arnan is a PR professional, who understands the importance of images. In order to sell his wares to the IDF and defense establishment top brass, he knows that he'll have to give Sayeret Matkal an image boost, even if the makeover is slightly superficial.

Arnan knows that the unit also needs an ethos, and this ethos will be no less important for the unit's survival and endurance than the quality of its weapons or even of its soldiers. This ethos will include a slogan, or a motto, a symbol, and a tradition. He copies all of this, word for word, from the British SAS, which he wants to emulate, not as much in terms of its mission as its image and glorious reputation as a fighting force. He picks a motto—"Who Dares Wins," Sayeret Matkal's motto till today— and a symbol, which for obvious reasons the soldiers are forbidden from wearing on their uniform. Both the motto and the symbol are secretly pilfered from the celebrated British commando unit.

Arnan starts developing a tradition for Sayeret Matkal, and any military unit's tradition is built first and foremost on its missions, as many and as successful as possible. And Arnan, bursting with emotion when he sees the unit he has been dreaming about for years taking shape, puts his mind to executing the reconnaissance missions that he has also been dreaming about—and it doesn't even cross his mind to commit Sayeret Matkal to operations that are not connected to reconnaissance.

But Arnan, after two stints as the unit's commander, must move onwards and upwards in the IDF and so must hand over his beloved creation to his successor. That's the way of the world and of any modern military. Dovik Tamari, appointed his successor in February 1964, is practically Arnan's diametric opposite: tall, chiseled, and with a magnificent track record in the Paratroopers. Arnan is a kind of prophet, an entrepreneurial, resourceful visionary of reconnaissance operations. Dovik, in contrast, is first and foremost a warrior. He will learn, of course, to navigate the labyrinth of the IDF Intelligence Corps, and will commit its intelligence doctrines to memory with a rigor and precision reserved only to a select few versatile and talented officers, but if you ask him, the most basic, supreme value is just to be a good soldier.

Dovik knows that no matter how hard his men train, even in conditions similar to real combat scenarios, he will never be able to distill for them the reality of a genuine combat experience, which in an instant transforms the awareness and reaction-style of any rookie soldier. It's clear that if the first time that bullets start whizzing past their ears is during a sensitive and secretive reconnaissance mission, it will end in disaster. They will have to get used to bullets flying around them in "regular" combat activity in order to acquire the necessary combat experience and internalize the most appropriate way of responding.

Therefore, in a boost to improve Sayeret Matkal soldiers' combat-readiness and give them the necessary combat experience, Dovik understands that he will have to get the unit involved in every possible IDF operation.

He has the right connections with generals in the operations departments and also the necessary leadership ability to head the Sayeret Matkal team attached to IDF forces in whatever their first joint mission will be. He won't neglect covert reconnaissance operations, of course—they're the reason for this whole unit's existence—but meanwhile, he will lead his men into several rounds of combat.

During Dovik's stint as the commander of Sayeret Matkal, therefore, his men join the IDF's "routine" night-time incursions into Arab countries for frequent sabotage operations. They gain experience that will be worth its weight in gold.

Chapter 3

THE BULMUS OPERATIONS— SUEZ CANAL, MAY 1969

By the time the War of Attrition with Egypt erupts in early 1969, Sayeret Matkal already has a respectable reputation in battlefield reconnaissance. The long-running battle over whether the unit is even necessary has ended with absolute victory for Avraham Arnan, the unit's hardnosed founder and first commander. Sayeret Matkal fails to get roped into a single battle or serious operation in the Six-Day War, despite the best efforts of its commander, Uzi Yairi. But since then, it has seen action in the Battle of Karameh against Palestinian militias in Jordan and a daring raid on Beirut International Airport in retaliation for a terror attack on an Israeli passenger plane. This triggers a groundswell of voices, within the unit's ranks and beyond, calling for Sayeret Matkal to play an active role in every possible war or battle, not just in reconnaissance operations—the original reason for the unit's existence.

During the U.S. Civil War, President Abraham Lincoln told one of his generals that if he did not want to use the army, "I would like to borrow it for a time." Just like that, Sayeret Matkal's young officers come knocking on Arnan's door at the IDF Intelligence Directorate, which still has Sayeret Matkal in its sprawling grip, and without beating around the bush, ask him something to the effect of: "If you're not using Sayeret Matkal, do you think we can borrow it?" These young officers simply can't accept that while the IDF is stuck in the mud of the Suez Canal, Sayeret Matkal is sitting on its hands and only getting a piece of the action when dispatched on reconnaissance missions.

Everyone, both these young officers and the generals in IDF intelligence, knows that Sayeret Matkal was founded for exactly these covert missions. It has proven its ability over the past decade to deliver priceless intelligence, and according to IDF intelligence chief Aharon Yariv, the IDF reaped the sweet fruits of this reconnaissance in the Six-Day War. On all this, there is total consensus. But this assessment ignores the times when the whole IDF is at war, whether a lightning campaign like the Six-Day War or a long slog like the War of Attrition. The young officers in Sayeret Matkal believe that their unit should not be consigned only to intelligence work but leveraged wherever the IDF is fighting, even at the cost of distracting from its original reconnaissance role.

In any case, Arnan goes ballistic when these young officers show up. No matter how many years have passed since he handed over command of Sayeret Matkal and moved up the ranks of IDF intelligence, he is still the unit's founding father. His name is still on the deeds, and no officer, however talented, should have the audacity to tell him what to do with "his own" unit. Arnan also possesses a considerable ego, and in his mind, meddling with the unit's mission statement means taking a one-ton bomb to the rules that he personally devised in the early 1960s.

But not even Arnan and his powerful lobby of generals can stop these young horses galloping into battle. Menachem Digli, who takes over from Uzi Yairi as Sayeret Matkal's commander in April 1969, is much more of a combat soldier than an intelligence officer, and he doesn't miss a heartbeat when he parachutes into the commander's seat. He is perfectly aware that he will never be able to explain to posterity why Sayeret Matkal was absent from the heat of the War of Attrition that progressed the Suez Canal, and he immediately starts devising its first operation: "Bulmus 3."

* * *

Operation Bulmus 3 is scheduled for the night between May 10 and 11, 1969 (despite the numbering, "Bulmus 3" is the first of the Bulmus operations). A Sayeret Matkal force of twenty-five soldiers is supposed to cross the Suez Canal, from the Israeli to the Egyptian side, around nineteen miles south of the northern mouth of the canal at Port Said, on inflatable Zodiac boats. There, it will lay three ambushes for Egyptian military vehicles on the road parallel to the canal, west of the city of Ismailia. An eight-man force from Shayetet 13, Israel's equivalent of the U.S. Navy SEALS, will ferry the commandos to the western bank of the canal and secure the passage from both sides while the Sayeret Matkal force completes its mission.

The collaboration between Shayetet 13 and Sayeret Matkal, which began in the days of Uzi Yairi, has deepened over the years, becoming practically routine. Sayeret Matkal understands that there is no way to operate around the Suez Canal, where the War of Attrition is currently raging, without the support of Shayetet 13, and Shayetet 13 recognizes that the road to ground operations in Egypt runs through Sayeret Matkal.

Shayetet 13 has long been scouring for its own distinct purpose and identity. Its commander, Ze'ev Almog, understands that to succeed, it will have to engage in real combat operations, including on land, and not just serve as a ferry service for other units, such as Sayeret Matkal.

Both Shayetet 13 and Sayeret Matkal reach the period following the Six-Day War with a ferocious will to prove themselves after failing, to their great frustration, to prove their mettle in the war. Sayeret Matkal, which was fully prepared for a mission to destroy Egypt's airfields, went into mourning when the Israeli Air Force did exactly that in the first few hours of the war, leaving the unit chasing crumbs. Shayetet 13, in contrast, took part in several daring missions, but they were spectacular failures, and it wrapped up the Six-Day War with its head in its hands.

A deeper partnership between the two commando units, one on land and one at sea, should benefit both of them and satisfy the IDF's growing need for deterrence against Egypt's incessant attempts to test its defensive lines along the Suez Canal. Sayeret Matkal commandos spend many weeks at Shayetet 13's base in Atlit, learning how to swim with flippers, navigate the seas, emerge from the sea with a gun that still works after immersion in water, sand, and salt, and a range of other skills developed by Shayetet 13 over the years and now methodically transferred to Sayeret Matkal. The naval commandos, for their part, spend months studying at Sayeret Matkal's base and engaging in joint training exercises for crossing bodies of water, especially the Suez Canal, with all the rules, problems, and challenges that such missions entail.

The technique that Israel's naval commandos have developed is for Shayetet 13 soldiers to swim quietly across the canal carrying a rope, clamber onto its stone-paved western bank, and stretch the rope between the two banks of the canal so that Sayeret Matkal's commandos can cross while connected to the rope and thus withstand the strong currents.

Digli, Sayeret Matkal's new commander, is not familiar with Shayetet 13 and its abilities, but he is a quick and creative learner. He concludes that in order to keep the soldiers' shadows as small as possible when they cross the canal, they should use small "Mark 1" rubber dinghies instead of the larger, standard "Mark 3" variety. Digli sends his men with the dinghies to the IDF Intelligence Directorate's technology unit, so that its inventors can quickly develop a manual pulley block for the back of the boat, to make the boat travel forwards or backwards. This will allow them to sail at a reasonable pace and in total silence across the Suez Canal. It's an impressive gizmo, as even the skeptical Ze'ev Almog is forced to admit.

Operation Bulmus 3 is therefore the first joint operation between the two Israeli commando units along the Suez battlefront, and its primary aim is deterrence: to prove to Egypt that the IDF is capable of pulling off sabotage operations deep inside Egyptian territory.

Like always, Sayeret Matkal insists on setting up a series of observation posts across the area of the operation, overlooking on the western side of the Suez Canal. For a few days, they do not detect any suspicious movements, and the operation is approved for execution on May 10, 1969.

The commander of the operation is Ehud Barak. Barak, who will rise to become one of Sayeret Matkal's most celebrated commanders, leading some of its most important covert operations, is Menachem Digli's deputy. The naval commandos swim across the canal in perfect silence, extending a rope from one bank to the other, and the thirteen-man force crosses in Mark 1 boats attached to the ropes, taking up position on both sides of the road. Before the operation, Sayeret Matkal ran drills for several scenarios in the scale model outside the unit's base, working on the assumption that Egyptian military vehicles would approach from the north or south, alone or in convoys, or maybe from both directions simultaneously.

First Lieutenant Uzi Dayan is in charge of the ambush along the road, and he is the first to spot an Egyptian truck coming from the south and approaching the "crate": the sterile zone that the Israeli forces have created, securing the perimeter against any unwanted intruders, where the action will happen. He can hardly contain the adrenaline pulsating through his body in the seconds leading up to the truck's arrival, when he can order his men to jump into action together. When the truck finally reaches the "crate," the stretch of road blocked by Sayeret Matkal's soldiers on both sides, Uzi utters the magic word, which encapsulates the dream of every commando participating in missions like these, practically a cry of joy: "FIRE!"

Long bursts of rhythmic gunfire shred through the silent night. The Egyptian vehicle takes a serious hit but keeps limping on, its tires and engine screeching, until it grinds to a halt some 160 feet later. Another hail of bullets, and Uzi picks his soldiers up off the floor and breaks into a sprint toward the truck.

Uzi is Sayeret Matkal's mile-run champion, and also much more determined and competitive than his men, and he closes the 160 feet between him and the bullet-ridden, smoldering truck in thirty seconds flat. Nobody cares about searching for the driver, who has disappeared into the dead of night: they are scouring for Egyptian soldiers, because the purpose of the operation is to prove to the Egyptians that the IDF can reach the Egyptian side of the canal and perform combat operations as easily as if operating on Israeli territory.

Barak rounds up his officers and soldiers and they make their way back to the rendezvous on the western bank of the canal, where the naval commandos are waiting. They quietly board the Mark 1 boats as if mounting warhorses and silently sail back east, to the Israeli side of the canal, a subtle smirk of victory indelibly smeared across their faces.

Who could possibly suppress a victorious smile after such perfect execution? And who can imagine that this exact same smirk will fatally undermine the success of the next mission, Operation Bulmus 4?

* * *

As Sayeret Matkal's commander, Menachem Digli revels in the success of Operation Bulmus 3. Even if the operation was somewhat modest, not exactly on the scale of the legendary rescue mission in Entebbe, which is still a few years away—a success is a success. However daring and inspirational as the unit's reconnaissance operations are, its combat missions are still in their infancy. And each success is a sure-fire guarantee that the next mission will get a go-ahead.

Bulmus 4 is launched three days later, on May 13, 1969, along the same stretch of the Suez Canal as the previous operation, under the watchful gaze of the commander of the IDF's armored forces in the Sinai.

Eighteen Sayeret Matkal soldiers, most of whom took part in Bulmus 3, set out on the mission. The idea is to replicate the same action plan as before: lying in ambush on the western side of the canal and then opening targeted fire at Egyptian military vehicles driving along the road.

Three "Mark 1" dinghies, each carrying six Sayeret Matkal fighters and one Shayetet 13 commando steering the boat, make their way to the western bank of the canal (the Egyptian side). But then they discover that few Egyptian soldiers are already calmly awaiting them at the exact point where the boats are supposed to make landfall. The presence of Egyptian soldiers, no matter how brave, is no reason to call off a Sayeret Matkal operation, and Digli decides to divert it half a mile to the south. In any case, the planned site of the ambush is dangerously close to the location of the previous ambush, just three days ago.

Shayetet 13's commander, Ze'ev Almog, takes little comfort from this mission's proximity to the time and place of Operation Bulmus 3. He is also worried that they have not devoted enough time to observe and study the Egyptians' routine, like the last time. The soldiers are also crossing the canal in the same boats they used three nights earlier, whereas swimming would have minimized the risk of detection by the Egyptians—and none of this contributes to the prospects of the commando units' second operation in one week.

Indeed, the troops quickly discover another Egyptian force waiting for them across the canal, in a camouflaged position on the western bank—and the Egyptians unleash heavy gunfire at the Sayeret Matkal force on the boats, right in the middle of the canal, from close range.

The first Israeli soldier hit from Egyptian fire is First Lieutenant Chaim Ben-Yona. He is killed on the spot, falls off the boat, and disappears into the murky waters. A Sayeret Matkal rescue force, situated on the eastern (Israeli) bank of the canal, responds with massive gunfire toward the Egyptian ambush, and thus the commandos on the boats find themselves caught in the middle, trapped in a ferocious gunfight. They are sitting ducks, drenched in the water spraying all around them and watching with horror as bullets rip through their rubber dinghies. There is nothing left for them to do in these bullet-ridden boats, so they dive into the water and retreat, swimming under Egyptian fire, to the Israeli side.

One of the soldiers wading through the canal, Benjamin "Bibi" Netanyahu, is not exactly an Olympic swimmer. With military gear loaded on his back and a weapon hanging around his neck, Netanyahu slowly starts to drown—putting him on track to become the second Israeli fatality that night. But two comrades in his team realize that he's in trouble and call in a naval commando to rescue him. Only the bubbles swimming up to the surface reveal where Netanyahu is drowning, and the naval commando rips through the water toward him. He dives down, throws Netanyahu's heavy backpack and gun off his back, and drags him back to shore. The naval commando who saves Netanyahu's life is seriously injured two months later in the raid on Green Island but returns to military service. And Netanyahu? As they say, the rest is history.

* * *

This whole stretch of the Suez Canal looks like an Independence Day fireworks party. Egyptian artillery fire gets closer and closer to the Israeli commandos on the shore, but their withdrawal is held up because nobody can imagine leaving without finding Chaim Ben-Yona's body. Almog, Shayetet 13's commander, orders his naval commandos to dive back into the water and search for the body. But there's no chance of finding it now. Digli rounds up his men and leads them in a brisk march east, through the swamps, to get away from the canal before first light, so they won't become target practice for Egyptian artillery. The strenuous march through the bogs, especially after such a grueling night, is exhausting and pushes most of the soldiers to the brink of collapse. At first light, they reach the sand dunes beyond the swamps and are picked up by Israeli armored personnel carriers and taken away to the area's HQ base to debrief after the hardest night of their service to date. But it will not be the most difficult night overall: the conquest of Green Island still lies ahead.

Chaim Ben-Yona's body is washed up by the powerful currents and discovered twelve miles south, on the Egyptian side, a few days later. Chaim is Sayeret Matkal's first-ever combat fatality. His parents are asked to cooperate with Sayeret Matkal and the army and never utter the name of their son's unit. The Egyptians return the body to Israel a few days later, and Chaim is laid to rest in his kibbutz in the Galilee.

Chaim Ben-Yona was born in 1947 in a displaced persons' camp in Germany and reached Israel with his parents after a long and arduous trek through hell. The difficulties of the journey must have been what made his parents separate when they reached Israel. His mother met and

married a man called Willy, who adopted Chaim as his own. After studying at the kibbutz school, Chaim performed a year of voluntary service
and then enlisted into Sayeret Matkal. Back in basic training, the staff
called him "the general" because he seemed to come straight from central
casting, thanks to both his physicality and unmistakable aura of leadership. Obviously he also caught the eye of his commander, who sent him
to officers' school even before finishing his fifteen-month training course.
Some of Chaim's comrades are convinced that the main reason he was
sent to officers' school early was that there was no room for another future
general in one squad, besides the squad commander. He was supposed
to go on vacation after finishing officers' school but preferred to join the
team that embarked on the luckless operation known as "Bulmus 4."

Chapter 4

OPERATION BULMUS 6—THE RAID ON GREEN ISLAND, JULY 1969

It's the summer of 1969, the War of Attrition along the Suez Canal is escalating, and the hot blood pumping through commanders' veins on both sides is stopping anyone from thinking straight. The blitzkrieg of the Six-Day War has given way to a grueling slog of erratic reprisals.

The War of Attrition is out of sight and out of mind, but it's claiming a heavy price. In less than a year and a half, 367 Israeli soldiers have been killed along the Suez Canal, the fatality rate of a bona fide war, while life in Israel continues as normal and hardly anyone on the home front, relaxed and sated, pays attention to the fact that the Six-Day War did not really end after six days of war.

Israel's wars during this period, like the First Lebanon War that will soon follow, are usually not initiated by experienced and knowledgeable prime ministers, but by generals or dominant defense ministers who used to be senior officers. They dictate the IDF's timetable, based not necessarily on a clearly defined military doctrine but often on their own personal whims and overinflated military egos.

On July 10, 1969, an Egyptian force raids the eastern bank of the Suez Canal, charges at the Israeli tanks parked on a pier south of Port

Tawfiq, kills eight Israeli soldiers, injures nine, and abducts one soldier (whose body is returned shortly afterwards). It is now clear to all the officers responsible for the IDF's deterrence—from Brig. Gen. Raful Eitan, the head of the Paratroopers and Infantry Brigade, and downwards—that Egypt needs to be given a taste of its own medicine. Or more specifically, that Israel must immediately rehabilitate its deterrence, which was struck a mortal blow in the surprise Egyptian incursion.

Military or diplomatic deterrence is not something that can be measured, and nobody can calculate it from the number of fatalities or attacks on enemy war materiel or infrastructure. But common sense, as understood by the IDF's generals and seen through Defense Minister Moshe Dayan's one working eye, states that in order to restore Israel's deterrence, won with blood, toil, and tears in the Six-Day War, they will have to plan and execute an operation unlike anything that has ever been seen in the Middle East, or indeed, the whole of military history.

Since the outbreak of the War of Attrition, every time the Egyptians have struck the Israelis in the gut, the aggressive IDF response to punch the Egyptians back on the nose has been led by a range of forces from different IDF units (such as the Paratroopers and Golani)—but Sayeret Matkal and the Shayetet 13 naval commandos have been getting increasingly large pieces of the action. Sayeret Matkal, because it is already involved on this red-hot front and wants to translate its abilities into missions that are not completely about reconnaissance. And Shayetet 13, because it is looking to make a unique contribution and understands that the Egyptian front along the canal is an excellent place to try.

When the War of Attrition erupts, Shayetet 13 has been around for nineteen years and is still searching for its calling and identity. It has an established training program, some of the finest soldiers in the IDF, and a long heritage as a fighting-fit military unit with commando capabilities, especially at sea. But according to its official mission statement, its main job is to dive into and penetrate enemy ports, so it is still missing proper fighting credentials. In the background, of course, is the memory of its failures during the Six-Day War, and unless it finds its true destiny, the unit is fated to wither away, unable to attract the budgets and resources from the IDF that any special forces unit needs in order to thrive.

Ze'ev Almog, Shayetet 13's eighth commander, assumes command with a strategic decision of immense significance: he must find a cast-iron mission for the unit, to express the full range of its abilities and of course make a mighty contribution to the IDF and Israel's national security in the wars that lie ahead, and in the intervals between them.

As fate would have it, the War of Attrition presents Shayetet 13 an excellent opportunity to implement Almog's ideas. When the war starts, its commandos perform several missions, mostly at sea, and transport Sayeret Matkal for land missions reached by crossing bodies of water. Almog insists on taking Shayetet 13 another massive step forward and transforming it into a unit that not only ferries soldiers into battle or infiltrates enemy ports in order to sabotage ships, but is also fit for combat engagements on land itself. This is supposed to be the winning formula that will finally give expression to its fighters' abilities: not just as frogmen, but as a dual-purpose commandos who can silently navigate through the water toward targets on land, discard their oxygen tanks, flippers, and flotation devices, slip out of their wetsuits, and transform themselves into a land force as good as any commando unit in the IDF, if not better.

Indeed, Shayetet 13 operates alone to pull off the raid on Al-Adabiya in the southern Gulf of Suez (Operation Bulmus 5) on June 21, 1969: a daring attack on an Egyptian guard post, in which twenty-five Israeli naval commandos manage to kill thirty-two surprised Egyptian soldiers. The Israeli force suffers only two light injuries. Obviously the success at Al-Adabiya gives Almog and his naval commandos a huge injection of vigor—and it bolsters the Israeli military's confidence in Shayetet 13's abilities.

All that's left for Almog to do is to keep beefing up these capabilities, to prove that its success at Al-Adabiya was no fluke.

Sayeret Matkal, in contrast, is perfectly tailored for reconnaissance missions. No man would dare to trample on its turf, and it has stood out for over a decade under the deft leadership of its vocal commanders. The challenge is how to transform it into a regular military commando unit, even at the cost of endangering its soldiers, who are constantly mobilized for reconnaissance missions by military intelligence and the chief of staff—instead of limiting it only to reconnaissance operations in the shadows, where despite the lack of sunlight, Sayeret Matkal already knows how to reap a precious harvest for which demand is insatiable.

Menachem Digli, who becomes Sayeret Matkal's fifth commander almost two years after the Six-Day War, brushes this question completely aside. If you ask him, the unit should be wherever there is live fire. Over the years, he has become something of a celebrity in the Israeli intelligence world, but he cut his teeth in the Golani infantry brigade, where he reached the rank of company commander before becoming irresistibly drawn to Sayeret Matkal and being its commander. For him, like Almog (his counterpart in Shayetet 13), the War of Attrition is a once-in-a-lifetime opportunity to give a serious shake to all the hackneyed old conceptions about the unit's mission and work.

Digli put his money where his mouth is. He shoves Sayeret Matkal into every possible commando operation along the Suez Canal and personally commands most of them. He also pushes the unit into a dizzying number of diverse operations all around the Middle East.

Almog and Digli see eye-to-eye, therefore, that the units under their command must be the tip of Israel's spear on the southern front. But besides an inspirational mode of leadership, each of them also has a massive ego that might easily blow up any collaboration to benefit their respective units and the IDF at large. Digli takes over as commander from Uzi Yairi, a good friend of Almog's from their university studies, and the personal chemistry between Yairi and Almog was a strategic asset in the burgeoning relationship between the two units. Nevertheless, although there isn't as much as a spark of love or even affection between Digli and Almog, they make sure on their short but bumpy ride together to maintain a relationship as chilly as the waters of the Suez Canal— but to avoid the sort of blow-ups that might scuttle their units' winning collaboration.

* * *

After the Egyptian attack on the parked tanks at Port Tawfiq, triggering a need for an appropriate and much more painful Israeli retaliation, the IDF, on the orders of Chief of Staff Haim Bar-Lev and at the suggestion of Raful Eitan and Ze'ev Almog, chooses Green Island as the next target for the rehabilitation of Israeli deterrence.

Green Island is an Egyptian maritime fortress, built on the edge of a cliff on the southern extreme of the Suez Canal, one and a half miles south of Port Tawfiq, near the town of Suez, as part of the British Army's efforts during the Second World War to defend the canal. Around the island is a breakwater, partially surrounding a reef, and several bunkers in order to defend the southern mouth of the canal from German attack by air or sea. The Egyptian military inherited the site from the British and fortified it, building a compound around 475 feet long and 225 feet wide. According to Israeli military intelligence, it holds anti-aircraft guns (with 85mm and 37mm shells), fourteen machine guns, a radar to monitor anti-aircraft fire, and a garrison of 80–100 Egyptian soldiers, mostly from one of the Egyptian military's most celebrated commando units. Penetrating Green Island will therefore be the toughest military challenge on the Suez front. If you ask the Egyptians, it's a target that an army whose commanders have their heads screwed on would never dare to attack.

And as confident as the Egyptians are that the island is completely impenetrable, the IDF's top generals—especially Bar-Lev, Almog, and Raful—are convinced that nothing like an attack on this island, of all places, will inflate Israel's deterrent power to proportions that will leave the Egyptians and the whole world in no doubt: you don't mess with the IDF.

When Chief of Staff Bar-Lev asks Almog whether he can take charge of this mission, Almog hesitates. Not because he is cowed by the magnitude of the challenge, but because he knows that he doesn't have enough men. Major General Ariel Sharon, the head of the IDF Training Department at the time, who still has a habit of meddling in every commando raid on the drawing board, whispers to Almog that first he should say, "yes," and only then find the forces to top-up his men. Sharon advises him to take the Paratroopers, but Almog is already used to working with Sayeret Matkal's soldiers and prefers to take them instead.

This time, despite the immense complexity and the unprecedented dangers, the raid on Green Island is Shayetet 13's job, including the intelligence, the planning, and the command in the field. But the high-stakes mission on Green Island will require, according to early planning, around forty soldiers, a supply that Shayetet 13 is still unable to produce, and so Almog and Raful agree that there is no choice but to call in Sayeret Matkal. Digli gives the decision an easy green light. He would obviously prefer for Sayeret Matkal to lead the operation, as it has led every operation it has participated in, but he also knows that he cannot refuse Raful's request, with the chief of staff nodding vigorously over his shoulder, because that would set back everything he has been doing to build up Sayeret Matkal as a targeted fighting force by several years.

Digli decides to contribute two teams to the mission: the most veteran team, which is just about to be released from service, headed by Shlomo Tirosh; and the youngest team in the operational division, Team Amichai. The three teams in the middle, engaged in the unit's reconnaissance missions on a daily basis, continue going about their intelligence work. That's on the explicit orders of none other than Chief of Staff Bar-Lev himself, who forbids them to participate in the raid.

From the moment that Sayeret Matkal understands that it is embarking on a dangerous, even lunatic mission, the men's adrenaline starts working overtime and the stubborn competition over a "good spot in the middle of the team" pushes all fears, concerns, and nagging doubts aside. That's what it's usually like with soldiers, and it's definitely the case with Sayeret Matkal, especially among its handful of officers.

Digli shows up at Sayeret Matkal's base on July 11, 1969. And when he tells his officers about the planned mission on Green Island, not only do they swiftly make their peace with the massive insult of being demoted from the leading force to the role of auxiliaries, second in importance to

Shayetet 13, but there immediately erupts a different battle: who will get to take part in the mission, and who will stay behind?

Hanan Gilutz, for example, is about to complete his military service and has already registered to start studying at the Technion, starting July 20. But when he hears about Green Island, he marches over to Digli's office, finds him sucking the end of the last cigarette in the box, and informs him that if there's a mission—he's in. Digli furrows his brow, shoots a glance at Hanan, sees the grit he loves so much, takes one last puff of his cigarette butt, and nods: "You'll join the mission as Shlomo Tirosh's deputy." Hanan, who has already seen a thing or two in his military career and knows that Green Island will be like nothing he has ever seen, is as thrilled as if he were told that he's the new commander.

The Sayeret Matkal force assigned to the mission comprises three squads:

Shlomo Tirosh's squad, including Hanan, Noam, Kuki, Nahum, Shuli, and Maayani.
Ehud Ram's squad, including Danny, Amos, Uri Gilboa, Yigal, and Uri Matityahu.
Amitai Nahmani's squad, including Shai, Yoram, Boaz, Nimrod, and Yuval.

* * *

There are eight days to go, and still no comprehensive plan for Sayeret Matkal and Shayetet 13. There are no joint drills and nobody has a clue who's meant to do what and how. All they have is the martial adrenaline frothing in the veins of Raful, Almog, and Digli, and the quiet approval of Chief of Staff Bar-Lev. It's a race against time, because any operation to restore deterrence should be pulled off as soon as possible, or else it will fail to achieve its full desired effect. That's how these things work.

They go to Shayetet 13's base: Digli, Ehud Ram, Shlomo Tirosh, and Hanan Gilutz. Shayetet 13 is still Sayeret Matkal's older and slightly shy sister. Its naval commandos have the sea and the Crusader fortress at Atlit, and of course they know how to dive, swim, and fight and have raised some of the finest and most celebrated warriors in the IDF—but the Israeli army still doesn't take it completely seriously because it lacks an impressive operational record or a concrete mission statement. As a result, the unit is seriously underfunded. That's why Sayeret Matkal ends up acquiring Zodiac boats, an upgrade on Mark 5 boats, for Shayetet 13 and completely transforms its ability to attack by sea. It also develops tracking systems for these boats, in the pre-GPS era, using radar-based triangulation technology from the Israeli Air Force. This technology will help to direct the vessels on their way to Green Island.

There are also profound cultural gaps. The naval commandos are used to operating deep underwater, two at a time at most, without any means of communication. Sayeret Matkal's forces have always worked in relatively big teams, mostly in perfect synchrony and coordination.

When Sayeret Matkal's officers step into Ze'ev Almog's office, they meet the Shayetet commandos who will join them for the mission. There is excellent chemistry between the soldiers in the two units, which has developed over the years in countless joint operations. The ego wars, as it happens, are raging one level above the soldiers, at the level of the unit's commanders, without tarnishing the friendly relations between the fighters themselves.

And if the two commanders, Digli in Sayeret Matkal and Almog in Shayetet 13, are still missing a tiny spark to ignite their impossibly tense relationship, Digli, an expert in conquests of every sort, deploys his famous charm against Almog's secretary. She has plenty of chiseled and tanned suitors, of the sailor variety, but this long-legged, handsome officer steals her heart on the spot. And when Digli struts into Almog's office, he has already conquered one small but envy-inducing target.

On Almog's desk is a model of Green Island. In hindsight, it turns out that the proportions of the structures and the distances between them are wildly inaccurate, nearly causing a massive disaster in the operation itself. But for now, the subsidiary targets on the island are divvied up between the squads, and they discuss the best ways to reach the island, building a training program in the short time they have left.

Shayetet 13 has just a few days to come to grips with a new challenge: to dive as a group, without polished and rehearsed protocols, in their IDF combat fatigues, wearing full battle gear and carrying their weapons. Once again, the hasty solution to this challenge given the crammed timetable will end up causing delays on the day itself.

Over the next two days, Shayetet 13 and Sayeret Matkal run separate drills on combat in built-up areas—and on Wednesday, July 16, the soldiers from both units set out to practice on a life-size model, using an old, fortified police station. This is a "wet run," using live fire with Kalashnikovs and RPGs, under the admittedly anxiety-inducing watch of Raful Eitan. During the drill, Shlomo Tirosh, the team commander and the most senior of the squad commanders, takes a hit from a piece of stone that ricochets off a wall, suffering an injury that will definitely put him out of action for this operation. As if Digli could see this coming, Hanan Gilutz, Tirosh's deputy, becomes the squad commander instead.

In the two days left until the operation, the soldiers are busy adjusting their webbing, waterproofing their gear, and as always in Sayeret Matkal, obsessively hoarding weapons: grenades, including phosphorus smoke grenades, and magazines loaded with tracer bullets, which carry a small pyrotechnic charge. Raful notices one of the soldiers carrying tracer bullets and forbids their use, so that the Egyptians on the shore won't realize immediately that the island is under attack. But Digli and Almog refuse to give up on the tracers, which are much more accurate in the heat of battle, and the issue is taken as high up as Chief of Staff Bar-Lev and Defense Minister Dayan. Israel's military and political leadership is deeply involved in preparations for the mission, perhaps because of a profound unease with sending men into such a well-guarded target with such little strategic significance for either Egypt or Israel. In any case, Bar-Lev approves the tracer bullets, and by the time he completes his order in his slow voice, the magazines are already loaded.

* * *

On Friday, July 18, the eighteen Sayeret Matkal commandos participating in this mission take off with Digli, their commander, to Rephidim, an Israeli airfield in the Sinai Desert, and from there travel by truck to Abu Rudeis in the western Sinai.

The next day, Saturday, July 19, the full teams from Shayetet 13 and Sayeret Matkal come together for the Chief of Staff's final briefing. Bar-Lev arrives to give the men a boost of morale but does the exact opposite. He tells the soldiers, in his slow and clear voice, leaving no room for doubt, that if the force suffers ten fatalities or more, the operation will be considered a miserable fiasco and the survivors will have to retreat at once. It's a chest-thumping pep talk that leaves the soldiers' jaws on the floor. Now they can't stop thinking about which of the forty soldiers in the room will fill the chief of staff's quota. All the men, from both Shayetet 13 and Sayeret Matkal, have seen their fair share of death-defying operations, including along the Suez Canal, and everyone understands that this one is much more dangerous than anything they have ever done. And they really don't need the chief of staff's body count to understand the magnitude and danger of their mission.

But this time, there's an added factor: even now, at the start of the War of Attrition, Green Island is accessible to Israeli fighter jets, and if needed, Israel can even send a squadron to obliterate the island or at least deal a crushing blow to its fortifications, weapons silos, and commandos. No fighter jets are scrambled, and in later years, people will ask whether Israel could have spared its soldiers' lives. But not right now. The soldiers and commanders preparing this raid have no dilemmas or doubts.

The IDF of 1969 believes that the psychological effect of landing Israeli commandos on the island and throwing them into face-to-face combat with Egyptian elite forces will be infinitely more effective than bombing the compound from the air. The chief of staff is upfront about the price that the IDF is willing to pay for the extra deterrence from a physical invasion as opposed to plain old airstrikes: ten men.

* * *

In the evening, Sayeret Matkal's men board the truck that will take them to their embarkation point at Ras Sedr. Hanan slips out of the cabin into the belly of the truck and opens the back door, to help his men hop out. On his left, he spots Danny. It's clear that everyone, without exception, is extremely tense and anxious, but there is something dark and gloomy in Danny's eyes, as if they can already see death—as if he has already received news of his own death, somehow, a few hours before it happens.

At exactly 16:00, the men sit down for their "Last Supper," as some of them jest with each other. Nobody can really manage to eat. Their nagging thoughts suppress their appetite. Yuval, a young soldier in Team Amichai, less than a year into his service, sits down between Amos and the older truck driver, a civilian employee of the military. "You got a ciggie?" Yuval asks the truck driver. "Give me one so we can enjoy the last smoke of our lives." The truck driver, a large-bodied man, quick to anger, can't get his head around this dark humor. "Don't you dare talk like that," he reprimands the young soldier. "A young and handsome guy like you . . . I'll give you a cigarette on condition you take that back." He whips a cigarette out of the box and flings it at Yuval, who grips it and lights it slowly, his expression gloomy, his eyes sunken as if swallowed deep into his head, and only the haze of white smoke wafting up to the clear skies of the Sinai seals the two men's unwritten deal.

Digli holds a roll call for his men on their way out. They must all jump on the spot with their webbing and backpacks, to check that their gear is completely silent and nothing will accidentally fall out. The commandos look like a small herd of buffalo: heavy, cumbersome, and drooping under their own weight. The moment of truth is approaching, and a mountain of doubts presses down on their shoulders, weighing them all down no less than the bulky satchels on their backs.

At 20:30, the whole force boards a dozen Shayetet 13 boats and sets out on its long voyage. Almog, the commander of Shayetet, guides them to the target using the tracking technology that Sayeret Matkal developed for this kind of operation. About two hours later, the boats reach a distance of a mile from the target. The boats carrying the Sayeret Matkal commandos—the "second wave," which is supposed to wash over the island only after the naval commandos in the "first wave" do their job—are tied to each other and bide their time out at sea. The boats carrying the Shayetet naval commandos advance another third of a mile, pour their twenty diving fighters into the water, and return to their original spot, to await the end of the fighting.

The naval commandos plop into the water and start swimming as a group toward their target, led by Dov Bar. The currents from the island are much stronger than expected, so they progress at a sea snail's pace. At a certain point, Dov decides to have everyone dive underwater, in order to not to keep getting pushed back by the strong waves, and also to minimize the risk of discovery. Shayetet 13 only came up with protocols for diving in such a large group a week earlier, so it is still not completely polished and this massively hinders the twenty naval commandos, who are used to diving with only one other partner.

The divers were supposed to reach the island at 00:30, to secretly create a breach in the barbed wire fence encircling it, and then to summon the Sayeret Matkal force to storm in, all guns blazing. But the Sayeret Matkal commandos have been waiting for over two hours in their boats, without any sign of life from the divers. Almog and later Raful try to contact Dov over the walkie-talkie but are met with radio silence. And the deeper the silence, the higher the top commanders' anxiety levels. The last opportunity to launch the mission, according to the official order, is at 01:30, and the second hands on Almog and Raful's blackened watches zip forward at the speed of light. That same night is the first-ever moon landing, and the commandos out at sea keep glancing at the sky, as if trying to make out Neil Armstrong and Buzz Aldrin in their white spacesuits taking one small step for man and one giant leap for mankind.

It turns out that Dov and his men were swept away by the undercurrents and were just one wrong move or two from missing their target altogether. Only Dov Bar's resilient and infectious spirit manages to overcome the arduous conditions. When he pokes his head out of the water and sees how far they have been swept away to the south, he yanks everyone above the water and whispers to them over the radio that failure is simply not an option this time, and together everyone manages to reach the bottom of the island, exactly to the designated point, in total silence and without getting detected, after a swim that feels like a dive through the seven circles of hell for three hours straight.

At this point, Dov is supposed to call in Sayeret Matkal, but inexplicably, he doesn't. The naval commandos start cutting through the fence in order for the forces to stream into the compound, when Ilan suddenly spots an Egyptian soldier right in front of him, unleashes a quick burst of gunfire from the hip, and kills him. Ilan's gun has the same effect as a conductor's baton, giving the signal for the concert to begin. Massive Egyptian gunfire erupts from every corner of the island, and Sayeret Matkal's commandos are still bobbing at a faraway point at sea.

Obviously Sayeret Matkal's unplanned absence from the island forces the naval commandos to fight alone and exhibit breathtaking levels of bravery. And Sayeret Matkal's soldiers, waiting for several nerve-racking hours on the boats with every imaginable nightmare scenario running through their minds, finally spot the red flares decorating the skies above the island, a surefire sign of the tracer bullets that Raful so forcefully insisted on banning.

The soldiers switch on the boats' engines at once and break out in a roar toward the island. They need to reach exactly the breach in the barbed wire fence around the island that the naval commandos opened just a few minutes earlier (with a delay of over an hour from the original plan), marked out for them with a glaring flashlight. It's hard to imagine the rush of adrenaline that pulses through the commandos' bodies in these few minutes, brusquely chucking their fears overboard.

* * *

The Shayetet force has already seized the top of the bridge on the island, and Sayeret Matkal's role is to cleanse the fortress. Ehud Ram's squad is supposed to empty the roof of the fortress, while Hanan Gilutz and Amitai Nahmani's squads are supposed to purge the two flanks of the yard—Hanan on the right and Amitai on the left. They leap off the boats at lightning speed and sprint toward the roof of the fortress, from which they will descend into the inner courtyard. One naval commando serves as a human ladder for Sayeret Matkal's men to scale the roof. Ehud Ram's squad, which reaches the roof using this human ladder maneuver, huddles near one of the adjacent artillery positions, when Ehud suddenly asks for a quick update. Digli, the commander of the Sayeret Matkal force, urges him to keep moving. Ehud, a tall man, slowly gets up, takes one step forward, maybe two—and immediately collapses. A hail of Egyptian bullets from the artillery position cuts his young life short.

Uri Matityahu, his deputy, who doesn't clock that his commander is down but realizes that Digli's order is not being executed, takes command of the squad and starts pushing it forward on the roof. When they start advancing on the next artillery position, a lethal burst of gunfire rips through them and kills Danny, who falls into the water, and another Danny from Shayetet 13. Uri keeps moving on the roof, chucking grenades ahead of him and shooting at every machine gun post and artillery position greeting him and what's left of his squad.

When Hanan, having also scaled the roof from the naval commando's broad shoulders, charges forward with his soldiers, it doesn't cross his mind that Ehud Ram, the first Israeli commando to climb up to the roof, has already been killed from a bullet to the head and that his deputy, Uri Matityahu, has taken over as the squad commander.

All around him is a pandemonium of gunfire and explosions, but Hanan is in the zone, calmly determined to achieve his mission, come what may. He takes his men—Noam, Kuki, Nahum, Shuli, and Maayani—to the right of the roof and is shocked to discover that the yard is tiny and looks nothing like the soccer pitch in the model on Ze'ev Almog's desk.

Hanan is worried that in this yard, only half the size of the penalty area on a soccer pitch, his and Amitai's squads might end up shooting each other. He lobs a grenade into the yard, to avoid any unpleasant surprises on their way down from the roof, and orders Maayani to scale down the metal ladder attached to the wall. One of his men has a split second of hesitation and Hanan sends him to provide cover and climbs down first into the yard, followed by the rest of his squad.

On the right is a room with a window looking out on the ladder. Nachum and another soldier enter the room and "cleanse" it, filling it with gunfire without even checking whether it is occupied. Before storming the next room, Hanan tells Shuli and Kuki to get into position on either side of the door. Kuki throws a grenade inside, and when they hear an explosion, they leap inside and immediately come under fire. But at that fateful second, Hanan realizes that the boom came from the room behind the wall in front of him, which belongs to Amitai's squad, and that Kuki's grenade is yet to explode. Hanan hollers at them to stop. The two buffalo, buckling under their webbing and backpacks, run back to the door and get stuck for a millisecond in the narrow opening, unable to budge in or out, until they finally manage to wriggle free, an instant before the grenade explodes. They enter again and cleanse the room.

Yuval and Nimrod are at the rear of Amitai Nahmani's squad. Nimrod first, Yuval second. They climb down from the roof into the courtyard and pass the first room, which should have been cleansed already. Shai is already there, and Nimrod draws his attention to a hunched figure in the room, trying to escape. Nimrod opens fire from a distance of three feet, sending the man flying back inside. Nimrod presses himself against the wall, Yuval joins him, and they both brace to cleanse the room just as they have practiced dozens if not hundreds of times.

After the grenade explodes, Nimrod shouts at Yuval to turn left, and he himself takes a right. But in the corner of his eye, he spots another grenade flying in an arc toward the doorway that they are about to enter in a couple of seconds. It's unclear who chucked it, but from the way it flies through the air, Nimrod thinks that there is no chance it will make it into the room, but will land on the floor right in front of them. Nimrod then crouches down, with his back to the ladder, hoping that his seawater-soaked sneakers, pressed to his face, will give him some basic protection from the imminent explosion. He bends over as low as he can, his hands shielding his head and groin, as a secondary layer of protection. Now he knows exactly what's going to happen, and he has no way of stopping it, besides the prayer that has only half escaped his lips when he hears the explosion. Yuval is closer than him to the site of the impact and is flung backwards, against the wall next to the ladder, the deafening roar of the grenade explosion suddenly putting an end to his anxiety—and to his life. There's no doubt: in his death, blocking the shockwaves and flying shrapnel, Yuval ends up saving Nimrod's life.

Nimrod realizes that his role in this battle is over, and that his job now is to get the hell out with Yuval's body as quickly as possible. He can't feel any pain—that will come later—but he understands that his left leg has been decommissioned. He gets up for a moment, strokes Yuval's head, and pulls his webbing and weapon off him. He's a medic now, a combat soldier no more, and he tries to haul Yuval on his back and to climb back up the roof. But this is far too tall an order for him now, and he shouts out for his comrades on the roof to climb down and extract him and his dead friend.

Hanan and his squad continue cleansing room after room along the right-hand wall of the yard. Some of the rooms are closed and Hanan shoots the locks on the doors to open them. Some of the rooms are occupied by Egyptian soldiers. They are all killed. While the rooms are cleared out, the gunfire from Amitai's squad's tracer bullets starts to get dangerously close to Hanan's soldiers, and he shouts at Amitai to stop.

* * *

The overall situation of the Israeli force is still unclear. Both Sayeret Matkal and Shayetet 13 seem to have a few men down, with many of the others injured in the initial stages of the raid on the island. Digli advises Almog to halt the fighting and start treating the many casualties. Raful, located out at sea in the floating command post, agrees and orders Almog to start evacuating the wounded. But in the meanwhile, Uri Matityahu's incomplete squad comes face-to-face with two Egyptian soldiers scrambling up from the yard toward the last artillery position. Uri orders his soldiers to start lobbing grenades at them, which blow up piles of ammunition at one of the artillery posts. A ferocious explosion rips through the island, unleashing a ringing noise in the ears of the soldiers on the roof—a noise that will accompany them for the rest of their lives.

Digli instructs the squad commanders to check that nobody's been left behind and shouts at Hanan through his megaphone to start packing. It turns out that Danny from Sayeret Matkal is missing. Amos tells Digli that he might have flown off the roof into the water, where the slope is steep and slippery. Digli walks around the perimeter of the roof, shining a flashlight in every direction and eventually discovers a soldier lying far below him on the edge of the water, his wetsuit covering his torso. It's Danny. Digli orders Yigal, Uri Gilboa, and Amos to climb down from the roof and take the fallen man's body to the boats.

Hanan and his squad unleash a heavy burst of gunfire at the positions on the roof, over on the far end, and start retreating. They scale the fortress roof and then go back down to the boats, back to Ras Sedr.

* * *

The time is 02:45. July 20, 1969. Slightly over an hour after the battle began. Over the radio, a cacophony of messages between the boats, and between the boats and the command center on the shore. And in the distance, behind them, a massive Egyptian bombardment of the island in a desperate bid to eliminate the Israeli force that has long since set sail in Shayetet 13's commando boats toward safe harbor. And then finally—an almighty explosion brings down some of the structures on the island, from the bombs set on a timer by the Israeli force before it fled.

When the first glint of daylight spills into the gulf, a pair of Israeli choppers appear over the horizon and lift an injured soldier off one of the boats.

Uri Matityahu, attached to one of the last boats leaving the ravaged island with the Israeli withdrawal, along with a few naval commandos, is sure that the hard part is behind him. But the Egyptians have other plans and keep bombarding the island and the surrounding sea. Shrapnel from one of the Egyptian artillery shells hits his boat, which quickly starts losing air. And Uri realizes just as quickly that for the rest of the journey, over three miles, he's going to have to swim. At least he still has his flippers . . .

The distress calls to the other boats in the area are no use. Nobody picks up that they're in trouble. Uri and the other commandos start swimming in along what they think is the quickest route to shore, but the ferocious currents in the Suez Gulf sweep everyone south instead of east, and at 04:45 they find themselves drifting further away from land, not closer. Luckily, someone alerts the command center to the presence of six soldiers in the water, and two helicopters are dispatched at once to rescue them with a "teabag maneuver," lifting them out of the water. All this happens under incessant Egyptian bombardment, in broad daylight. It's not a simple task to spot the swimmers in the water, and they split into two trios, to make it easier for the pilots to track them. After a few misses, the choppers manage to lift the six soldiers to safety.

At 06:15, the boats sail into Ras Sedr—and into the open arms of Chief of Staff Bar-Lev and Defense Minister Dayan. But they arrive bearing bad news, of dead and injured men. The big-boned truck driver from the soldiers' "Last Supper" stands among the generals on the beach, trying to find the blond soldier to whom he gave a small cigarette and a big telling off, the one who said that it was the last cigarette he would ever smoke. The driver gazes helplessly at men as they disembark, to prove to himself and to the world that it was *his* cigarette that saved the soldier's life. Amos, who witnessed this little scene before the mission, walks up to him, his legs failing him. "He's dead," Amos tells the driver.

"Who's dead?" asks the driver.

"The guy you're looking for," Amos replies.

The driver falls to his knees, throws his head between his massive palms, and screams at the heavens: "Oh God, oh God! I told him not to say that!" He can't stop crying, and his tears leave a small puddle in the sand.

The force suffers six fatalities: three from Shayetet 13 (Haim, Yoav, and Danny) and three from Sayeret Matkal (Yuval, Ehud Ram, and another Danny). Two of the six fatalities are from Kibbutz Ein Harod in the Jezreel Valley, which also contributed a third soldier to the same mission: Shai. And these two men have something tragic in common: Haim's younger sister happens to be Danny's girlfriend. In one impossibly difficult and bitter night, Tamar Shturman loses both her brother and her boyfriend. It's a sad, painful, and all-too-Israeli story.

Haim is the third fallen soldier in his family, the third of three audacious warriors to fall in battle. His grandfather, Haim Shturman, after whom he was named, was one of the founders of the HaShomer defense organization in Mandatory Palestine, who was killed in 1938 while searching for a site for two new kibbutzim in the Beit She'an Valley. Chaim the naval commando's father, Moshe Shturman, was killed ten years later in the War of Independence, when the young Chaim was one year old. And now the family grieves the loss of the third Shturman.

Hanan approaches a small hut on the outskirts of the military compound at Ras Sedr and opens the door. He is greeted by the sight of six bodies still wrapped in their black wetsuits, which will soon be swapped for white shrouds. Six young men who contributed to the chief of staff's quota, storming their target in boats and returning home in coffins. And none of their families will dare to ask the questions that are begging to be asked, about whether this operation was truly necessary. That's Israel in 1969, which accepts the loss of life with sorrow but pride.

On Sunday, July 21, the State of Israel bows its collective head at the funerals of the six fallen soldiers from Green Island. The rhythmic melody of the gun salute reminds the survivors of the barrages that rang in their ears just the night before, and a flicker of a smile of satisfaction with this operational success overcomes the tears that fill up in their eyes but refuse to drop, because tough commandos from Sayeret 13 and Sayeret Matkal aren't supposed to cry. At least not in this day and age.

And when the bereaved families are invited to visit Shayetet 13's base in Atlit, and Yoav's mother starts weeping bitterly, a woman walks up to her: Atara Shturman, the grandmother of Haim Shturman, who also fell in the same operation. "I too am allowed to cry," says Mrs. Shturman, "but despite everything I've been through—I won't. Crying doesn't help. Please stop crying. Get ahold of yourself and toughen up."

But not even Mrs. Shturman's eyes can remain dry when another of her grandsons, Amir, is later killed in a military operation near Egypt's Great Bitter Lake. Not even Atara Shturman, as hard and unbreakable as a rock, can stop the tears when the fourth generation is killed in combat.

Chapter 5

OPERATION ISOTOPE—THE SABENA FLIGHT HOSTAGE CRISIS, MAY 1972

The following chapter somewhat deviates from the rest in its language due to the personal involvement of one of the authors—Avner—in the operation described henceforth. Avner's unique optics therefore manifests itself in first person.

It's May 8, 1972, and we, Team Itamar,[1] are heading back from shooting practice at a range near Sayeret Matkal's base in the early evening. The base is dark and empty. All the other squads are training somewhere else.

This is a period of relative calm. It has been two years since the end of the War of Attrition, and no other war can be seen on the horizon. Terrorist organizations are in the grips of a protracted crisis: the IDF's closure of Israel's borders, and pressure from Arab countries not to use their territory as a base for attacks, is making it hard to pull off terror attacks on Israeli soil. The IDF believes that this situation will lead to spectacular attacks beyond Israel's borders, such as airplane hijackings.

---

1 Avner Shur, one of the authors of this book, was one of the soldiers in this squad.

On September 6, 1970, terrorists from the Popular Front for the Liberation of Palestine hijack two passenger planes: an American TWA flight from Frankfurt to New York, and a Swiss Air flight from Zurich, also to New York. The planes are forced to land at the Dawson's Field airstrip in Zarqa, Jordan. The terrorists also try to hijack an El Al flight from Amsterdam to Israel but fail. (One of the hijackers, Patrick Argüello, is shot by security guards, and his accomplice Leila Khaled is arrested and handed to British authorities in London.) Two of the terrorists, having failed to board the El Al flight, hijack a Pan Am flight instead and fly it to Beirut and then Cairo. Three days later, a British-owned BOAC flight from Bahrain is also hijacked and forced to land at Zarqa. The three aircraft forcibly landed in Jordan are blown up on the ground after the passengers are taken off.

In light of this, the IDF puts together a plan called Operation Isotope, which aims to thwart attacks on the international airport at Lod or on other Israeli targets using hostile aircraft—unidentified planes, booby-trapped planes, or hijacked planes full of kidnapped passengers.

In the case of hijacked airplanes, the plan contains two main components: forcing the plane to land, and then eliminating the hijackers and seizing control of the aircraft. The IDF command centers that are supposed to take part in such an operation all study the plan in intimate detail. Some units also perform drills, so that by May 1972, the plan is clear to most of the actors who will have to execute it if the time comes.

* * *

On the night of May 8, 1972, Second Lieutenant Shai Agmon comes running to our tent and shouts, "Where's Itamar?!" We point toward Itamar Sela's room in the officers' quarters and send him there. Barely thirty seconds go by, and Itamar shows up at the encampment and orders us to take all of our personal gear and board a truck to Lod Airport, as Ben-Gurion Airport used to be called. A hijacked airplane has landed at Lod, he briefs us—and we're going to liberate it.

It is clear to everyone that we, the fearsome Team Itamar, after a year and a quarter in the IDF, can and must free the hijacked plane, and God help anyone who tries to take this operational treat away from us. It is also clear that an infinite number of questions are going to hitch a ride with us to Lod Airport, along with a cacophony of doubts. Because after all, Sayeret Matkal has older and more experienced squads, not to mention the dozens of on-duty and reserves officers who inevitably pop up from every corner of the earth at moments like these, each demanding his fair share of the action. Not this time. This operation is ours—it belongs to Team Itamar, and nobody is going to push us aside.

The D-400 truck speeds toward the airport, the driver ignoring the traffic lights and "STOP" signs along the way, and comes to a screeching halt at the entrance of the terminal. A quick-footed photographer from the *Maariv* daily newspaper is already lying in ambush and snaps pictures of the heroes from Sayeret Matkal. The grit and confidence that they will project from the front page of Israel's highest-circulation newspaper will definitely help to steady the Israeli public's nerves.

As far as we're concerned, and as newspaper readers will agree, the squad plastered over the next-day's front page is a winning team. It is an image that's worth over a thousand words and a hundred daring deeds.

In the business lounge of the departures hall, we immediately recognize a swarm of people from the newspapers and TV. Defense Minister Moshe Dayan, much shorter and thinner than we imagined him, wearing khaki pants pulled almost all the way up to his chin, give him the look of a dwarfish duck. IDF Chief of Staff David "Dado" Elazar, meanwhile, is much more impressive in reality than he looks in newspapers. Rehavam Ze'evi, the head of IDF Central Command, is also there, and so is "our" Ehud Barak, the commander of Sayeret Matkal. He is only a young major and still has a boyish face, but nobody in the VIP lounge that moment has any doubts about who is running the show.

When Yoni Netanyahu arrives, the commander of our company, he takes us immediately to one of the hangars behind the terminal building in order to hold a drill of the operation to seize control of the plane.

The Boeing-707 plane operated by Belgium's Sabena airline took off from Brussels at 13:34 en route to Lod, via Vienna. On board were ninety-nine passengers, half of whom were Israelis, and another ten crew. The hijackers boarded the plane in Brussels, three of the terrorists boarding together and sitting in the same row, and the commander of the cell boarding separately and sitting somewhere else. Until they were identified as terrorists, they called each other by the Israeli names written in their forged passports, albeit in Arabic accents.

After a refueling stop, the plane took off from Vienna at 14:30, and in the late afternoon, in the skies of Yugoslavia, the hijackers seized control. Midair, the hijackers sent a message that they planned to land the plane at Lod and threatened that unless terrorists were released from Israeli detention, they would blow up the plane—with everyone inside.

At 19:05, Sabena Flight 571 landed at Lod.

The operation had been planned in Beirut by senior Fatah commanders, using the code name "Black September." Operating out of the Lebanese capital, the cell contained two men and two women: the commander, Ali Taha Abu Snina (a.k.a. Abu Nidal, but in the radio dispatches he called himself Captain Rafat); Abed al-Aziz Atrash, who traveled on a forged passport under the name Zakariah Graid; Rima Isa Tannous ("Zakia"), with a passport under the name Sarah Biton; and Theresa Halsa ("Samira"), who flew under the name Miriam Hasson.

It's 20:00, and Yoni starts to lead a dry-run on an El Al plane in the hangar. We are supposed to run in two columns behind the plane and along both sides, clamber onto the wings by giving each other a leg up, and after quickly opening the emergency doors above the windows, break into the plane, one column turning right and the other left. Both teams are supposed to purge the terrorists with Uzi submachine guns, firing from the hips.

The drill leaves us shocked and speechless. Having fired our fair share of Uzi bullets, entering a plane full of hostages with such weapons is like trying to hit two individuals in a stadium full of spectators: the terrorists will die in the end, but it's hard to believe passengers won't also be hit.

Ori Tabenkin suggests, with Team Itamar's signature dry sarcasm, taking over the plane with a recoilless rifle, a lightweight artillery system. If we're going to war inside an airplane, then let's go all the way!

The serious look in Yoni's eyes, and in those of all the other commanders flooding the area, immediately extinguishes our doubts about the operation and sends us to practice again, and again, seizing control of the empty El Al plane. But the more time goes by, the more our undisputed status as the team that will lead the takeover becomes, well, disputed. A gentle but steady trickle of soldiers and officers from higher-ranking squads starts streaming into the hangar. When they heard about the hijacking, they all instinctively got in their cars or hitched a ride and came to the airport in order to push us to the back of the line. And if that were not bad enough, every El Al plane landing in Lod in the meanwhile has had at least one ex-Sayeret Matkal sky marshal on board, and they were naturally ideal candidates for the mission thanks to their rich firearms experience and intimate familiarity with aircraft mechanics.

We can't stop running calculations in our heads, how many of us will get to take part in the mission in the end, and slowly but surely, with each new military hero who struts into the hangar, we understand that this time, the glory—if any exists—will be hogged by others.

* * *

In the meanwhile, on the runway, the pilot of the Belgian airplane starts reading through the plane's radio a list of 317 terrorists jailed in Israel, whom the hijackers are demanding be released.

During that evening, the Israeli government decides not to release terrorists. In order to buy time, it orders the plane to be grounded by deliberately sabotaging its landing gear.

At around 21:00, the Belgian ambassador and one of his aides roll up at the airport. The IDF intelligence chief, Major General. Aharon Yariv, sends an envoy to welcome them, reassure them, and convince them to go back to their offices, in order not to add any unnecessary pressure.

At 21:30, the head of the IDF Operations Directorate, Major General. Israel Tal, who is commanding the whole operation from the terminal, orders the head of the Infantry and Paratroopers Corps, Rafael "Raful" Eitan to go to the runway and command the forces on the ground.

Starting around 21:15, for about an hour, IDF intelligence director Aharon Yariv negotiates over the radio system with "Captain Rafat," the chief hijacker, either through the pilot or directly with him. He acts cautiously and stresses the difficulty of rounding up terrorists from prisons on different sides of the country in such a short time, as the hijackers are demanding. During the negotiations, the terrorists demand a generator and a refueling tank. El Al's deputy CEO explains that without electricity, they will lose radio signal with the plane, so it is decided to accept the terrorists' first demand. They are also sent a refueling tank, but it stands untouched under the plane's right wing until the end of the operation.

Soon after 22:00, a team of airport technicians accompanied by Sayeret Matkal soldiers are dispatched to the plane, in order to cause a leak of hydraulic fluid from the front wheels and thereby ground the plane, at least for a while. After that, the pilot announces that he can feel the plane sinking slightly to the left. The hijackers hope that the problems will be fixed quickly and pressure the pilot to take off. But it's impossible.

At 22:20, the hijackers announce that they have activated a time bomb, which will explode within the hour. Soon thereafter, IDF intelligence chief Aharon Yariv hands over the negotiations to Victor Cohen, a senior interrogator at the Shin Bet, who appeals to the terrorists in fluent Arabic and tries to persuade them not to set off the bomb.

At 22:30, the Belgian pilot manages to hint over the radio that the emergency hatch in the cockpit is open. It's the first clue that he is expecting some sort of initiative by Israeli forces, which is not far off: once it becomes clear that the negotiations are going nowhere, it is decided to prepare a night-time mission to seize the plane. After consultations, the IDF chief of staff orders operations chief Major General. Israel Tal to ready a team from Sayeret Matkal, which has already practiced for similar missions. At the same time, senior IDF officers and an El Al engineer inspect a similar plane to the hijacked aircraft and report to the defense minister and army chief that in their assessment, an operation to rescue the hostages is absolutely possible.

The head of the IDF Operations Directorate instructs Ehud Barak, the commander of Sayeret Matkal, to study this similar plane in the hangar and prepare a force to take over its hijacked counterpart. Two options are prepared. One, to launch the operation when the chief of staff gives the green light. Two, to launch it on the orders of the head of the Infantry and Paratroopers Corps if the kidnappers start killing hostages.

Barak's plan to seize control of the plane is as follows:

The forces will drive as far as the staging ground, some 650 feet behind the plane, and from there, they will advance on foot in two columns of twelve soldiers apiece. They will move, of course, through the hijacked plane's blind spot, so they won't be seen. The soldiers will climb onto the plane's wings from both sides using ladders and will break in through the emergency doors and the escape hatch under the cockpit. Inside the plane, part of the force will advance on the cockpit, and another part will advance on the tail, shooting the hijackers on the way.

At midnight, Ehud Barak and Itamar Sela show up at the hangar and we go outside with them to plan the takeover of the hijacked plane. By now, it's clear that we won't be in the first team breaking into the plane. And in truth, we find that slightly reassuring. The thought of seizing control of a passenger plane with Uzi submachine guns is unsettling, but we still play the game till the end. Barak, beaming incredible self-confidence and spouting IDF jargon that nobody completely understands, looks exactly like the ultimate military leader with whom we would want to embark on a mission. On any mission.

We board two army pick-up trucks and take a long detour through a nearby village in order to reach the airport runway exactly behind the plane, so that the terrorists won't be able to see us. The pick-up trucks stop over a mile behind the plane, and then we lie down on the hot asphalt and wait. The pressure and tension accumulate, as expected, in our bladders, and every few minutes someone gets up, crawls around thirty feet away, and crouches to empty his bladder. The small artificial lake by the side of the runway, "Lake Sabena," slowly widens.

At 02:00, we receive news that Defense Minister Dayan is about to visit our post. He arrives almost alone, with a single bodyguard, and is immediately whisked a few steps ahead of our force so that Barak and Itamar can update him on the first option for the assault, with the Uzis, which everyone already understands is impractical and won't go ahead.

In cases like these, the option currently on the table remains the only option until replaced with a different, better option, and for Dayan, the defense minister of the State of Israel, this is the operational plan that he is being asked to approve. He tries to shorten his diminutive shadow as much as possible and lies on his back in the warm puddle, the manmade "Lake Sabena," which has been filling up as the night goes on. Dayan speaks fluent Arabic, and the Arabic curse words that escape his lips can be heard almost as far as the plane. A smile spreads across his face for the first time, revealing his pearly white teeth in the dark, moonless night.

By the time Dayan leaves the site, dripping a yellowish liquid that definitely isn't water, we know for sure that we are not invited to the party that will begin sometime soon. And when dawn breaks over the runway and the Sabena plane, leaning slightly to one side, the thrill of adventure that kept our senses sharp overnight gives way to the unpleasant sensation of the asphalt heating up beneath us and the searing embarrassment at having missed such a golden opportunity.

* * *

And as we lie down on the asphalt, battling sleep and thoughts about fading glory, the diplomatic and operational channels are working overtime. Fearing that sunrise will give away the presence of our forces and make a secret, surprise takeover of the plane impossible, Barak, Raful, and Major General. Tal ask the chief of staff several times for permission to break into the plane—but in vain. Since there is no green light from the government, Barak receives an order at 04:00 to retreat to the staging ground and leave only a small security team and lookouts from our team by the runway, including a sniper.

Why does the Israeli government not approve a night-time raid? The reasons seem to have been threefold: the growing possibility that the hijackers might agree to leave Israel, completely exhausted from the events of the last two days; Moshe Dayan's assessment that there is still no immediate or tangible danger to the passengers; and finally, the ever-present desire to try to exhaust every diplomatic option before embarking on a military operation that might end in multiple fatalities.

Since there is no meaningful progress in the night-time negotiations with the hijackers, and since the terrorists—contrary to Dayan's threat assessment—keep threatening to blow up the plane and demanding the arrival of the Red Cross, compounding the pilot's gloomy reports, it is decided to send a representative of the Red Cross to the airport. At around 05:30, two Red Cross representatives arrive at the terminal and report for duty to the defense minister, Moshe Dayan.

Dayan, who has decamped in the meanwhile to the terminal manager's office with the chief of staff and other senior officers, explains to the Red Cross representatives that their only role is to relay messages between the two sides: they must not take any initiative or stake a position. The defense minister also emphasizes repeatedly that they were called here at the request of the terrorists, not the State of Israel.

* * *

At 06:00, one of the Red Cross representatives is sent to the airplane in order to receive the kidnappers' demands. He drives there in his own car, a Red Cross flag on the roof, with an airport vehicle traveling ahead of him as far as the beginning of the quiet runway. From there, the Red Cross representative continues alone, and at 06:25 he reaches the plane. At 07:00, the go-between returns to the terminal holding a new list of demands from the terrorists: the release of 317 terrorists, as before; the release of another nine terrorists whose names they "forgot" to convey in the original list; the repair of the airplane; and free passage for the hijackers to Egypt. The Red Cross envoy emphasizes that the hijackers, who did not let him enter the plane (they spoke while he stood on top of the refueling vehicle), seem tough and completely serious.

Dayan instructs the Red Cross officials to return to the plane and check with the hijackers how exactly they want Israel to satisfy their demands. By the afternoon of 9 May, the Red Cross envoys make another few round trips to and from the airplane. Israel explains that is ready to negotiate with the terrorists only about getting them out of the country, but the hijackers refuse and insist on the release of all 317 jailed terrorists (conveniently forgetting their earlier demand for the extra nine).

In the second round, a Red Cross representative is allowed to board the plane, to approach the entrance to the cabin, to see the terrorists, and to convey a message over a loudspeaker. He tries to reassure the hostages, telling them that the Red Cross is concerned for their safety. When the envoy returns to the terminal, he updates the Israelis that a "really grim mood" has gripped the plane. Some of the Israeli forces on the ground—not Barak's team, of course—are visible, and the terrorists are demanding that they move away from the plane.

Then, the commander of the Israeli Air Force, Major General. Motti Hod, has an idea: the hijackers are offered a three-way "package deal." Israel is willing to discuss, through the Red Cross, the release of Palestinian terrorists jailed in Israel in exchange for the release of Israeli prisoners of war in Egypt and Syria. The hijackers ask for time to convey the proposal to their headquarters. Their initial response is positive, but after a while, they backtrack.

At 11:30, after liaising with their headquarters in Geneva, the representatives of the Red Cross announce that they will not return to the plane. Later, they also demand a formal commitment that Israel will not use force as long as they, the envoys of the Red Cross, are still in the field. Dayan makes it clear to them that Israel has no intention of using force, but the situation might develop in a way that demands a military operation in order to save lives. At that point, a member of the airport's ground operations crew announces that the fuel in the generator provided to the plane is about to run out, and that the aircraft is about to lose its electricity and ability to communicate over the radio.

* * *

Even earlier, at 07:15, after Dayan hears the hijackers' demands through the Red Cross, he decides to prepare a daytime assault to seize the plane. Ehud Barak is called over to the IDF chief of staff, who gives him his instructions. This is when the head of Central Command suggests disguising Sayeret Matkal's forces as aircraft technicians, wearing white overalls.

The unit's soldiers, who have poured into the airport in a steady stream from every corner on the planet, have been training all morning for the possibility of a daytime assault. For target practice, they are using a Boeing aircraft purchased by Israel Aerospace Industries from TWA, an American company. The drills take place inside an El Al hangar. The unit's plan is totally different from the night-time plan, not least the addition of ladders and the fact that the option of breaching the plane through the hatch beneath its nose is no longer the main line of action.

For all this time, the Israelis still have no real-time information about what is going on inside the plane, besides reports from the lookout team watching from the south and the knowledge that there are apparently four hijackers on board, not three as originally thought (the pilot dropped a hint at 05:00).

At 12:08, after the head of the IDF Operations Directorate manages to persuade the Red Cross envoys to embark on one final mission to the hijackers and offer them a replacement generator, one of them surprises everyone by returning with the plane's pilot, Captain Reginald Levy. It turns out that the pilot was sent by the hijackers with an explosive belt, in order to illustrate the credibility of their threats to blow up the plane.

The pilot supplies invaluable information about the plane and the hijackers, including the following facts. The hijackers are two men, armed with pistols, and two women, armed with explosives and hand grenades. These grenades do not have safety pins, and have to be passed carefully from one terrorist's hands to the other's so that they won't accidentally explode. The two male hijackers, who occasionally take possession of the hand grenades, are stationed around the cockpit. One of the female hijackers is located with a bomb in the front-left section of the cabin and her accomplice is at the back. The pilot is unaware of her precise location. There are no seats behind the emergency exits. The hijackers are tense and restless and seem to be deadly serious about blowing up the plane if their demands are not met. The pilot also corroborates what can be seen from the outside, that the plane's back doors are occasionally opened for air circulation.

Captain Reginald Levy sketches a detailed map of the interior of the plane and the location of the hijackers. "You've got no choice but to give them the answer they want to hear," he says, adding in the same breath, "I know you can't actually do it, but I want you to promise them that they'll be able to get the terrorists jailed in Israel, and then they'll be willing to accept your conditions."

After Moshe Dayan and IDF Chief of Staff David Elazar return from consultations with their men, Dayan tells the pilot that he may communicate the following message to the hijackers: Israel will release the jailed terrorists; the released terrorists will be sent to Cairo on a plane belonging to a different airline. If the hijackers wish, they may be shown the plane and the released terrorists. When the released terrorists reach the airport, the women and children aboard the hijacked plane will be let go. As a condition for the implementation of this deal, the hijackers will allow food and water to be delivered to the hostages; at the same time, they will receive a replacement generator and the plane will be fixed and refueled.

The pilot informs the hijackers, through the radio in the control tower, that he has reached a deal with the Israelis and promises to return to the plane after confirming its details. The hijackers believe that a bargain has been struck.

* * *

In light of Captain Levy's fresh information, there is a sudden change in the plan to seize control of the aircraft. The new plan, the third of its kind, is guided by the belief that Sayeret Matkal's soldiers can simply walk straight up to the plane, using deception: by dressing up as technicians. The plan dictated to Ehud Barak is based on a force of sixteen Sayeret Matkal soldiers, under his command, who will reach the plane disguised as technicians and start "repairing" it. On the commander's signal (blowing a whistle), the soldiers will breach the plane through the emergency exits (two on each wing) and the two main doors on the left of the plane.

As for the force that will break into the plane, Barak deliberates whether to send Bibi or Yoni Netanyahu, and obviously neither brother wants to back down. In the end, he decides to send Benjamin "Bibi" Netanyahu, because the force contains soldiers from his squad. The force also includes four experienced El Al sky marshals, mobilized from the four corners of the earth and El Al planes landing at the airport during the crisis. Among the four is Moti Rahamim, the hero of the rescue of the El Al flight in Zurich in February 1969. In addition, the Paratroopers will prepare a force of fifty soldiers, who will wear prison uniforms and play the newly-released detainees if the terrorists insist on seeing them. A sapper squad will be on standby to check the plane and defuse bombs.

This is the first time that Sayeret Matkal has had to free hostages held by armed terrorists, and Barak is convinced that he must build the most experienced team he can get his hands on. And that's how we, Team Itamar, get pushed aside to the substitutes' bench and even further back.

There are two more issues at play. The plan is to seize the airplane using handguns, and only the most veteran members of the unit have practiced with them—and then there's the question of seniority. There is no way the commanders of the longest-serving teams, who have streamed into the airport in the meanwhile, will relinquish their piece of the action.

Barak runs the plan past the force and explains the method of breaching the doors and the division of labor inside the plane, running drills and giving the men the right gear. The two main maneuvers that they practice are how to breach the plane by opening the doors and how to storm down the aisle. The men are supposed to break into the plane using ladders, through the high-up doors at the front and back on the left side of the plane and the four emergency exits, two on each wing.

Opening the doors from the outside requires special preparation. The ladders must be steadied at a very specific angle in relation to the plane, both to allow the doors to be forced open and to take account of how they open outwards, so that the soldiers on the ladders won't be sent flying by the opening doors. In order to open the emergency doors on the wings from the outside, they will have to climb onto the wings, which are close enough to the ground to be mounted without ladders, and give the doors an extra-strong kick at a specific point in order to blast them open.

The men practice their technique for advancing down the aisle and battling the terrorists inside the plane while giving each other cover and identifying their targets, based on the knowledge and experience of El Al's sky marshals.

The soldiers who will break into the plane wear El Al mechanics' overalls, change shoes, and remove any identifying military symbols. They arm themselves with handguns from El Al security unit, hidden in the pockets of their overalls or underneath them, while the liaison and lookout teams take submachine guns and Kalashnikovs.

The team of "released detainees" from the Paratroopers are distributed brown prison uniforms from the Prisons Service. Under the "watch" of soldiers from their own brigade, they are boarded onto two buses and wait—alert and ready to go—near the terminal.

Two helicopters, a Sikorsky CH-53 Sea Stallion and an Aérospatiale SA 321 Super Frelon, with medical teams on board, land in the plaza opposite the terminal, on standby to evacuate the wounded. The ambulance and fire truck teams are briefed and sit in their vehicles, waiting for the signal.

After the drill aboard the TWA plane in the hangar, IDF Chief of Staff David Elazar briefs the men who will breach the plane's doors. Elazar instructs the men to break into the plane through the emergency hatch under the plane's nose as well. He climbs up to the control tower, to lead the operation from there. IDF operations chief Major General. Tal hitches a ride with the head of Central Command in his jeep, which will move behind the strike force in a way that will not cast suspicion on the "technicians" but will allow them to join them as soon as the gunfight starts.

* * *

At around 15:00, as a first step toward meeting the conditions of the deal, crates of food and tanks of water are sent to the plane under the supervision of a Red Cross official, but the hijackers refuse to allow the supplies onboard until the technicians come to fix the plane. The delayed arrival of the "technicians" has made the hijackers suspect that Israel is not living up to its side of the bargain or is deliberately dragging its feet.

At 15:30, the strike force starts moving toward the plane. We, Team Itamar, are still lying embarrassed on the hot, prickly asphalt behind the tail of the hijacked plane. The hot air of bravura that filled us with pride just a few hours earlier has long since been blown away. All that remains is massive disappointment and red marks all over our skin from the pieces of gravel on the asphalt.

The strike force advances on two tow-trucks with small El Al carts, along with another truck for the toolboxes and another small one for the ladders. It moves ahead at a snail's pace to the beginning of the quiet runway. Behind the force, slightly more than a mile away, are Major General. Ze'evi's command-and-control jeep and the bomb disposal unit.

When the strike force mounts the quiet runway, it crosses the Red Cross envoy on his way back from the plane. The Red Cross official stops the force, because there are seventeen technicians, not fifteen as agreed, and he insists on checking the matter with Dayan over his walkie-talkie. Dayan explains that the two extra men are the drivers and warns him not to delay the "technicians," because this will only make the hijackers mad. After Dayan hints to the Red Cross official that he might find himself responsible for the detonation of the plane or the cancelation of the agreement, he is convinced and the technicians proceed on their way.

At 15:40, the hijackers are informed from the control tower that the first group of "detainees" has reached the airport, with a TWA plane at their disposal. The hijackers are asked whether would like to speak with the "detainees" and whether the TWA plane can be brought any closer to the hijacked aircraft—and they respond in the affirmative.

At 16:05, the TWA plane that is supposed to fly the "detainees" is towed along the runway to a point nearly a mile northeast of the nose of the hijacked plane, close enough for the hijackers to see it but still at a sufficiently safe distance, as far as the terrorists are concerned.

At this point, the force stops, and the Red Cross representative approaches the plane, where he signals for the force to advance to a distance of just over 100 yards away. Here, he stops the force again. He and one of the plane's crew convey the hijackers' demand that the technicians approach the plane one by one and open their overalls, so they can show that they are not armed. Ehud Barak therefore clearly instructs his men that anyone with a handgun on his belt must hide it as best as possible. If someone opens fire during the inspection, the whole force must storm the plane, jump onto the wings without using ladders, and breach the emergency doors.

Having received these instructions, the "technicians" start walking one by one toward the plane. One of the hijackers sits holding a handgun by the open window of the cockpit and the plane's crew, standing on the tarmac, start frisking the "technicians." The crew discover that the men are armed with pistols but none of them react, apart from one. When he asks why the technicians are armed, he is told that the weapon is for self-defense and nobody is planning on using them unless they have to.

The soldiers, disguised as technicians, quickly assume their positions under the plane and start "repairing" it. At 16:24, after the terrorists' commanders confirm that they are ready to go ahead with the deal, Barak blows his whistle—giving the agreed signal to begin.

At once, all the soldiers in the strike force start working in unison. At the same time, the medical emergency vehicles and fire trucks speed toward the plane.

The rescue operation has begun.

* * *

The first duo that manages to break into the plane, through the front emergency door on the left wing, is Motti Rahamim and Danny Brunner, who smashes the door and opens it for his comrade. The door is breached, and the Abed al-Aziz Atrash, standing practically in front of them, opens fire. Bronner and Rahamim take shelter on both sides on the door, from the outside. Rahamim takes a shot at the terrorist—but misses.

While Atrash is shooting at Bronner and Rahamim, Omer Eran and Danny Arditi break through the back emergency exit on the left wing. Atrash is shot and killed.

Right now, Benjamin Netanyahu and Marco Ashkenazi break through the front emergency exit on the right wing and run into the hail of bullets that Rahamim is spraying at Atrash from the other side of the plane. They mistakenly assume that this must be enemy fire and immediately take shelter outside by the sides of the doorway.

Uzi Dayan's squad doesn't hear Barak's whistle and he has to order them specifically to jump into action, so at this stage they are still busy climbing up the ladder and trying to open the plane's back door. Danny Yatom's men clamber up a ladder to the main door at the front. Itzik Gonen tries to open the door, and Captain Rafat, the chief kidnapper, fires two shots at him from inside the plane, injuring him in his arm. Danny Yatom also takes a hit to the arm before he can enter the plane.

Ehud Barak is still on the tarmac, between the left wing and the back door, overseeing his squads' operations. Hezi Cohen, at the top of the ladder, manages to breach the back door in the meanwhile. Uzi Dayan storms in first, quickly checks the toilets at the back of the plane, and when he confirms that they are empty, he advances with Hezi toward the middle of the plane. Yuval Galili, the third man in this squad, stays behind and provides cover against any threats from the direction of the toilets. The squad's first task is to locate Rima, the terrorist who might have a bomb at the back of the plane. But she's not there.

A passenger sitting a few rows ahead signals to the Sayeret Matkal squad that the terrorist is sitting right next to her. Barak, who has boarded the plane in the meanwhile, orders Uzi to go and check this tip-off. Uzi moves ahead and the passenger points at the terrorist, Rima, sitting on the floor and holding a grenade without a safety pin. The startled terrorist begs, in English, not to be shot. Uzi orders her to open her hand, holding the grenade, finger by finger and takes the grenade into his own hand, finger by finger, so that the lever that activates it never leaves his grasp. With the grenade in his possession, he marches the hijacker to the back door and Galili takes her off the plane. Uzi and Hezi press ahead toward the middle of the plane, scanning the passengers as they move.

At the same time, Uri Koren from Danny Yatom's squad starts crawling up through the hatch in the plane's nose underneath the cockpit, when he suddenly sees a leg above him—a leg that he later discovers was Captain Rafat's. Koren shoots at the leg, and from the howl of pain piercing through the air he understands that he hit his target. He guards the opening and occasionally fires a bullet in the direction of the leg but avoids climbing into the cockpit, for fear that the hijacker is still watching the narrow and dangerous hatch above his head.

After eliminating Atrash, Motti Rahamim moves into the passageway between the seats and starts advancing on the cockpit. Suddenly, Rafat opens indiscriminate fire toward him from the cockpit (it turns out that he was not seriously wounded from Koren's gunshot). Rahamim advances on the cockpit, shooting all the way. Halfway there, he runs out of ammo and takes shelter behind a seat in order to swap magazine. By now, Danny Bronner is just behind him.

Itzik Gonen, with an arm injury, shoves his pistol through the narrow opening that he has managed to make in the front door and fires three bullets inside. Then he climbs down the ladder and tries to infiltrate the plane through the hatch in the nose. He soon gives up on this idea and moves to the back door, reporting to Barak that he has been hit. Danny Yatom stays on the ladder propped against the front door of the plane.

Omer Eran and Danny Arditi enter the plane and advance on the cockpit, following Bronner and Rahamim. Marko and Netanyahu, outside the doorway until now, also enter the plane and advance behind Arditi.

Uri Koren, still underneath the cockpit, fires a bullet in the rough direction of the chief hijacker. While Motti Rahamim reloads his pistol, Rafat leaps out of the cockpit and into the adjacent bathroom. Rahamim lurches forward and shoots at him, as does Bronner. Rafat is killed.

Uzi Dayan and Hezi Cohen advance on the middle of the plane from the back, performing a visual sweep of the seats in order to try to discover more hijackers, but they come up empty. They start helping to evacuate the hostages from the plane, women and children first.

Gonen, boarding the plane through the back door, hears from Galili that the back of the plane has not yet been swept. Despite being injured, Gonen checks the toilets, the kitchen, and the storeroom in the tail of the plane, but he too comes back empty-handed.

Netanyahu, Marco, and Arditi keep advancing on the cockpit and scanning both sides of the aisle, searching for the fourth terrorist and the bomb, which they know should be somewhere here. When they approach the end of the aisle, one of the passengers shouts that there is another female terrorist behind them, toward the tail. Hearing this, Netanyahu runs back and finds the fourth terrorist, Theresa. He frisks her clothes and bag to find a grenade or a bomb, but for now finds nothing. Theresa is manhandled forward, to the passageway between the seats and the toilets, for a more rigorous body search. This time, Rahamim finds a transistor battery—the power source for a bomb—in her bra. The soldiers try to speak with her in English, French, and Arabic in a bid to squeeze information out of her, but they receive no reply. It turns out later that she speaks Hebrew perfectly.

* * *

After the elimination of Rafat and capture of Theresa, Bronner and Rahamim's squad searches for Danny Yatom's squad, which was supposed to breach the front door but isn't there. Rahamim hears Yatom's gunfire from outside, shouts at him to hold his fire, and opens the door from the inside. Yatom scrambles onto the plane and asks whether the cockpit has been searched. After being told no, he opens the cockpit door and goes inside with Bronner.

Uzi and Hezi continue searching above and below the seats and helping to evacuate the passengers from the plane. Gonen advances on the middle of the plane and also sweeps the seats. In the first seat on the left, he spots a kind of explosive belt with a series of flat cells containing explosive charges, with two conductors poking out. Next to the belt, he finds piles of cigarette boxes. The boxes are searched, ruling out the possibility that they might contain explosive material.

After Theresa is seized, some of the passengers report that there might be another terrorist on board—a fifth one. Two facts support this theory. One, the soldiers heard gunfire from the front of the plane (in hindsight, this turns out to be a bullet discharged from Marco's pistol when he is forced to slap Theresa as she resists being hauled off the plane—injuring Netanyahu and Theresa herself). Two, they heard gunfire from the cockpit (this was from Koren beneath the cockpit, but since no one has made contact with him yet, nobody knows he was the shooter).

Ehud Barak, convinced that there is a fifth terrorist onboard keeping his identity a secret until the moment of truth, orders another sweep. Uzi and Rahamim therefore start searching the plane from the middle toward the back. Near the back of the plane, they bump into Gonen, who tells them about the discovery of the explosive belt. Uzi Dayan inspects it and neutralizes the charge by pulling the explosive material out of one of the fingers of TNT. He does all this while still holding the safety pin-less hand grenade he took off the terrorist Rima, firmly clutching the lever in order to prevent it from accidentally going off.

Meanwhile, Marco is sweeping the seats from the place where Theresa was captured, down to the middle of the plane. When he reaches Atrash's body, he spots a hand grenade lying next to him. He picks it up carefully and hands it to one of the soldiers standing in the doorway, so he can get it out of the plane. The other squads keep looking for the "fifth hijacker" and any other bombs, but there are none to be found.

* * *

The elimination of the hijackers on the plane takes precisely ninety seconds. The initial sweep of the plane takes a similar amount of time. During the sweep, the soldiers find two pistols, two hand grenades, and one bomb (a second bomb is found the next day, in a search around the plane). During the battle, some fifty bullets are fired by Sayeret Matkal, and around ten by the terrorists. In the gunfight, the two male hijackers—Rafat and Atrash—are killed, and one hijacker, Theresa, is wounded when Marco Ashkenazi's pistol accidentally discharges. In addition, two Sayeret Matkal soldiers are injured—Gonen, while at the top of the ladder by the front door, and Bibi Netanyahu, from Marco's stray bullet. Two of the hostages are seriously wounded. One of them, twenty-two-year-old Marie Holzberg, succumbs to her wounds about ten hours later.

And we, Team Itamar, lie on the burning asphalt, gazing longingly at the new heroes who stole our glory. And only when we hear gunshots do we sprint toward the plane, to help evacuate the wounded and maybe catch a heroic photo-op on the wing.

It's pandemonium outside the airport, as if the whole country has arrived to hail its latest heroes. When the crowds huddled at the airport's entrance start applauding us as we leave, exhausted and confused, we start to think that maybe we did play a small role in this success after all.

The whole of Israel is in a state of euphoria. The initiative, creativity, derring-do, and stunning execution inject a double dose of morale into the national bloodstream, and for the first time in history, Sayeret Matkal comes out of the shadows. Not officially, but in practice.

On the Friday after the operation, I travel to Kibbutz Asdot Ya'akov to see my girlfriend. When we enter the dining room, the whole kibbutz gets on its feet, giving me a standing ovation, applauding for the hero of the mission, Avner Shur, whose face was plastered over the front page of *Maariv* along with two other comrades. I discreetly ask my girlfriend to tell them that I didn't actually take part in the mission itself. "Stop being so modest," she snaps back in a whisper.

Chapter 6

OPERATION CRATE—THE ABDUCTION OF SYRIAN OFFICERS IN SOUTHERN LEBANON, JUNE 1972

On April 2, 1970, in the twilight of the War of Attrition on the northern front, an Israeli Phantom fighter jet flown by pilot Gideon Magen and navigator Pini Nachmani is downed over Syria. Two months later, in June, the Syrians down a Mirage fighter jet flown by air force pilot Boaz Eitan. The three men are taken into Syrian captivity and brutally tortured.

Sayeret Matkal, under Ehud Barak's command, sees itself as the obvious candidate to free the pilots and exclusively responsible for doing so. This sort of task appears nowhere in the unit's job description, but especially under Barak, it has become an integral part of its mission. Sayeret Matkal was founded as an intelligence unit with a very specific reconnaissance role, but every commander has striven to push it into commando missions—to harness its soldiers' capabilities for sensational missions that do not necessarily have anything to do with reconnaissance.

Barak is Sayeret Matkal's sixth commander and the first to have started his military career in the unit and gone the whole nine yards to the top. He is also the first commander to explicitly define the unit not only as a reconnaissance unit, whose actions are all top-secret, but also as a commando unit that should always be the IDF's top choice for commando operations on enemy soil or inside Israel, such as hostage rescue missions. As a young soldier, he learns that in the IDF, in order to turn a dream into an action plan, he would have to be forceful and assertive, and even slightly manipulative, which comes easily to him. Blessed with political instincts, Barak understands that there is no point submitting his plans for the unit for lengthy deliberations in the General Staff and dooming them in a long and fruitless decision-making process. Instead, he will simply present Sayeret Matkal's abilities and operational plans at every opportunity that pops up. Like this one.

Barak is a kibbutznik and begins his military service in a munitions unit attached to the Infantry Corps. Someone on the kibbutz gives him a tip-off that there is a new, super-secret, one-of-a-kind unit that is looking for creative, enterprising soldiers who can think out of the box, and Barak would surely fit the unit like a glove.

Ehud Barak arrives for a meeting at Avraham Arnan's home in north Tel Aviv. Both men are as short as their egos are large, and a large ego can often get in the way of a beautiful friendship. Not this time. The two men fall in love, not like father and son, but more like brothers in arms. This romance will experience many ups and downs in the future, but for now Barak, who steps into Arnan's garden as a junior munitioner, emerges an hour later as a potential future commander of Sayeret Matkal.

Barak has never been much of an athlete, just like Arnan, but he knows how to compensate for it with a whole arsenal of stellar qualities. From his first day in Sayeret Matkal, he stands out for his courage, his navigational instincts in the field, his leadership ability, his abundant creativity and of course his boundless self-confidence. In a unit that works in small groups, where each squad commander is a "chief of staff" unto himself given the circumstances, self-confidence is an indispensable resource, sometimes even more so than an actual weapon.

Moreover, even as a young soldier in Sayeret Matkal, Ehud Barak is a masterful politician, who looks up at the heavens and picks a place of honor for himself among the stars. He has always thought far ahead, and in every role, he has aimed not just for the next role but two or three steps ahead, if not more.

By 1963, aged just twenty and a half, Ehud Barak has already commanded Sayeret Matkal's first significant reconnaissance operation and shown off the resourcefulness, confidence, and courage that are only ever seen in division commanders and upwards. Failure in this mission would have spelled the end of the road for Sayeret Matkal and Arnan's long-running dream. But the operation is a huge success and Barak, practically still a child, learns to walk around like an equal with the chief of staff, head of the command, and intelligence chief, who all were biting their nails together in the command-and-control center, unable to believe until the very last minute that he could actually pull it off.

Less than a year later, Barak commands another unfathomably complicated, first-of-its kind mission, which is also a massive success—thus making him the commander of two of Sayeret Matkal's first missions, of supreme importance in the unit's formative years.

* * *

In the summer of 1972, Ehud Barak is wrapping up his first year as the commander of Sayeret Matkal. He submits a few options to Chief of Staff David Elazar for how Israel can free the pilots from Syrian captivity. Some of them look like they were lifted straight out of James Bond movies, and they are all turned down with a smile. "It's a non-starter," Barak is told.

Uzi Dayan, a senior squad commander, decides to pull off a maneuver and circumvent the chief of staff, going straight to his uncle, Defense Minister Moshe Dayan. The defense minister politely welcomes his nephew and Barak, his commander, and they tell him about the possibility of rescuing the pilots by storming the Mezzeh Prison on the outskirts of Damascus by helicopter. Some of the men in Sayeret Matkal soldiers know the three MIAs personally, and freeing them from captivity is not just a national mission but a personal calling and act of friendship.

But Uncle Moshe is not particularly impressed by Sayeret Matkal's grit and derring-do, either. He explains to the two young men that the captives are alive and healthy, that an opportunity will surely arise at some point to swap them for Syrian captives, and that a mission like the one they are proposing will only lead to more casualties and maybe even more captives, so there is no point launching any operation at this point.

But as fate would have it, the chief of the Syrian military decides to organize a series of tours for senior officers from his operations directorate along the Israeli-Lebanese border in order to study the terrain, for both defensive and offensive purposes. Word reaches an Israeli intelligence agent, and from him it reaches Barak and his officers, who receive the news with intense interest and excitement.

An operation to abduct senior Syrian officers from the northern border is definitely realistic and stands a shot of getting the chief of staff and defense minister's approval. And if they're lucky and the Syrian "fish" who fall into their net are sufficiently rich in rank and role, they might just be suitable payment for the Israeli pilots rotting in a Syrian jail.

* * *

The first patrol, it turns out, is planned to take place on Mount Dov (what the Arabs call the Shebaa Farms), on the foothills of Mount Hermon, and a Sayeret Matkal force sets out to conduct observations and choose an exact location for the ambush. In the end, they pick a turning in a dirt track scaling the mountain on the Lebanese side. They assume that the Syrian convoy will slow down at this bend, giving them a chance to stage an assault and catch the officers.

The codename chosen for these abductions is "Crate," and what is later numbered as the first one goes ahead on June 14, 1972. The Sayeret Matkal force, commanded by Ehud Barak, positions itself at night around the bend on Mount Dov and eagerly awaits the Syrian officers. But then they receive an order to pack up, and the team is forced to return to base embarrassed, even though Barak is convinced the cancelation was arbitrary and unnecessary.

A few days later, it turns out that the Syrian patrol has moved to the westernmost stretch of the Lebanese road along the border, parallel to the Israeli road running along its northern border. And thus, on June 19, 1972, Operation Crate 2 is launched, once again commanded by Barak and his deputy Yoni Netanyahu. For the Netanyahu family, this is a family event, because Yoni's younger brother Iddo is a soldier in force pulling off this incursion. It's unclear whether anyone in the IDF's high command is aware of this snafu—two brothers from the same family are not supposed to participate in the same operation on enemy soil—but these are the days before the Yom Kippur War, and the army and the unit are not as sensitive about these cases as they will soon be. The third brother, Benjamin "Bibi" Netanyahu, completed his military service a few days ago and is getting ready to go to and study in the United States.

This time, there is a strong sense in Sayeret Matkal that "we're gonna do it," and whenever this happens, there is always a stampede of commanders demanding to take part in order to secure their own slice of the glory that will surely follow the operation. And when they lie in ambush overlooking the Lebanese road, someone suddenly lights a cigarette. Tzvika, the operations officer, simply can't fight the urge. Ehud Barak, wedged behind a Lebanese boxthorn, snaps at Tzvika's partner, "Omri, tell him that if he doesn't put out his cigarette at once, this is the last time he'll ever light a cigarette in his life."

A goodhearted Lebanese shepherd stumbles on the area of the ambush with his flock of sheep and quite easily spots the Sayeret Matkal commandos bending over behind the bushes that have not quite grown enough to hide the bulky muscles popping out of their camouflage. Iddo Netanyahu grabs the shepherd and signals to him, slicing his hand across his throat, what will happen to him if he dares to even open his mouth. A fellow soldier, sharing the same bush with Iddo as cover, crouches to shoo the shepherd and his flock away, and the team hunkers down again between the bushes.

Even before the shepherd and his flock disappear over the horizon, the soldiers hear the sound of vehicles approaching from the north. Less than a mile away from the ambush, the Syrian officers' convoy comes to a halt, and behind them, a complete surprise: an armored Lebanese vehicle, equipped with a cannon. Yoni reports this to Barak, who passes this on to Chief of Staff Elazar, sitting in the command-and-control center. Elazar consults with the head of Central Command, Motta Gur, and the pair astonish Barak and his men by ordering them to scrap the operation because of the Lebanese back-up. Stunned and disappointed, Barak goes berserk over his walkie-talkie and tries to convince Elazar that it will be a walk in the park to overpower both the Syrian officers and the armored vehicle. One of the soldiers taking part in the action who is from Team Bronner, in charge of the recoilless rifle, jumps into the conversation and reports that the armored vehicle is sitting right in his crosshairs. But Elazar, a stubborn and coolheaded man, puts his foot down and refuses to authorize the abduction given the latest developments.

The commandos lock their weapons and watch helplessly as the convoy passes right under their noses on the road. It turns out, and this too comes as a surprise, that the chief of the Lebanese military is also in the convoy—hence the addition of the Lebanese armored vehicle.

The Sayeret Matkal force regroups in a forest near Akhziv, back in Israel, to debrief with the chief of staff and head of Central Command. Barak, used to strutting around with chiefs of staff and other VIPs as if they were buddies since he was a second lieutenant, takes an axe to the military hierarchy and starts bluntly and loudly berating the chief of staff and the head of the Northern Command, because he thinks the command-and-control center didn't understand the conditions on the ground and the cancelation was ridiculous and totally unnecessary. Uzi Dayan backs him up, promising that the next time, the force will have to report back "untruths" and proceed with what seems eminently doable on the ground.

To everyone's astonishment, despite his superior rank and perhaps because of his affection for Barak and the unit, Chief of Staff Elazar responds with a restrained smile. "I want to tell you a story," he says. "Two bulls, one old, one young, reach a green pasture. From a distance, they see a herd of plump cows enjoying the sunshine and the grass. 'Let's each take a juicy cow and get down to business,' suggests the young bull. 'No, my friend,' says the old bull. 'We have all the time in the world. We'll get through the whole herd, cow by cow, until we get through them all.'" The joke fails to land, and the disappointed commandos get in their vehicles and return, dejected, back to base for the second time, without the cows of Elazar's imagination and definitely without the Syrian officers.

* * *

Sayeret Matkal's frustration is short-lived, however. According to concrete intelligence, another tour of Syrian officers is supposed to take place in another two days, on June 21. The operation to abduct them will be called "Crate 3" this time, and the preparations are the most serious and comprehensive of all the Crate missions.

The feeling in the unit is that it's now or never.

Sayeret Matkal, true to form, occasionally beefs up its forces regardless of its specific operational needs. In Crate 1, the team sets out on foot; in Crate 2, it also sets out on foot, in much greater numbers; but this time, the unit practically sends a whole battalion, commanded by Yoni Netanyahu and his deputy Uzi Dayan. Ehud Barak decides to stay back in the command-and-control center this time with the chief of staff and his generals, to make sure a Crate-2-style cancelation won't happen again.

Besides all their regular gear, the IDF equips the commandos in Operation Crate 3 with a whole fleet of tanks, stationed on high alert on Israeli soil, and for the sake of mobility also two half-tracks. The idea is to pull off the ambush with vehicles this time, instead of on foot like the previous times, and so Sayeret Matkal's main force boards two vehicles. One of them was captured from the Jordanian army during the Battle of Karameh a few years earlier and reassigned to Sayeret Matkal; the other is Itzik the quartermaster's own personal car.

The ambush is supposed to take place near the Lebanese village of Ramyeh, at a point where the Lebanese road parallel to the border almost touches its Israeli equivalent, with only an old rickety fence between them. The Sayeret Matkal force moves into position at night on the Israeli side of the border, hiding its vehicles among the trees of Moshav Zarit's groves, while Yoni approaches the fence with his squad to see how and where they can step over it and send in the troops as soon as the convoy appears.

At around 07:30, the force receives a "red-hot" alert that the Syrian officers are approaching the area of the ambush. The vehicles, which are supposed to be the tip of the spear of the attack, move into position next to a faucet near the fence in the grove, and the soldiers, in order to disguise their intentions, pretend to be repairing a broken pipe. Meanwhile on the Lebanese side, the territory between the road and the border fence starts filling up with Lebanese villagers who have come to work their fields. The two drivers, Omri and Avner, already have their heavy right feet on the gas when a crackly update comes in over their radio systems, canceling the alert. But Yoni asks his drivers to keep their engines running. He senses that this time it's going to happen, come what may.

It turns out that one of the many Lebanese villagers over the fence tipped-off the convoy about the suspicious movement of unfamiliar vehicles in the area, and the supremely cautious Syrians are trying to turn around and drive back in the direction they came from.

But not this time. The two Sayeret Matkal vehicles come to life with a roar of the engine, mount the road, and speed toward the road on the Lebanese side of the border. Only 550 yards of Lebanese territory stand between them and the enemy convoy of three vehicles: a Lebanese jeep, a blue Austin police car (probably also Lebanese), and a luxury Chevrolet Impala. Crammed inside the Chevrolet are seven senior Syrian generals: one brigadier-general (*eamid*), three colonels (*eaqid*), and three lieutenant-colonels (*muqdam*), two of whom are pilots.

When Uzi Dayan and his two vehicles cross the border and reach the convoy, the Lebanese soldiers escorting it and some of the Syrian generals are already standing outside their cars, weapons drawn. Their bewildered expressions attest to their complete confusion, trying to make sense of this rapid chain of events, as two strange vehicles screech to a halt right in front of them and an armed posse spills into the road. The element of surprise, when combined with grit and artful aggression, makes all the difference. In a flash—one second, maybe two—the Syrian officers start to understand the dramatic turn their lives are about to take.

Dayan leaps out of the car first, even before his driver Avner manages to find the brakes with his trunk-like leg. He runs around from the right, another soldier taking the left flank. Dayan yells in Arabic, which he learned from the Arab workers on his family farm, "Stand up and hands in the air!"—and is astonished to see the men running away in shock. He shouts again for them to stop (maybe they didn't understand his Arabic?), but they keep retreating, inviting a brief and unfriendly gunfire right at their feet.

Dayan's gunfire gives the signal for the battle to commence. The force comes under fire from behind the Lebanese jeep, aimed at Dayan and his men. In an instant, a row of Israeli Kalashnikovs comes flying up to shoulder level, like wind instruments in an orchestra, bringing down three Lebanese gendarmes. The others all disperse to the four winds once they understand that only by fleeing or surrendering can they stay alive.

"ONE MAN DOWN!" comes a cry in flawless Hebrew. Zadok, a reserves soldier, is lying by the side of the road after taking a piece of shrapnel to his right thigh. The blue Lebanese Austin manages to quickly maneuver around the commotion and escape along the road, to the east. Dayan believes that he can catch it sprinting, but it's no use.

Yoni Netanyahu and Dayan approach the Chevrolet Impala and order their drivers to pull the Syrian officers who are still there out of the car and tie them up. Only the brigadier-general, wanting to set a personal example for his men, stubbornly refuses to play along with his captors until he realizes the sheer size, in width and height, of the mountain of a man looming over him and understands that sometimes you can play the role of David, but not when the man playing Goliath is *that* big.

Zadok is given first aid by Dr. Shmulik Katz, the unit's in-house medic, who then goes over to treat two Lebanese gendarmes. One of them returns his soul to his creator the moment the doctor's angelic hands touch him.

Muki Betser arrives with his team aboard two half-tracks and sets out to sweep the area north of the road. Suddenly, the force comes under fire from the south. Muki and his men jump out of their vehicles and move into position, but the enemy is nowhere to be seen. It turns out that the bullets came from Danny Bronner's team, trying to catch one of the Lebanese gendarmes, who was running away. Muki's team is ordered to search for the blue Austin, which escaped into the village, but the men can't find it and loop back to the site of the conflagration.

Two Syrian officers—one colonel, who is the head of Syria's combat intelligence, and another lieutenant-colonel—managed to escape on foot through the thicket around the road and disappear. Sayeret Matkal's commandos load the five remaining Syrian officers, one Lebanese captain, and four surviving Lebanese gendarmes into the Israeli vehicle, and off they go back to Israel.

Danny Bronner gives the order to shoot the tires of the Syrians' luxury Chevrolet Impala and leave it as a memorial on the Lebanese road, but Dayan is horrified by the thought of giving up on such a fancy car, gets the engine running, and drives it like an off-road vehicle into Israeli territory, for Sayeret Matkal to use. This car will serve the IDF Intelligence Directorate for many years to come in hosting foreign delegations—and not necessarily ones from Syria.

And just as this colorful and eclectic motorcade stops to refuel on its way back to base, it is announced on the radio that an IDF force on a "routine" patrol in southern Lebanon randomly bumped into a group of Syrian officers and brought them back to Israel for interrogation.

When the gas station attendant hears the news on the radio, staring at this bizarre column of cars waiting to refuel, he is so astonished that his jaw hits the floor and so does the pump in his hand.

Years later, at Team Bronner's annual reunion, as the men reminisce about three "Crate" operations, two misses and one hit, and as their stories of battlefield bravery embellish each other's, they pull out four classy

Browning Hi-Power pistols bearing the imprint of the Lebanese Army—flashy souvenirs from the third operation. And only Danny Castel, an honest and unassuming man, cries out, offended: "But they told us to hand over the guns when we got back to base . . ."

* * *

Soon after the abduction, Israel offers to exchange the Syrian officers for the IDF captives and to do so quietly, without causing the Syrian regime too much embarrassment. Damascus rejects the offer and demands the officers' unconditional return, arguing that they were kidnapped and are not prisoners of war. The Lebanese government files a complaint with the U.N. Security Council over Israel's violation of its sovereignty.

In the months after the abduction, Israel and Syria hold negotiations through mediators until they finally strike a deal for a prisoner swap. On June 3, 1973, nearly a year after Operation Crate 3, the three Israeli Air Force officers return from captivity. In return, Israel hands back to Syria the officers abducted in Operation Crate 3 and another forty-one Syrian captives. The Lebanese men captured in the same operation are also released and a pardon is issued for a resident of the Druze village of Majdal Shams, who was sentenced to twenty-three years behind bars in May 1972 for spying for Syria.

And when Pini Nachmani, the navigator, returns from captivity, he recalls telling his fellow MIAs, "Just you wait, the guys from Sayeret Matkal won't forget us." After the abduction of the Syrian officers, his wife Ruchele writes him a letter, sent to the prison: "The guys went fishing and came back with a few fat fish." So at least for the last year of their captivity, they had a reasonable hunch that freedom was near.

With this, Sayeret Matkal honors the unwritten agreement that is practically a pillar of Israel's national security doctrine: every soldier must know that if he falls into captivity, the State of Israel will do whatever it takes to bring him home.

Chapter 7

OPERATION SPRING OF YOUTH— BEIRUT, APRIL 1973

When Amitai Nahmani walks up the staircase in a building on Rue Verdun in Beirut, a few seconds before Kamal Adwan, a senior Fatah commander, is assassinated in his bed, he is fighting two battles at the same time: in one, he's climbing upstairs, his senses as sharp as a hedgehog's spikes. The slightest hesitation, the smallest absent-minded mistake, will be critical for his own life and the lives of the three Israeli soldiers hot on his heels. The second battle, confounding his senses, is with himself: he can't stop thinking about the morality and necessity of killing a man as he cuddles his wife in his sleep. This isn't how Amitai imagined his service in the IDF's most elite commando unit.

He stands in front of the door he was assigned in the briefing and orders one of his men to retrieve an explosive charge to blow it off its hinges. Another soldier signals that it would be best to leave the explosive and just kick the door in, soccer-style. He raises a heavy leg—and off flies the door, together with the doorframe. Through the gap is a dim light, enough to be able to discern Adwan, a Kalashnikov in his hands, socks on his feet, gray pants, and a white shirt that will soon turn red. Amitai suddenly realizes that his own life is in danger and preempts

Adwan, shooting from the hip and emptying four bursts of gunfire into the Palestinian terrorist leader. The first hail of bullets eliminate Amitai's own doubts; the next three pierce through Adwan's head and torso.

Ordering the rest of his squad to enter their assigned rooms, he steps into Adwan's bedroom and switches the light on. Adwan's wife is still in bed with her two children. They will live to grieve him, while Amitai and his men conduct a rapid search of the apartment and run outside with two suitcases full of documents. The soldier who inspects Adwan's Kalashnikov will later report that it was cocked but not loaded. A tenth of a second, even less, was all the difference between Amitai's life and Adwan's.

* * *

A few months earlier, Sayeret Matkal commander Ehud Barak and his intelligence officer Amnon Biran sit down for a meeting with a senior Mossad officer. His name is Romi, and he is the chief intelligence officer of Mossad's Caesarea branch, which runs undercover missions in Arab countries. For months, he and his fellow operatives have been working night and day to plan and pull off this operation by themselves. Only after examining the mission from every possible angle does Mossad understand that it can't pull off this complex mission alone—hence the decision to ask Sayeret Matkal's commanders for assistance.

Romi pulls out a series of photographs from a folder. They show Kamal Adwan, Kamal Nasser, and Yusuf al-Najar—all commanders in Fatah, a Palestinian terror group operating out of Lebanon. Al-Najar is Arafat's deputy, the commander of Fatah's military branch, and one of the masterminds behind the kidnapping and murder of eleven Israeli athletes at the Munich Summer Olympic Games. Romi presents other photographs showing the exterior of the three men's homes in two apartment blocks on Rue Verdun, in the heart of the Lebanese capital. Barak and his intelligence officer would struggle to think of any combat mission more tempting than vengeance against the Fatah commanders who planned and executed the brutal abduction and killing of Israeli athletes.

In Israel's long-running war with terrorist organizations, few terror attacks have been as demoralizing and painful as this one. Israel has seen even more barbaric terrorist killings, but the Olympic Games—which are all about bringing nations together—were the last place where Israel expected its citizens to be kidnapped and butchered. To add to the horror, the entire tragedy unfolded on the soil of Germany, whose moral obligation to the lives of Israelis and Jews was supposed to be immeasurable.

IDF commanders are supposed to carry out their missions with equanimity and restraint. Not in this case. The burning hunger for revenge, especially for anyone in an IDF uniform, or with a beating Jewish heart, is a more powerful force than any military training about the virtues of restraint and cool, clear-headed logic.

Ehud Barak is one of the least emotional commanders in the IDF, and his instinct for vengeance, if it exists, is concealed behind heavy layers of analytical sophistication. But when he gets a whiff of an exhilarating commando mission, God help anyone who tries to get in his way.

And when the photos of the three architects of the Munich Olympics massacre are pulled out of Romi's folder at Mossad HQ, the well-oiled cogs in Barak's head start whizzing at breakneck speed. In his own mind, he starts conjuring up forces and missions, access routes to the target, and most importantly—a flurry of creative ideas to get him and his men into the Fatah commanders' apartments in the middle of the night, without getting detected on the way. Barak and Biran bombard Romi with operational questions and he writes everything down, promising to turn their queries into an EEI ("essential elements of operation") document.

A month goes by in the blink of an eye, without a hint of progress, until Barak bumps into a general who tips him off that military intelligence has identified a target in Beirut, one that Mossad already had its eyes on: the apartments of Fatah leaders. He says that IDF Chief of Staff David "Dado" Elazar loves the idea, but will only consider approving it on two conditions: the presentation of a detailed operational plan, and the selection of at least two or three other targets in the area, so that if there are operational mishaps in the apartments, at least the force won't return empty-handed. Elazar assigns the task of finding additional targets and building a comprehensive operational plan for the whole mission to Emmanuel "Mano" Shaked, the chief of the Paratroopers and Infantry Corps.

Immediately, Barak asks Biran to check whether fresh information has come in from Mossad, and Biran confirms that it has. Barak calls the IDF General Staff's operations department and is told that there is already a lot of "meat" in terms of intelligence material, but the chief of staff is not happy with the preliminary plan presented by the Paratroopers and Infantry Corps. This plan would involve a squad of around fifty soldiers launching a convoluted raid better suited to a fortified target or built-up compound, not for surgical operation in the beating heart of Beirut targeting no more than three Fatah commanders.

Barak is thrilled with the news. Now, not only will he and his men get to perform this cardinal mission in Beirut, if it goes ahead as part of a broader operation, but he will also be able to flaunt his and his unit's special knack for planning. Barak is an expert at the sensitive politics at the peak of the IDF pyramid. He therefore goes to the same general and explains that with the existing intelligence, he would be delighted to present a plan for the chief of staff's approval. He is speaking, of course, only about the Fatah apartments. This mission is his "baby."

* * *

And thus, a group of officers headed by Barak and his intelligence officer Biran sit down and start building the operational plan in painstaking detail. But another two weeks go by, even three, and Barak and his men hear nothing from anyone about the mission. In the last week of March 1973, Barak goes on vacation in Eilat. On Saturday, March 31, as he swims at leisure in the pool, a message arrives for him at the reception desk. Barak goes up to his room. On the dresser is a note, stating that he is requested to speak urgently with his unit. He calls the secretary on duty at the unit, and she "orders" him to get back to Tel Aviv at once.

On the phone, Barak is also asked whether the plan he mentioned two months ago about the trio of Fatah commanders in Beirut is still viable. Certainly, Barak replies at once. "So you'll pitch it to the chief of the Paratroopers and Infantry Corps right now," he is told, "and an hour later—you'll run it by the chief of staff."

Barak is a chief-of-staff-in-waiting and has long been strutting around as an equal in the company of the IDF's top generals. "Why the hell should I report to the chief of the Paratroopers and Infantry Corps before the chief of staff?" he protests down the phone. But Emmanuel "Mano" Shaked, the commander of the Paratroopers and Infantry Corps, is already on his way to Sayeret Matkal's base to review and approve the plan before it climbs up to the chief of staff.

Shaked is older than Barak and outranks him. He is aware of Barak's somewhat clunky attempt to overtake him at top speed, but since the IDF has such a prime target on its radar, he keeps a lid on his high-ranking ego and manages to collaborate with Barak. He approves Barak's plan and they travel, each in his own car, to meet the chief of staff.

IDF Chief of Staff David Elazar is enthralled but keeps his cool. He asks Barak to start training immediately for his unit's mission and instructs Shaked to come back the following morning with plans for additional missions in and around Beirut.

Barak returns to Sayeret Matkal, assembles his officers, and puts them on immediate war footing. On their bucket list: getting on top of all the latest intelligence from Mossad, down to the tiniest details; launching joint combat procedures with the Paratroopers and Infantry Corps; getting final approval for all the plans from the General Staff; coordinating with Mossad about the landing beaches in Beirut; and training and conducting drills at Israeli sites that look similar to Rue Verdun in Beirut.

While Barak and Biran's original plan is constantly fine-tuned, Barak starts working on the composition of the force for this operation.

Barak and Biran plan the operation from back to front, that is—from the moment their forces meet the three arch-terrorists in their apartments, maybe even in their beds, and backwards. One of the key conditions for the mission's success will be an absolute surprise, so Barak and Biran come up with the idea of dressing the squad in civilian clothes, disguising them as the targets' Lebanese neighbors. The force will also need to be relatively small, in order not to raise suspicions and to reach the Fatah commanders' homes as quickly as possible.

Besides the size of the force, the idea of dressing up as civilians leads to two other conclusions. First, the "civilian" team must be mixed—men and "women": burly commandos in costume. Walking in pairs, or groups of three, men and women together, will not raise suspicions. Second, all military gear—from guns and explosives to walkie-talkies—must be concealed in the men's suits, the elegant ladies' bags, and the James Bond briefcases that some of the men will carry, so that they can whip them out quickly.

Now, having decided on a walking route to the target, Sayeret Matkal has to work out how to get to Rue Verdun in Beirut in the first place. It is decided that the commandos will reach Lebanese waters on an Israeli Navy gunboat, which will anchor far from shore; they will then switch to Shayetet 13's Zodiac boats and sail to the rendezvous point on the beach. On the shore, Mossad operatives await them, equipped with rental vehicles and accurate prior intelligence about the quickest and safest route to the Fatah commanders' homes.

And once Barak and his men know how to reach their target, they have to start brainstorming possible scenarios and responses, with the unit's signature precision. Covert intelligence operations usually only go ahead after everything—but *everything*—is ready, and this attention to detail can become a long, debilitating nightmare. But in such complicated kinetic operations, so far from Israel's borders, there is usually only a narrow and rare window of opportunity. Missing that window will usually lead to the cancellation, not postponement, of the operation.

Barak fully understands that an infinite number of surprises might pop up in the middle of a metropolis like Beirut and that it's impossible to prepare for every possible scenario. Sayeret Matkal will therefore need to take a few calculated risks. The Sayeret Matkal team's main worry is getting stuck in a busy Lebanese street at the end of the operation, unable to use Mossad's cars to get back to the beach. This might happen as a result of roadblocks, gunfire at the "Israeli" vehicles, the surprise appearance of the Lebanese Gendarmerie, or—or anything else.

In this case, Barak is convinced that the streets of Beirut can be transformed into something out of an action movie for a few minutes, in the style of *Die Hard 2* (which is yet to hit movie theaters for many years). He believes that nothing in the world can stop eighteen Sayeret Matkal soldiers from seizing a few Lebanese cars, even in the heart of the city, scaring off the drivers by threatening them with guns, and looping back to the beach. He is certain that in civilian dress, with the unit's trademark resolve, this strike force—armed, focused on its mission, and armed with the element of surprise—will always be one step ahead of its foes.

Another question that requires long discussions and countless drills is how to act in the stairwells of the apartment blocks where the Fatah commanders live. Should they take out the concierge? Should they switch the light on in the stairway? Should they even take the stairs, or the elevator? Should they shoot anyone walking in the other direction and take the risk of waking up everyone in the building—not all the soldiers will have silencers—or should they let them pass and take the risk of raising their suspicions? Should they conceal their weapons or expose them? No less importantly: How should they break into the three apartments at exactly the same second, so that smashing down one door will not wake up the other Fatah commanders in other apartments?

Barak and his officers work around the clock planning for countless possible scenarios in this thoroughly non-military, and therefore unfamiliar, environment. And when the planning moves into the final stages, not because all the questions have been answered but because the moment of truth is approaching and it's nearly time for Barak to make final decisions, the handpicked elite force starts training for the mission.

When it comes to building a strike force, a range of not always professional factors gets taken into account, and this creates tensions both within and between the regular squads, and also between the men and their commanders. Officers are always overrepresented on these missions: they are more senior than their soldiers, more experienced, and also—you've got to admit—they "deserve" it more. Because for those who sign on for extra time after their mandatory service, all they want is to be given the rare opportunity to take part in an operation straight out of Hollywood like this one, Operation Spring of Youth, and to step out of the shadows where they normally live at least once. There's no point denying that in every Sayeret Matkal soldier, even the most determined peaceniks among them, lurks a daredevil, vengeful warrior who dreams of putting into practice, if only once, everything he has trained for over the years. The sorry saga of the murder of the Israeli athletes in Munich has seeped into the bloodstream of all of Sayeret Matkal's fighters, and nobody is willing to miss a once-in-a-lifetime opportunity to settle a score like that.

* * *

The elite team put together by Ehud Barak, who is both a coach and a player, includes Barak himself as the field commander together with Amiram Levin, Yoni Netanyahu, Muki Betser, Amitai Nahmani, and a few other squad commanders, all battle-hardened Sayeret Matkal officers, as well as Dov Bar, the Shayetet 13 officer escorting the force (the recipient of a Medal of Distinguished Service for his role in the raid on Green Island), and Dr. Shmulik Katz, the medic.

When Amitai Nahmani, the commander of the operations division, who has been tasked with commanding one of the hit squads that will kill the three Fatah leaders, understands the exact details of the plan, he starts to have deep, gnawing doubts. He's the kind of person who has an absolutist moral compass, which guides him in every step he takes and decision he makes. In his own handwringing way, he challenges Barak with his moral dilemmas about taking out Fatah commanders in their sleep as opposed to the battlefield, as they have always done. This, Amitai believes, is a complete change of the rules of the game. Barak knows Amitai well and knows this isn't a flight of fancy that he can bat away, but a serious issue that demands an honest operational and moral answer. Otherwise, he knows, one of his top commanders might start entertaining doubts—putting himself and his men in tangible danger.

Barak explains, in his own mellifluous way, that this approach is supposed to minimize risk, and therefore not only is the whole matter justified, but there isn't even a moral question to begin with. But Amitai is an experienced and esteemed commander, who serves as Sayeret Matkal's conscience, and there is no way he will quietly accept such a vague answer, even from an upstanding commander like Barak. Amitai tells Barak that he respects his arguments but would like to receive a more detailed answer from someone at an even higher rank, preferably the chief of staff himself.

David Elazar always treats such questions from soldiers on their way to dangerous operations on enemy soil with gravity and humility. "These subjects have got to die for their role in planning the murder of the Israeli athletes in Munich," Elazar explains to Amitai in a meeting scheduled especially for this. "They belong to the PLO leadership in Beirut, and Yasser Arafat himself attends meetings in their apartments. Finally, the operation itself is based on sophisticated ruses, which will allow us to minimize risk and increase the chances of success." That's his final word. It's hard to say whether Amitai is truly convinced, but this supreme military seal of approval is enough to eliminate his doubts and reawaken the fearless warrior inside him.

The training drills are divided between the part at sea—or more specifically, the arrival from the gunboat to the beach in Beirut—and the part on land. The part at sea includes a practice beach landing in Shayetet 13 commando boats and then speedy practice runs with the Mossad operatives who are supposed to welcome the soldiers ashore. The Mossad operatives rush straight from the training grounds to the airport, to catch flights that will take them all around the globe before finally landing in Beirut with enough time to spare before the operation. Mossad's six operatives/drivers—three for Sayeret Matkal and three for the Paratroopers—are assigned different tasks to perform that night: they are supposed to blend into Beirut for a relatively long time, rent local cars in which to take the Israeli forces to their targets, closely study all the access routes, and conduct detailed observations of the field of action.

Once the Mossad operatives leave Sayeret Matkal's base and Israel, the training for the ground operations continues. At first, the drills take place around a model "house" built of tent cloth on the unit's base. The purpose of these exercises is to give the soldiers a dry run of entering the buildings, branching off to the apartments, and reacting to surprises.

In the second stage, the soldiers go through a "wet run" in abandoned police stations from the British Mandate era, where they can practice with live fire, hand grenades, and blowing doors open with explosives.

In the third and final stage, the Sayeret Matkal force starts training in apartment blocks under construction in a residential neighborhood in north Tel Aviv and finally, the day before the operation, it holds a "dress rehearsal": a full run-through starting at Tel Baruch Beach in Tel Aviv, involving hired cars that pick up the soldiers arriving from sea and take them to the target area, walking in pairs or threes from the parking spot to the target, breaking into the "terrorists' apartments," and killing them. The Israeli forces are even dressed up, just like in the real operation, but the exercise is not completely lifelike because they cannot use live fire in the model buildings. But such are the constraints of the time and place, and the soldiers must now pack these constraints into their backpacks and sail with them to Beirut.

* * *

And thus, on April 9, 1973, as soon as night falls, an Israeli gunboat jam-packed with an eighteen-man force from Sayeret Matkal and other units departs from an Israeli Navy base in Haifa. Joining the elite commando unit are two squads from the Paratroopers, one commanded by Amnon Lipkin-Shahak and the other by Amos Yaron, tasked with blowing up Fatah warehouses on the outskirts of Beirut. They are also joined by a Shayetet 13 force commanded by Shaul Ziv, the chief of Israel's naval commandos.

Soon after midnight, the Israeli gunboat anchors in the middle of the sea, just off the coast of Beirut, and the forces disembark onto rubber dinghies, which will take them to different targets on the beach.

The Sayeret Matkal force lands, exactly as planned, on the beach of a local hotel. There, in the hotel parking lot, the men are awaited by three large rented American vehicles, inside which are three Mossad operatives, whose sighs of relief when they spot the Israeli forces can be heard as far as Damascus. There are three beautiful "women" among the soldiers, who settle into their seats and try to expunge the taste of saltwater from their voyage on the commando boats. Barak, in costume as Muki Betser's date, is wearing a black wig (not blond, as the legend goes) and a well-padded bra, stuffed with army-grade cotton socks. He is wearing flared pants, the peak of fashion at the time, and with the beautiful make-up applied by the secretaries on the base, and with his diminutive, curvaceous stature—no Lebanese gendarme, however eagle-eyed, could possibly spot the commander of Sayeret Matkal in the tarty lady strutting through the streets of Beirut, hand-in-hand with the lanky Muki Betser in a shiny black suit expertly tailormade to match his slender physique.

Amiram Levin, a short man, is dressed as a brunette in high heels. The other men in the strike force are dressed and made up as ordinary Lebanese civilians. Even a well-trained eye would struggle to detect the Uzi machine guns, variety of hand grenades, and a war chest of explosive charge underneath their jackets.

The rented vehicles cruise through Beirut's seaside promenade, the Corniche. On both sides of the road are hotels and embassies. The soldiers have all been abroad before, although for them, "abroad" means total darkness and radio silence, not passports, duty-free shopping, and chartered airlines. But none of them have been abroad in the way people are in the twenty-first century, staring at a foreign country through the windows of moving cars.

The Muslim quarter of Beirut, including Rue Verdun down the middle, is an attractive neighborhood of tall apartment blocks with concierges at the front and glass doors allowing passers-by to see their luxurious lobbies. The whole area is illuminated with fluorescent lighting and is bursting with life even late at night. Sayeret Matkal has never trained for or experienced this elegant setting. It has always thrived in the darkness, tiptoeing in and behind the shadows. Even in military operations, the unit always prefers quick forays out of the dark, exposing itself for just a few seconds before slinking back into the shadows.

* * *

The cars stop on the corner of Rue 60, an alleyway off Rue Verdun, and Barak gets out first and immediately falls into Betser's long arms. They will lead the force, which trails behind them in pairs and groups of three, looking like unimpeachable Lebanese ladies and gentlemen, keeping around fifty feet between them. The alleyway is extremely narrow, and when Betser embraces Barak, they take up the whole sidewalk on their way to the target, barely leaving any room for the Lebanese gendarmes heading their way to pass them. In the tense few seconds before this unavoidable encounter, Barak signals to Betser not to make way for the police officers on the sidewalk, thus making them step onto the street without taking another look at the lovebirds walking by. Betser is supposed to lead his squad to the home of Yusuf al-Najar ("Abu Yusuf"), Arafat's deputy, who is the number-one target in this whole operation.

Barak and Betser reach the building with Abu Yusuf's apartment. Based on the intelligence, there should be security guards outside the building and the front door should be locked, with a concierge behind it. But these three obstacles have simply vanished, providing a virtuosic overture for the concert that should begin in two or three minutes. They enter the building and take a left and a right. The lobby is empty and completely quiet.

Meanwhile, Yoni Netanyahu arrives with two more men. This trio is Muki Betser's squad, which is supposed to climb up to the sixth floor to wake up Abu Yusuf—not particularly gently or politely.

Amiram, the deputy commander of the force and the head of the squad that stays downstairs to guard the street, doesn't appear behind them as he is supposed to, making Barak slightly anxious. Barak searches for him through the building's glass door and happens to spot a Renault Dauphine lingering by the entrance. He calls Amiram on his Motorola device and tells him that someone is sitting inside the car. The man in the Renault must realize that something is happening right under his nose, because he steps out of the car and whips a pistol out of his suit—but immediately absorbs a hail of bullets and lurches back in the car.

Muki Betser walks past Barak's squad in the building's opulent lobby and sprints up the stairs to the sixth floor. His men are hot on his heels, all on their way to Abu Yusuf's apartment. They reach the door and Betser orders one of them to attach explosive charge. They can hear a battle downstairs, and Betser is convinced that Barak and his men got into trouble in the street, so he has to complete his mission pronto and go down to help.

With the explosive charges firmly attached to the door, Betser taps three times on his Motorola and waits for Barak to tap three times in response, giving him the final green light to break in. Barak's three taps give the signal, and the explosive charge detonates with a deafening roar, sending the door flying like a piece of paper. Black smoke billows in Betser's doorway, and he takes a right towards "his" room in order to wake Abu Yusuf up. But the man is already awake and opens his bedroom door wearing underpants and a pajama shirt. The light is on in the room behind him, so his tall silhouette occupies the frame and a hail of bullets can be emptied into him before he can come to his senses and raise his gun. Betser joins in with another burst of gunfire, shooting from the hip, and Abu Yusuf collapses to the floor.

One of the commandos skirts past him on his way to the second room, Abu Yusuf's trembling hand grabbing his leg and trying to trip him up. Betser adds his own brief bursts of gunfire, and Abu Yusuf's soul departs to the great courtroom in the sky. He's definitely got some explaining to do. Betser manages to check that the dead man in front of him is missing a pinkie on his right hand, a telltale sign that he was really Abu Yusuf, and now he needs to grab documents from the apartment, with the recently departed's wife and children still there—but the non-stop gunfire he hears downstairs, from the street, is a message to dart back downstairs and come to the defense of Barak and his men.

* * *

Exactly at the millisecond when Barak taps three times on his Motorola, signaling for Betser and his men to break into Abu Jihad's room, the commander of the third squad, Tzvika Gilad, and Amitai Nahmani's squad are standing at Kamal Nasser and Kamal Adwan's front doors, respectively. The building with these two apartments is next door to the apartment block where Abu Yusuf lives—or rather, lived.

Tzvika Gilad has picked two men from his own squad for the task. He trusts his soldiers with his eyes closed, and there's no way he'll bring other officers into his team. He's just not sure that they can sing from the same hymn sheet that he and his men know so well.

When Amitai Nahmani darts toward Kamal Adwan's apartment, his counterpart Tzvika Gilad also runs up the stairs, two steps at a time, with his men behind him, into Kamal Nasser's apartment. Running upstairs, they hear muffled gunfire at the Renault Dauphine, and adrenaline starts pumping through their veins. When Gilad reaches "his" door, he looks back. Only one of the commandos is there, and he retrieves an explosive charge from his backpack and starts attaching it to the door. The other commando gets held back for a moment when he spots the security guard in the lobby and shoots him with his pistol, and that's why he's slightly late. And as he is busy attaching the explosive to the door, they can hear someone shouting from inside, *"Min hada?!"*—"Who's there?!"

Gilad decides that there's no time to wait for Barak's signal and orders him to detonate the device at once. The explosion sends the door flying. It also blows the next-door neighbor's door off its hinges, and even the door of the fridge inside, and the boom can be heard all the way down the street. The open doorway fills up with billowing smoke and dust, and Gilad jumps headfirst through it into the apartment. In the entrance he comes across two women, one lying lifeless on the floor and the other standing up. He turns immediately toward Nasser's bedroom and shoots his first burst of gunfire into the empty bed. The other commando heads for the balcony, quickly scans it, and doesn't find anything. He goes back into the apartment. And while Gilad is still in the living room, emptying a few short rounds into the piles of furniture blown over in the explosion, they scan the kitchen. Suddenly, they hear someone shout: "I've been hit!" Gilad opens a hail of bullets in the direction of where the soldier was shot from and then spots Kamal Nasser sprawled in a pool of blood. They shoot him again, to double-check he's dead, and the trio sprint back downstairs. The first soldier was shot in the leg but pushes on with the Sayeret Matkal force, without receiving medical attention just yet.

* * *

While Muki Betser, Amitai Nahmani, and Tzvika Gilad climb upstairs to the three apartments, Amiram and his perimeter team, who have remained downstairs in the street, are engaged in a gun battle with the Lebanese Gendarmerie, which has been called to the scene. The reverberations of the gunfire can be heard all the way down the street, echoing in the ears of all the local residents. This gunfire is the reason why the soldiers have no time to finish searching for the documents and to bring them to Israel.

When Amiram and his men are the last to reach the front of Abu Yusuf's building, they find out that the Renault Dauphine is still there, and it looks like the driver hasn't been shot after all. Maybe he's just frozen, glued to his seat in shock. Barak orders them in a whisper to shoot him, and this time dozens of bullets from Barak, Amiram, and the other soldiers' submachine guns leave nothing to chance. His head slumps on the steering wheel, setting off a loud honk that blares throughout the rest of this operation.

At exactly this point, a Land Rover pulls up toward them. The soldiers spot it and unleash long bursts of gunfire at the driver. The driver leaves the engine running and flees for his life. But Land Rovers in Beirut have an odd habit of cloning themselves—and just after the first one, along comes a second. Amiram and his men open fire at it and become the targets of indiscriminate gunfire from the gendarmes sitting in the second Land Rover.

* * *

In the meanwhile, Betser shows up with his men in the street, having killed Abu Yusuf, and a moment later Amitai Nahmani and Tzvika Gilad stream into the same area with their men. All three squads have accomplished their missions.

By now, the street is swarming with people and bullets are whizzing through the air from every direction when Ehud Barak quickly ushers his men into Mossad's three cars, which have come right up to the door of Abu Yusuf's building. And at the exact moment Barak finishes counting his men and starts giving the order to step on the gas, a third Lebanese Land Rover appears at the end of the street, facing the unidentified force running rampant through the streets of Beirut.

The first Mossad car, which has already started moving, comes to a halt. Betser jumps out and chucks a grenade, which falls on the middle of the roof of the Land Rover, slowly rolls down, slips off the car, and throws the Land Rover and all its passengers into the air with an almighty explosion. Another Lebanese man suddenly shows up, waving his gun, and sprints toward the stairs of the building before being downed by the precise gunfire of the Israelis sitting in the first hired car.

The whole force, in the three vehicles, cruises down the coastal road to the point where Shayetet 13's commando boats should be waiting for them. The boats, which have been bobbing a quarter of a mile off the coast, quickly close the gap at Barak's request and with the help of Dov Bar, the naval commando representative on the ground. As the soldiers board the boats, the medic performs first aid on the soldier who took a 9mm bullet to his kneecap.

The Israeli force sails in the commando boats to the gunboats waiting for them far out at sea. There, they meet Emmanuel Shaked, the commander of the operation, and the other Paratrooper and Shayetet 13 forces, as well as the bodies of Avida Shur (the brother of one of the authors of this book) and Haggai Maayan, two soldiers from Amnon Lipkin-Shahak's team who were killed in the raid on the headquarters of PFLP founder Nayef Hawatmeh in another part of Beirut, and of Yigal Pressler, a company commander in the 50th Battalion of the Nahal Brigade, who was seriously wounded in the same operation and flits between life and death for the whole, long voyage back to Israel. His life is saved, and he goes on to become the prime minister's counterterror advisor.

The gunboats, packed with soldiers, an elite mission from the IDF's special forces, docks at Haifa's military port at dawn and is welcomed by Chief of Staff David Elazar and a rabble of jubilant generals. Such operations, pulled off with such success, are an excellent reason for a massive gathering at the finishing line. More people can rightfully claim credit for this operation than anyone can possibly count.

Never till now has the IDF ever undertaken such a complicated mission, so far from Israel's borders, integrating so many branches of the military. But the operational success is only part of the story. It is based on a perfect picture of the intelligence, thanks to years of Sisyphean work by Mossad's multitalented spies—including a brave female operative who lived in Beirut before, during, and after the operation—who manage to track down the Fatah commanders' apartments and bring Sayeret Matkal forces on a specific night when all three senior figures are at home and tucked into bed. Don't forget that each of these terrorist leaders had several apartments and kept flitting between them.

Of course this young country, which will celebrate its twenty-fifth Independence Day in a month, goes out of its mind with joy and pride, despite ridiculous shroud of secrecy under which Sayeret Matkal tries to keep the operation. In fact, the unit's existence is still top-secret, and none of the commanders knows how exactly to treat this heroic mission. On the one hand, nobody wants to forgo the glory and the songs of praise emblazoned on every newspaper front page, nor can they; but on the other hand, it's clear to everyone that too much exposure for Sayeret Matkal might cause irreversible danger to its future intelligence capabilities. And thus the information doesn't just leak out—it gushes out and is immediately met with a mealy-mouthed denial. Sayeret Matkal saturates the newspapers but retains a certain foggy aura of mystery.

Israeli national pride, cutting across all parts of the nation, becomes intermixed with an impulse for revenge. Israel inflates its collective chest, knowing that the masterminds and terrorists behind the Munich Olympics massacre were killed in a daring and sophisticated operation. That's how Israel builds national pride and honor.

And Sayeret Matkal proves to itself and the IDF that it can initiate, push for, and plan audacious and elaborate military missions, and pull them off in such perfect fashion. Operation Spring of Youth becomes a critically important milestone for the unit, transforming Sayeret Matkal into the obvious top candidate for similar missions in future. And it looks like this is a major milestone not just for the unit but also for Ehud Barak personally, who was the main driver pushing this operation forward and turning it from a fantasy scenario on a drawing board into a real, surgical, and successful mission. Barak's self-confidence, much like the self-confidence of the whole unit, skyrockets.

Chapter 8

THE RESCUE OF ISRAELI PARATROOPERS FROM THE PEAK OF THE HERMON—NOVEMBER 1973

T he Yom Kippur War begins to limp toward its sad and smoldering demise with the IDF stationed on the Syrian side of Mount Hermon and just sixty-three miles from Cairo, its weapons loaded but locked. Sayeret Matkal, shellshocked, counts its dozen fatalities, its morale at an all-time low.

We, the most veteran Sayeret Matkal team on active service, spend the dying days of the war at Air Field Fayid, a military airfield near Ismailia on the western side of the Suez Canal, on alert for potential operations. As soon as the ceasefire goes into effect, we return from Egypt to Sayeret Matkal's base in a desperate, practically futile attempt to return to the same sort of routine as before the war. A heavy black cloud of misery traps the unit in its shadow and seems to make everyone sluggish and somber, dulling the joy of their reunion and return to their base, and drawing a solid, impassable line between the world before and the world after.

We go back to the warm, familiar embrace of the team that has become, and there's no avoiding it, our favorite hideout and our only human shield against the terrible consequences of the war. Only someone seared by the same horrifying experiences of war can understand the basic, primordial, and intensely human need to be surrounded by people who were partners in exactly the same experiences.

On November 1, a week after the ceasefire finally takes hold, Yoni Netanyahu, by now the deputy commander of Sayeret Matkal, bumps into team commander Rami Lapidot in the yard at the unit's base. Sixty reserve paratroopers are stuck at the top of Mount Hermon in the Golan Heights, he tells him. They were part of the force that conquered the peak of Mount Hermon, on the Syrian-Lebanese border, from Syria in the last days of the war. Now, they are trapped in a terrible snowstorm that is making it impossible for helicopters to rescue them. Some of them have already succumbed to frostbite, he adds, and Sayeret Matkal is being called to apply its singular expertise to Mount Hermon: to reach the paratroopers on foot and help them escape this frozen disaster zone.

Rami calls over Doron, a sergeant in his team, and orders him to draw up a list of equipment and soldiers and to start preparing for a helicopter flight up Mount Hermon. Exactly then, Avi from Team Itamar bursts into a room with five team members who have managed to get back from a quick home visit, and tells them that they need to get organized at once to head out to Mount Hermon and rescue the frostbitten paratroopers. The force will comprise the whole of Team Rami along with five stowaways from Team Itamar and a few other men on base.

Dragging their feet to the warehouse, they hear cries urging them to hurry up from all around. Sayeret Matkal's high-pressure, single-minded, heavy-handed machinery starts spinning into action, quickly jumping out of its slumber and coming back to life.

Rami and Itamar's teams—experienced, skilled, and obsessive about detail—know for sure that the safest way to the mountaintop, freshly conquered from Syria, which gazes down mockingly at its baby sister on the Israeli side of the Golan Heights, runs through meticulous and rigorous preparations, and if not a detailed study of the route there, then at least packing top-grade layered clothing, checking all the unit's mountain-climbing gear and making sure all the soldiers get the right sizes, and dry runs with everyone walking around the base in all this gear, to make sure it all fits perfectly and thus avoid any chafing.

Every additional minute of preparations, as the most veteran soldiers can tell you in their sleep, will save at least ten minutes of arduous mountain-climbing while fiercely battling the sadistic weather, which is among Sayeret Matkal's most brutal and despicable foes.

But right now, the voices of the paratroopers trapped in the blizzard are sawing through Yoni's head, and he urges us to disregard our rich mountaineering experience, skip all the necessary preparations, and just storm the helicopter, whose deafening roar we can already hear.

The process of kitting ourselves out is practically a religious ritual, and it too contains arbitrary elements, such as matching the colors of our undershirts and thermal underwear, but also supremely important operational elements, turning the whole thing into a frantic mess with people running around and grabbing whatever they can. The foul winds of war are still blowing in Sayeret Matkal, sweeping away the habits, old and new, that everyone has acquired over the years.

* * *

The helicopter gobbles up Rami and his men, the five stowaways from Team Itamar, and the others. The flight to Mount Hermon is the last opportunity to try to turn the piles of equipment haphazardly hoarded from storage into outfits that will offer effective protection against the cold but also allow the men to walk up impossibly steep inclines. But this attempt, after the earlier hastiness, is doomed from the start.

The helicopter tries to land on the peak of Mount Hermon on the Syrian side and thus to save the commandos the long climb, so they can reach the trapped paratroopers more quickly. But an impenetrable black wall of clouds mocks the IDF helicopter, blocking any aerial access to the peak. Eventually, the helicopter lands at the bottom of the Mount Hermon ski lift, in a clearing still empty of snow, into a ferocious, deafening wind.

Fifteen soldiers line up facing Yoni Netanyahu, waiting almost in horror for his decision. He announces that only a dozen soldiers and one commander—Rami—will be needed for the mission, passing a pointed finger over the agonized faces of the soldiers and selecting the hikers. Rami's team constitutes the bulk of the force and is armed with its own commander, so his eight men will obviously join the rescue force. Iddo Netanyahu, Yoni's brother, is also selected to join the hikers, along with a veteran medic, whose presence in the force is an absolute necessity.

Yoni is left with five soldiers from Team Itamar, from whom he must select two. It's hard to describe the gut-wrenching, tense feeling of watching Yoni's pointed finger selecting the next in line. Those who have already hiked up Mount Hermon countless times before in the harshest weather can't help but feel horrified at the thought of an impossible confrontation with the mountain's wrath. Yoni points at Omri, an old high school classmate of Yoni's brother Benjamin "Bibi" Netanyahu, who reached the unit thanks to Bibi's warm recommendation. Yoni can't ignore these bona fides and lets Omri benefit from this family connection by joining the force. Then his finger continues slicing through the icy air until it lands on Uzi. The three remaining men from Team Itamar must of course pretend to be hugely disappointed at not being selected for this mission, but they can barely disguise their smiles of relief and satisfaction.

Even before the soldiers selected for this mission board the Hermon Brigade's half-tracks, which will take them as far as they can up the mountain, to a point from which they will have to hike, Rami tells Yoni that they haven't eaten anything in nearly twenty-four hours and that the hasty preparations could end up being fatal. They need at least an hour to get all their clothing and gear ready before they can start walking. It's early evening now, and Rami desperately tries to buy another ten or twelve hours, till first light, in order to try to study the route and prepare accordingly. But the storm shrieking in their ears drowns Rami out, and Yoni keeps gesticulating wildly, telling the force to board the two half-tracks and get a move on.

And thus, some of the soldiers set out wearing unsuitable pants, either because of a shortage or the mad rush, and others are missing several vital layers of clothing for the weather that has already come close to defeating the sixty Israeli paratroopers stranded on the mountaintop.

At 18:30, the force gets off the two half-tracks near an Israeli military outpost and starts making final preparations for the hike.

Forty-five minutes later, at 19:15, they start moving.

* * *

Meanwhile, Yoni picks up the three representatives of Team Itamar chosen for the mission and sets out with them toward Mount Avital, which will function as the command center for this operation. A genuine, close, jokey friendship with Yoni is not in the cards for us in Team Itamar, even at the end of that terrible war, which had a tendency to bring people together, soften them, and make them drop their defenses. We have come a long way with Yoni. First of all, in the unit's slang, he's our "grandpa." Itamar, our commander, used to be a soldier in Team Yoni. After that, Yoni headed the training company during the whole of our team's training and invested mighty efforts in our military education, much more than in other teams. But this relatively long shared history does nothing to soften our personal relationship and Yoni. He is a closed book, an introvert, a serious man who never reveals any of the thoughts and plans that are surely running around in his brain.

The terrifying winds at the departure point, with raindrops as sharp as knives lashing through the pitch darkness, make it extremely hard for Rami to identify and pick any route to the paratroopers. The signal with the command center on Mount Avital is perfect—luckily—and they also have a clear line to the stranded paratroopers. The ground is wet and slippery but completely snow-free. The force advances at a shockingly slow pace, a third of a mile an hour, bravely battling the fierce westerly winds keeping them firmly planted in place. Rami walks ahead with an open compass, stopping every half an hour to open a map and call over Lonny, the force's informal deputy commander, and together they decide on how to continue. Lonny also holds an open compass as a permanent back-up to Rami's, which is quickly filling up with water. At every stop, the soldiers drink hot tea out of polystyrene cups brought from the base, but the tea gets colder and colder as the night goes on.

The relationship between the soldiers in Team Rami and their commander has known more downs than ups during their service together, characterized by an oppressive chilliness, a kind of bitterness and coldness similar in ferocity perhaps only to the biting cold from which they are suffering together now on the slopes of Mount Hermon.

Rami's role in this mission is therefore much more difficult, with eight critical pairs of eyes piercing his back like laser beams. Team commanders, despite the title and authority, are first and foremost human beings, and in missions like this they must grapple with exactly the same physical and mental difficulties as their subordinates. Rami must also care for his soldiers like a kind of Mother Teresa, navigate a practically unnavigable route, and make, at any given moment, dozens of decisions that might prove fateful for his soldiers' lives, and also for his own.

At a very early stage of the hike, the Israeli commandos understand something that should be obvious to anyone who has ever braved the trails up Mount Hermon: the clothing grabbed in a manic hurry is unsuitable for the treacherous conditions at the top of the mountain. The ferocious rain permeates through their raincoats with ease, and the combination of water pummeling down and icy winds makes the soldiers feel like they are being stabbed all over, and disaster awaits.

The initial reports that the force sends the command center on Mount Avital are deeply disturbing. Rami sends Yoni coded descriptions about the situation. It's hard to convey a precise picture in intricate military code, but Rami's voice betrays the first hints of hesitation and disappointment. This is not how he expected to lead his elite troops up to the paratroopers, dying and desperate to be rescued, on the mountaintop. Even the terrain, the likes of which Sayeret Matkal's officers and soldiers have defeated hundreds of times before through diligent and rigorous study, is in open mutiny. Yoni, supremely experienced and sensitive, hears these voices, picks up on these early signs of serious distress and the rapid ebbing of confidence and bombards the force with heavy barrages of encouragement and determination over the radio system.

At point two on the route, as marked out in Yoni's briefing, Rami is updated that Shai Shacham's rain pants are torn. Then he receives another report from the rear of the force, that Iddo Netanyahu's pants are also beginning to tear. Rami reports mournfully to Yoni at the command center that "one of the matches" is struggling to walk and is holding the force back. If this "match" keeps walking without rain pants, with the rain and wind battering down on his naked flesh, it can only end in disaster. Shai is a strong and tough guy. Nobody could have imagined that *he* would find it hard to walk even in the most unbearably harsh conditions.

The force continues nevertheless, walking slowly from the east to the mountain ridge, seeking the best possible shelter from the brutal wind. Rami doesn't have a clue about their exact location, because they are walking through visibility of just three feet, maybe six. At what they think is point four on their map, based on Rami's understandings with Yoni in their hasty pre-departure briefing, the force sits down to rest—and finds it agonizing to get back up and continue walking.

And right then, Yoni's command center receives an equally astonishing and awkward dispatch: the besieged paratroopers suddenly appear over the IDF's radio system and report that they are in excellent shape, protected inside a large cave, shielded from the cold, and that there is no reason to rush to their aid. The earlier reports about gruesome cold injuries were a complete fiction, as the commanders' imaginations ran wild in the fog of war. There is no comparing the gleeful, upbeat tone in which the stranded paratroopers report on their supposedly desperate condition and the depression of the team coming to their rescue.

A long and scathing discussion erupts on the radio system between Yoni and Rami about the possibility of packing up, retreating from the mountain, and calling off the mission. But there's no chance of that happening. Not on Sayeret Matkal's watch. Rami looks at the broken "match," fading in front of his eyes, listens to Yoni's chest-thumping rhetoric with unimpeachable patience, and knows that no good will come out of this adventure.

Shai walks and falls over, picks himself up and falls over again. "What's going on?" Rami asks him. "My backpack's wonky," replies Shai. Rami gives the order to transfer Shai's backpack to another soldier and asks another man to keep an eye on Shai.

"Try to send in a helicopter," we, Team Itamar, suggest to Yoni Netanyahu in the command center, hoping to reach the luckless rescue force and bring it back. And indeed, an IDF chopper is quickly dispatched to the mountain, detects a faint first light, and starts a hesitant ascent toward the peak. The pilots think that they might stand a chance but they are quickly disappointed. A black and impenetrable fortress of clouds surrounds the peak of Mount Hermon, blocking any possibility of landing the helicopter. Yoni exhorts the pilots to find a hole in the clouds, come what may. Not this time. The helicopter returns, dejected, to its base—and Rami's team loses its last scintilla of hope.

* * *

Shai keeps tottering and toppling, and the other men in the force are not doing much better. Rami drags the force beyond the mountain ridge, to a place that he thinks is protected, and discovers to his astonishment that Shai is not even wearing a tracksuit under his torn rain pants. The medic tries to wrap Shai in a thermal aluminum blanket to warm up his legs, but it tears quickly, and his hands freeze in the meanwhile. Rami tries to close Shai's rain pants with a safety pin so they won't fall down while walking. Doron opens a smoke grenade to try to warm Shai's legs, while Rami presses his face to Shai's to stop the smoke reaching his nostrils or mouth. Shai reacts well to the grenade's warmth and he says that he can bend his legs again. The men open a second grenade at once and wrap Shai's legs in a bandage. Shai is fully conscious and says he'll be alright and the force can press ahead.

Meanwhile, in the command center, tensions are skyrocketing. Everyone listening in to the communications and familiar with the special circumstances of the mountain and the season has every possible nightmare scenario running through his mind.

Rami and the force get up and keep walking. On the eastern side of the ride they find a rock wall to hide behind. Shai lies down at once and the others form a circle around him, covering him again in the slowly-disintegrating aluminum blanket. They light two candles in tin jars by Shai's legs and try to give him the little lukewarm tea that is left, but to no avail. They also feed him "rescue sweets," a highly nutritious kind of candy developed especially for long stays in the field. He sucks them for a short while, then spits them out. He's clearly losing consciousness, because he no longer recognizes his friends. Rami orders the men to bring rocks, to try and build a wall on the east and shield Shai from every direction. His barely audible order is swept onto the rock wall and dissipates into the air, without any response from the men around him.

Rami is patched through to Dr. Alex Betler, Sayeret Matkal's doctor, over the comms system, who instructs the force to warm Shai up and let him rest, to drink as much as possible, and to keep walking in order to stay warm. What else can he advise them from hundreds of miles away, when the force has zero suitable equipment for cases like this?

Day breaks over the mountain and faintly illuminates the group of soldiers, in a physically and mentally disastrous state. Shai falls asleep. They mustn't let him sleep. What should they do? Omri and Lonny are also showing the first signs of frostbite. They cannot stay put, because they'll get hypothermia, but they cannot go anywhere, either. Rami understands that it is more dangerous to stay in one place than to keep walking, hard as it is, and urges everyone to get up and persevere. He also orders the men to carry Shai in pairs and even in threes.

The rain stops for a moment, but the wind intensifies, its terrifying shrieks swallowing Shai's last grunting, groaning breaths.

"The match is out," Rami tells Yoni over the walkie-talkie, his words freezing the whole atmosphere over the Golan Heights. Yoni and the soldiers in the command center go pale, even whiter than the snow on the peak of Mount Hermon. And up there, on the mountain, Shai's friends stand around him, in the biting cold, their tears freezing in their eyes. The tears will stream down their cheeks, but only later, when their brains manage to communicate the terrible news to their hearts. Their heartache and physical agony dissolve into a slurry of sorrow and despair, which will seep into their muscles for many years to come.

* * *

The attempts to resuscitate Shai continue for forty-five minutes, while the paratroopers, hearing everything over the radio system, start making their way down to Rami's force. They are fully kitted-out, wearing the perfect clothing for Mount Hermon, and in fine spirits. Rami sends three soldiers up the mountain ridge to fire shots in the air and mark out their location for the paratroopers. Omri and Lonny's situation continues to deteriorate.

The quick link-up with the paratroopers is one of the most frustrating episodes in Team Rami's military service: on the one hand, it's clear that this encounter will save their lives, simple as that. But on the other hand, the fact that the paratroopers they set out to rescue are in such fine shape blows to smithereens the unit's last shreds of morale.

The paratroopers untie the frostbitten commandos' webbing, make a huge bonfire out of them to warm them up, and surprise them with their refreshing camaraderie: there are more important things than soldiering in a place completely devoid of enemy forces. They lead Rami's force into the cave on the mountaintop, and their frustration only grows. Who the hell sent a Sayeret Matkal force in such a rush to rescue paratroopers who were so safely and warmly ensconced in a cave, kitted out with the most weather-appropriate gear, in fine spirits, and in no discernible danger?

The paratroopers' regimental doctor immediately gives Lonny and Omri a lifesaving infusion while the rest of the force enjoys a hot drink, food, and new, warm clothes. And as if by magic, as soon as everyone settles down in the warm cave, the heavy cloud cover slowly dissipates and the helicopter that set out on a fool's errand earlier lands right outside the cave and whisks Omri and Lonny away to the hospital in Safed. After that comes another chopper, to evacuate the rest of the force to a helipad near Kiryat Shmona, in northern Israel.

Here, in a nutshell, Sayeret Matkal flaunts many of its signature characteristics: steadfast determination, courage, sacrifice, and an obsession to constantly prove *something* to *someone* all the time. Always pushing the boundaries of possibility; tempting the forces of nature; exhibiting extreme persistence, come hell or high water, and also a certain hastiness, as a side effect of everything else. When suffused with the foul, lethal winds of war, the results of all this can be catastrophic.

And when the whole force is evacuated, all that remains trapped in the icy winds of the slopes of Mount Hermon is Shai Shacham's carefree smile, gleaming in his friends' minds for the rest of their lives.

Chapter 9

THE MA'ALOT MASSACRE— MA'ALOT, MAY 1974

The Ma'alot massacre was one of the greatest traumas in the history of Sayeret Matkal, and indeed of the State of Israel. Even while writing this chapter, forty-five years after the attack, we veterans of the unit find it hard to drive down Route 89 by the town of Ma'alot in northern Israel without getting goosebumps when we remember that terrible day: May 15, 1974.

On Sunday, May 12, 1974, at around 22:00, three terrorists from Nayef Hawatmeh's PFLP sneak into Israel through the Lebanese border, not far from the village of Zar'it. The infiltration is detected by a patrol of the Border Police, but the manhunt goes nowhere.

On Tuesday, shortly before midnight, near the village of Tzuriel just east of Ma'alot, the terrorists open fire on a pick-up truck taking workers from Kiryat Ata to their homes in the Arab village of Fassuta. One of the workers is killed and seven others are injured. The wounded truck driver manages to keep driving to the village of Elkosh and alert the local security officer, who reports the incident to the police. The IDF launches another sweeping manhunt, but the three terrorists get away.

Nobody can imagine that the nightmare is just beginning.

On Wednesday at 03:30, the night between May 14 and 15, the three terrorists reach Ma'alot in the upper Galilee and enter the home of the Cohen family on the northern edge of the town after presenting themselves as police officers searching for the terrorists. They murder the father, forty-five-year-old Yosef Cohen, the mother, thirty-five-year-old Fortuna, and their four-year-old son Eli. Before she is murdered, Fortuna manages to hide their infant child Yitzhak, and since he is both deaf and mute, he makes no sound and is therefore saved from the three terrorists' insatiable barbarity.

From the Cohen family home, the terrorists continue in the direction of the Netiv Meir School. They plan to lie in ambush for the schoolchildren showing up in the morning. Even in their wildest dreams, the terrorists could not have imagined stumbling so soon on an Israeli school full of children, who in a short while will become their hostages. But the string of bad luck threading through events from the moment the terrorists infiltrated Israel has now become the start of a terrible tragedy.

As fate would have it, the Netiv Meir School just happens to be providing accommodation that night for the annual outing of a religious Jewish school in Safed. One hundred and two students from ninth to eleventh grade, headed by their teacher Yona Amroussi, have embarked on a two-day hike through the Galilee. When they set out, it is already known that there is a terrorist cell roaming free around Israel and that security forces are on high alert. Yona, the "commander" of the outing, acts responsibly and called the police in Acre to check whether he and his students have authorization to head out on this trip. He is given a green light, along with instructions not to veer off the main roads.

On Tuesday at 17:00, the children reach the Netiv Meir School by coach and started preparing for bedtime. The boys will sleep in the corridor on the first floor; the girls, in the corridor on the second floor.

On Wednesday at 04:00, Shimon Kadosh, a janitor from Ma'alot, sets out for work and bumps into three men who seem lost in the town's quiet streets. After he bids them peace, as he always does, they ask him in Arabic and broken Hebrew how to reach the nearest school. Shimon gives them precise instructions, and instead of thanking him, they shoot him, gravely injuring him. The three terrorists walk toward the school and there, outside the building, they come across Pinchas Vaaknin, a teacher, sleeping in the car that has escorted the school children from Safed. The terrorists order him to give them his car keys, and when he can't find them because of stress and confusion, they walk straight into the school.

One terrorist stays by the entrance, and the two others go up to the first and second floors, where the students are sleeping. The brother of one of the schoolgirls, an IDF soldier who has joined the outing as a chaperone and is sleeping on the ground floor, wakes up, understands what is going on, and escapes the building behind the back of the terrorist stationed at the door. His sister is trapped in the building with all the other boys and girls. In the meanwhile, Mr. Vaaknin leaves his car, slips into the school without the terrorist spotting him, and starts running upstairs, screaming, "Terrorists! Run for your lives!" Most of the students are convinced it's a prank, but the sound of gunfire ricocheting down the corridors makes it clear the expedition is over. And not just that.

Seventeen students, two teachers, one soldier, a rabbi, and a bus driver manage to run to the window of one of the classrooms, jump down, and save themselves. The terrorists notice that the children are escaping en masse and jump into action. They round up everyone still in the school—eighty-five children, two medics, and two teachers—in a single classroom on the second floor and booby-trap the room, the staircase, and the corridor. Later, when the negotiations begin, the hostage-takers will demand the release of twenty terrorists in Israeli prisons, whom they want to be flown to Damascus. If this does not happen by 18:00, the terrorists warn, they will blow up the school with everyone inside it.

The commander of the cell is twenty-two-year-old Ziyad Rahim, who speaks fluent Hebrew. His accomplices are Ali Ahmed Hasan Linou, aged twenty-seven, and Ahmed Salah Harbi, aged nineteen.

* * *

Giora Zorea was appointed the commander of Sayeret Matkal in April 1973 after ten years of service, most of them in the unit, making him the second commander after Ehud Barak to have been conscripted into the unit as a young soldier and to have risen the ranks after holding nearly every command. His deputy is Amiram Levin, who will also command the unit one day. Both men, singularly unflappable, operate as an outstanding pair of commanders in perfect professional synchrony.

In their outward appearance, they look like Don Quixote and Sancho Panza: Giora is tall and lanky, Amiram is short and stout, but both are utterly fearless, lead by example, and know to get the best out of their subordinates without ever transgressing the bounds of impeccable interpersonal relations. This ability, to squeeze the best out of their men without crushing them or becoming hated by them, is nothing to sniff at.

At 05:00 on Wednesday, May 15, Giora receives a report that over eighty schoolchildren are being held hostage at a school in Ma'alot by three terrorists, and he is asked to rush Sayeret Matkal to Ma'alot as quickly as possible. The helicopter that lands at the unit's base can take only thirty soldiers, with all their gear. The main force sent over to the hostage crisis comprises Tzvika's team and a rabble of soldiers and officers who happen to be on base that morning.

Amiram Levin reaches Ma'alot even before the helicopter, straight from his home in Haifa, and starts studying the lay of the land and possible access routes to rescue the hostages.

Sayeret Matkal's commanders and soldiers know well that it doesn't matter how many rounds of negotiations there are with the terrorists: in the end, the unit will have to free the hostages by force. With a lot of force. No incident in which terrorists held Israeli captives has ever ended with the flutter of a dove's wings. Every Sayeret Matkal soldier dressed in full battle gear and whisked to the scene of the hostage crisis knows, therefore, that he is going to risk his own life in order to save the lives of others. In this case: of eighty-five children and four adults. All the other adults—security guards, teachers, and drivers—have fled for their lives, leaving the children they were supposed to be watching to their own devices, startled and frightened, with three fanatics with Kalashnikov rifles watching their every move.

At 04:45, Prime Minister Golda Meir's military secretary, Israel Lior, wakes her up and gives her a brief report on events in Ma'alot. Golda, who has already lost much of her personal strength and fortitude after the humiliating fiasco of the Yom Kippur War, picks up the phone to Moshe Dayan, who is still her defense minister despite having lost the titanic reputation as "Mr. Security" with the outbreak of that ruinous war in October 1973. Dayan lands in Ma'alot at precisely 07:00 with his military secretary at the exact same moment as another helicopter: that of IDF Chief of Staff Motta Gur, recalled only a month earlier from his role as Israel's military attaché in Washington to replace David Elazar, who resigned. Three more helicopters circle the skies of this sleepy town, signaling with the furious rotors that a major incident is underway.

Sayeret Matkal commander Giora Zorea and his deputy Amiram Levin join forces with Muki Betser, a senior reserves officer in the unit, who has also shown up at the scene. That's what it's like with Sayeret Matkal officers, on active duty or in reserves: they all have a fifth sense that tells them whenever there's a terrorist attack underway, and then they drop everything to run to the scene of the crime in order to get a slice of the action at any price, including risking their own lives.

The three officers start planning how to seize control of the school, fully aware that this is an extremely difficult and unprecedented event. In order to prepare properly to raid the school, in full coordination with other security forces, they are going to need time. They will need to study the internal layout of the school, monitor the three terrorists' routine, and tailor their missions to the teams that have already arrived from Sayeret Matkal. But Defense Minister Dayan is pressuring them to wrap up as quickly as possible and be ready to enter the school, in case the terrorists start massacring their hostages.

Giora, Amiram, and Muki interrogate the school principal, who arrives on the scene, and one of the teachers, who managed to flee, and they inspect the blueprints of the school, supplied by the municipal engineer. It's a three-story edifice built onto the side of a hill, so the first floor from the west side is on columns. On both the second and third floors, there are four classrooms. The sports hall, north of the main school building, gives them a direct vantage point and line of fire to the windows of the classroom where the children have been corralled—the easternmost classroom on the second floor. Inside the classroom are two terrorists, one wearing a red shirt; the other, black. Most of the children are wearing khaki, which will make it easier to identify them during the raid.

* * *

According to the plan in the works, the main effort will come from the west, where the incoming forces will be hidden from the terrorists' view. The main problem vexing Giora and Amiram is that storming the building from the west will require climbing stairs, and it will take a relatively long time to get from the entrance of the school to the classroom with the hostages. There is also a major concern that the classroom, and maybe even the staircase leading there, is boobytrapped. They examine the possibility, therefore, of climbing up to the second floor on ladders, breaking in through the northern window, just a few feet away from the terrorists, and catching them off guard.

Giora is deeply skeptical about the operational feasibility of the ladder option because it has never been tried, and nobody has a clue how exactly it will go. The approach that wins out, therefore, is to storm the building from the west, through the staircase, but to have another squad enter through the window on the second floor on ladders at the same time.

Dayan is still the dominant figure on the ground. These events are his bread and butter and give him back some of the confidence and leadership that he lost somewhere in the Sinai Desert and Golan Heights just a few months earlier. He summons Victor Cohen from the Shin Bet, who handled the negotiations with the Sabena hijackers two years earlier, to the scene. The defense minister is convinced that he can replicate the success of the Sabena crisis using the same negotiations team and special forces unit that ultimately rescued the hostages from the airplane.

Inside the school, and in the absence of most of the counselors, teachers, and chaperones, it is the young and unassuming schoolboy Yaakov Kebla who takes command, reassures his friends, and even defiantly demands that the terrorists bring them food and water.

At 11:45, the Israeli cabinet convenes and decides to accede to the terrorists' demands and free the prisoners. The government's surrender is announced on the news at 14:00 and triggers an outpouring of joy, from both the terrorists and the schoolchildren, who can start smelling the intoxicating fumes of freedom. But the road to freedom will still be long, and who knows whether they will even make it to the end.

Giora is undoubtedly the man with the greatest responsibility on his shoulders—the practical and operational task of rescuing eighty-nine hostages—and he must invoke all his experience to build the best plan.

When Sayeret Matkal and the IDF establish their command-and-control center in a building behind the school, there are already three lookouts positioned in the area. In just a few moments, there will be a brusque changing of the guard, and they will be replaced by Sayeret Matkal snipers, whose main mission is to report on the terrorists' movements and, if the time comes, to shoot them. One squad, under Rami Lapidot, assumes position south of the building with a view of the window where Rahim, the chief terrorist, occasionally stands. A second squad, under Yoni Raz, takes up position north of the building, in front of the classroom windows. A third squad, under Alon Shemi, takes up position west of the school at an angle that will make it hard to watch and shoot at the windows of the western classroom, where the hostages are held.

The raid is supposed to be conducted by two forces:

The first force, under Amiram's command, will storm the main access point through the front gate and up the stairs to the second floor. Amiram has already commanded dozens of covert and overt operations, and there is probably no one else in the IDF who has taken part in as many missions where the difference between life and death is being a millisecond or a millimeter away from a flying bullet. And in any event with so much gunfire, Amiram will always lead the main force and stand—or run—in the heart of the danger. As far as he and his commanders are concerned, things couldn't be any other way.

The same is true of Muki Betser, the commander of the second force. Team Muki will try to scale the building on ladders up to the windows of the floor where the hostages are held, shoot through them, smash them in, and storm the classrooms. Team Muki is also joined by Uzi Dayan. He's sick today, but there is no way he'll miss the action. He also has unrivaled connections: his uncle, Defense Minister Moshe Dayan, whose word is law.

In the end, after all the patrols and consultations, two alternatives are proposed: if the three sniper squads catch glimpse of the three terrorists through the windows at the same time, they will take them down. If they see only one or two of them, they will shoot them, and the gunshots will be the signal for the two forces—Amiram's and Muki's—to storm the building and eliminate the surviving terrorists.

At this stage, Moshe Dayan is the most enthusiastic cheerleader of the idea of storming the building and rescuing the hostages. This situation is topsy-turvy. Usually, the army presses for the military option—that's its job—while the political echelon tries to tone it down. But this time, Motta Gur, the new chief of staff, his uniform still spotless, who has just come back from service in Washington as the IDF attaché, is pushing to exhaust the negotiations with the terrorists at any price. Who knows? Maybe there will be a miracle, and the incident can be wrapped up without casualties.

Dayan takes off in his helicopter to Jerusalem for a cabinet meeting, to receive the government's blessing for military action. But the government's decision does not exactly give him succor, and he returns to Ma'alot to meet his nephew, Uzi Dayan, and unburden his grievances on him.

* * *

Meanwhile, Israel's top negotiator Victor Cohen is speaking in flawless Arabic through a megaphone with chief terrorist Rahim and feels that his words are fluttering through the air like feathers in the wind. Rahim doesn't know that Victor handled the negotiations in the Sabena hostage crisis, but he is probably familiar with the event and knows that this eloquent man's only objective is to create a convenient atmosphere, mentally and physically, for an Israeli military operation that will undoubtedly lead to his death and that of his fellow kidnappers.

At 14:45, Dayan informs the government that one opportunity for a rescue mission has already been scuttled and asks for authorization to launch it once the conditions ripen. At 15:15, Dayan receives permission to order Giora to eliminate the three terrorists, but Chief of Staff Motta Gur is still hesitating and asks for more time to exhaust negotiations.

All three arenas—the hostages inside the school, the terrorists, and the soldiers in the large force surrounding the building—begin to feel the effects of tension and fatigue, rapidly eroding everyone's alertness and readiness. This tense and nerve-racking standoff has been dragging on for twelve hours, and morale among each of the three groups has ebbed and flowed with each morsel of information. Nobody knows how this tragic event will unfold—or, to be precise, how tragically it will end—but past experience teaches that the civilians murdered by the terrorists even before they took over the school will not be the only victims.

At this critical stage of the division of labor, there is always a nerve-racking process between Sayeret Matkal's commanders, and between the commanders and their soldiers. When Giora gathers his officers around and asks, "Who's going in first?" the question giving every officer a sinking feeling in his stomach is whether to jump in immediately and volunteer to join the first force, exposed to the greatest danger, or whether to pause for a second and let someone else take the bait. Counteracting this basic, raw human fear is the social pressure and immense embarrassment of revealing this fear or even the slightest bit of doubt in the company of battle-hardened officers, who are not just brothers in arms but also genuine friends.

The ability to volunteer and run headfirst into a fire runs completely counter to human nature and demands tremendous mental wherewithal. If you have never charged into a hail of bullets, certainly at a range of just a few feet, you can never hope to understand the crippling terror. Only the absolute taboo of being seen as a coward by their friends and the innate human tendency among combat soldiers to save the lives of others at any price, even at the price of endangering themselves, ignites the fuse in their brains that sends them storming into carnage and danger.

* * *

Outside the school, Motta Gur is still holding the operation back. Perhaps his long stay in the United States as Israel's military attaché has made him forget some of the behavioral norms of the Middle East. He still believes, with all his heart and soul, that a miracle will happen and the fabled dove of peace will swoop into Ma'alot and help the two sides reach an understanding that will make military action unnecessary.

Victor Cohen from the Shin Bet is still trying to exhaust the terrorists and buy time, but they keep repeating their ultimatum that at 18:00, they will blow up the school with everyone inside.

At 17:15 even Motta Gur, the last holdout of resistance, understands that there is no choice and orders a military operation. The order is immediately conveyed to Giora, the commander of Sayeret Matkal, who updates his forces: Amiram and Betser's teams, who will storm the school, and the three sniper squads around the perimeter.

At 17:25, a sniper in Rami's squad, hiding south of the school, fires the first shot. He is considered Sayeret Matkal's finest sniper at the time, and the lone bullet that he fires into the window splices through Rahim's shoulder but fails to kill him. The bad luck haunting this crisis from the outset continues to bedevil the force pursuing the terrorists. Rahim is still fit for action, despite his gunshot wound—a fact that will quickly prove lethal.

The sound of the first gunshot catches most of the terrorists off guard, since they were expecting a raid on the building. The repeated delays of the raid, along with the pent-up fatigue and general chaos around the school, have dulled the absolute alertness that is necessary for such a mission. But the sniper bullet is the starting shot for the forces to jump into action, sending them streaming into the school.

Tzvika is the first to storm the building at the head of a squad of three men. The quartet, part of Amiram's force, storms up the first nine-step stairway. Yuval, the commander of the second squad in Amiram's force, joins Amiram's force on the move and thereby dooms himself to a serious injury.

Rahim is fully aware that the bullet that cut through his shoulder will soon be followed by armed soldiers. He waits for them exactly at the top of the second staircase, which leads to the classroom with the hostages, and fires a long hail of bullets at the five men running up the stairs. He manages to hit Yuval in the leg and another two commanders.

Meanwhile, Tzvika responds with his own hail of bullets in Rahim's direction, pulls out a grenade, yanks out the safety pin, and chucks it at the terrorist. And once again, the goddess of bad luck fires a poison arrow, and it turns out that Tzvika lobbed a white phosphorus smoke grenade, not a regular shrapnel grenade, and he fills the corridor with a thick, almost impassable wall of smoke. The phosphorescent smoke, a solid wall of soot and dust, blinds Amiram as he leads his men up the stairs, and when he reaches the second staircase, after which he must turn right to the classroom with the hostages, he accidentally takes a left, up to the third floor. Once again, they lose a few priceless seconds, critical for the survival of the hostages. Amiram realizes his mistake as soon as he reaches the middle of the third staircase, turns around, and runs straight back down the stairs toward the classroom.

Despite his shoulder injury, Rahim manages to dodge Tzvika's bullets and grenades and dives back into the classroom with the hostages and opens wild, indiscriminate fire at a huddle of terrorized schoolchildren crawling between the tables and chairs in a desperate bid for shelter. Some of the children storm the windows and leap out of them, toward freedom and life.

The salvation that might have come from Muki Betser's squad, which was supposed to climb a ladder into the second-floor windows, can be written off. For some reason, the order to jump into action never reaches them, or they don't hear it. Only the first sniper bullet and the noise it unleashes send the first man in the squad, up the ladder to the window through which the force is supposed to raid the school. But when he starts climbing, he comes under a burst of targeted gunfire from an unidentified source, and he jumps back down to the ground. The gunfire stops and he starts climbing the ladder again. This time, one of the terrorists chucks a grenade at him through the window, and he jumps off the ladder again. And when he starts climbing the ladder for the third time, he sees children jumping out of the windows and understands that Team Muki's job in this battle is over.

In the corridor leading to the hostages' classroom, Amiram's team proceeds with caution and disastrously slowly. Itamar Sela, the commander of one of the three squads in Amiram's force, together with a wounded Yuval and Tzvika, finds two explosives at the top of the stairs, connected with an electric cable. He disconnects the wires in order to neutralize the improvised explosive device, but the phosphorescent smoke is everywhere, a heavy cloud that burns their eyes and nostrils and impedes the soldiers' progress—helping the terrorists, who are massacring the helpless children in the classroom in the meanwhile.

And in all this chaos, when nobody has a clue who is supposed to go where, one of the commandos leaps headfirst into the classroom with Tzvika just behind him, to be greeted by a horrific scene. Only the groaning and muted sobbing of the injured disturbs the silence. Rahim, wounded, is leaning against the blackboard, a weapon in his hand, but his brutal and lethal gunfire stops for a moment, apparently because he runs out of ammo. To the left of the doorway through which the Israeli commando entered stands another terrorist. The commando empties a hail of bullets into the two men at a short range and then spots another young man, practically a child, in the corner, wearing military webbing, armed with a pistol and holding a grenade. He is briefly confused by the man's young, childlike appearance, but his military logic wins out and the last terrorist is eliminated point-blank in a long hail of bullets.

* * *

The battle is over. And so are the lives of twenty-two hostages: eighteen girls and four boys. All students at the school in Safed. All brutally massacred. And Sayeret Matkal, for all its virtues, here in Ma'alot, here where it most needed to succeed, has failed miserably.

The classroom fills up with dozens of soldiers and medics, pouring in to treat the wounded and evacuate them to hospitals. Those who bore witness to the gruesome hostage scene at the end of the battle will never forget it. Those who stepped in puddles of children's blood will never be able to wipe it off their feet, nor will they be able to erase what they saw from the depths of their hearts and souls until their dying days.

Chief of Staff Gur and Defense Minister Dayan immediately order a preliminary investigation of the classroom where the children were held. The stench of blood and death lingers in the air, making it difficult to breathe. Giora Zorea and his men, who join the investigation, are still struggling to wrap their heads around the magnitude of the disaster. From the initial inquiry, it is clear that the bad luck plaguing this crisis from the outset, when the IDF received a report of a terrorist infiltration but failed to catch the culprits despite the trail of blood they left behind them, continued taunting Sayeret Matkal at every turn. In hostage rescue missions, mere seconds or even milliseconds make all the difference between success and failure. This time, the seconds ebbed away in a series of infuriating delays, leading to this terrible catastrophe.

The defense minister and chief of staff try to reassure Giora and his officers, perhaps in an effort to reassure themselves. Because in the end, blame for the failure will shimmy up to the top. That's the way of the world. But Giora is a man of unvarnished truth. It's hard to butter him up, and he understands every word that is said and reads between the lines. This time, Sayeret Matkal under his command screwed up. There's no other way of putting it. None of the long and impeccably logical explanations about the operational necessity of their actions will bring single child back to life, and nobody can go back and shorten the eternity between the sniper's first bullet and the moment the soldier who eliminated the terrorists stormed the classroom. Giora understands all of this perfectly well.

It is obviously impossible to blame Giora and his men, who risk their lives time and again to save hostages in crises like this. Not only that—they even fight for the privilege of risking their lives. But in the end, Sayeret Matkal is judged by its success in saving as many lives as possible while eliminating the terrorists in its path. In Ma'alot, the objective conditions for the unit were unbearably grim. And still, there is no doubt that the unit could have stormed that classroom more quickly and maybe even saved more children's lives. This horrible feeling, in total contrast to every hostage rescue mission before and after Ma'alot, will haunt the men who participated in this battle for eternity.

The long litany of events on this dark day, whether caused by bad luck or genuine cock-ups, is hard to digest: the sniper managed to hit Rahim, the terrorists' commander and apparently the most barbaric of them all, but the bullet didn't kill him, allowing him to continue on his aggressive murderous rampage; the order to open fire was insufficiently clear and caused a fateful delay of several seconds; not only did Tzvika's white phosphorus smoke grenade not inflict any damage on the terrorists, but this grave screw-up seriously delayed the raid on the classroom; running to the classroom, Amiram mistakenly continued running upstairs to the third floor. This mistake was also mainly due to the smoke grenade, which filled the staircase and caused another delay; this was compounded by the inexplicable hesitation of Amiram's men in the corridor leading to the classroom, apparently a result of confusion and misunderstanding about the full action plan. Moreover, Muki Betser's squad, which could have saved the day, failed to reach the window on the second floor, either because of inadequate determination or because of a misunderstanding, and thereby saved the terrorists from the critical surprise that might have totally transformed the results of this operation.

Sayeret Matkal knows how to deal with its successes with humility and should therefore also be able to cope with failures with tough investigations and an honest lessons-learned process, without fear or favor. But the thought that they could have saved more innocent boys and girls who were slaughtered will never let go of the men who fought that day, or their many brothers in arms in the same unit.

The Ma'alot massacre will go down in infamy in the history of Sayeret Matkal's operations and in the long, blood-soaked history of hostage-takings and attempted rescue missions. But Sayeret Matkal, headed by Giora, is able to convert the major fiasco of Ma'alot into a long, intensive, and painful journey of learning lessons and building a new operational doctrine that will take it to new heights in terms of its ability to react to similar crises in the future.

The morning after the massacre in Ma'alot, Giora launches a process that in hindsight, and maybe even in real time, is nothing less than revolutionary. For several weeks, all the unit's officers and soldiers design a diverse series of drills in order be able to contend with any scenario that might arise in the course of a terrorist attack, especially hostage crises. Giora takes his men to all sorts of buildings, planes, buses, trains, and even various seacraft. For each arena, the unit devises precise protocols with dozens of scenarios and responses for each kind of event.

At the same time, Giora and his officers develop guidelines for kicking the unit, or special standby teams, into action at a moment's notice. Sayeret Matkal soldiers are placed on high alert to respond to any scenario twenty-four hours a day, seven days a week.

The doctrine that Giora and his men, unable to get the dead children of Ma'alot out of their minds, develop during this period stands in complete contrast to the Chief of Staff Motta Gur's flaccid stance in Ma'alot. The new doctrine is to enter hostage scenes as quickly as possible, eliminate the terrorists, and save as many hostages as possible. And this intensive period, following the fiasco in Ma'alot, is likely what guarantees the unit's success in the many crises that will soon follow.

Avraham Arnan, the founding father and the Unit commander 1958–1960 and 1962–1964. A man of vision and praxis.
Photo: private collection

Dov (Dovik) Tamari, Unit commander 1964–1967, expanded the Unit operational capabilities and added active combat ones to the existing clandestine intelligence operations.
Photo: private collection

Uzi Yairi, Unit commander 1967–1969.
Photo: private collection

An aerial photo, of Green Island, the Suez Canal area, as published on the back cover of *Ha'olam Haze* weekly after the raid, July 1969.

The Green Island raiders, minutes before boarding their Zodiac rafts.
Photo: private collection

Menachem Digly, Unit comman
1971–1973, making a speech dur
ceremonial passing of the torch
Ehud Barak, April 1971.
Photo: private collection

Ehud Barak riding a camel during exercises in the early sixties. Barak is the first Unit commander who began his service as a soldier in the Unit.
Photo: IDF Spokesmen

Preparations for passing the torch ceremony
from Digly to Barak. Seen from right Digly
Barak, Avshalom Horan, Amiram Levin and
Slomo Israeli, the mythological master sergean
of those years.
Photo: IDF Spokesmen

Combatants carry a wounded comrade on a stretcher during Operation Crate, June 1972.
Photo: IDF Spokesmen

Combatants during Operation Crate, June 1972. Five high-ranking Syrian officers were abducted, then later exchanged with three Israeli POWs.
Photo: IDF Spokesmen

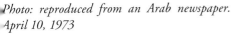

The cars rented by Mossad combatants that were used to drive the Unit team to their Beirut destinations during operation Spring of Youth, April 1973. Ignition keys were left intact.
Photo: reproduced from an Arab newspaper. April 10, 1973

Adi Golad (left) and Ori Tzafrir with the wig Lonny Rafaeli put on during the Spring of Youth in Beirut, Lebanon.
Photo: private collection

From left: Yusuf Al-Najjar, Kamal Adwan, and Kamel Nasser, Operation Spring of Youth targets. All three participated in or planned the Summer Olympic massacre in Munich, September 1972.

Photo: Reproduced from an Arab newspaper. April 10, 1973

Residence of the Popular Front's terrorists in Hartum St in Beirut, Lebanon, the morning after the raid in April 1973. The building was attacked by a paratroopers unit led by Amnon Lipkin-Shahak.

Photo: Reproduced from an Arab newspaper. April 10, 1973

A Lebanese Land Rover that was hit during the Spring of Youth raid in Beirut, Lebanon, April 1973.

Amitay Nachmany.
Photo: Yuval Anabi

Rami Lapidot, commander of Team Rami, commanded the rescue of Israeli paratroopers from the peak of the Hermon mountain, November 1973.
Photo: private collection

Giora Zorea, Unit commander from 1973 to 1975, who led the unit during the Yom Kippur War.
Photo: private collection

Shai Avital, Unit commander 1982–1984, led t
unit during the 1st Lebanon War, Summer 1982
Photo: private collection

Uzi Dayan, Unit commander, 1980–1982.
Photo: private collection

Omer Bar-Lev, (right), Unit commander
1984–1987, with Amos Ben-Avraham, Unit
commander 1991–1992. Photographed in 1985.
Photo: private collection

Muki Betzer, a platoon commander in the
Unit during the early seventies and then
the founding father of the SHALDAG
Commando Unit, pictured here during
Operation Litani, April 1978.
Photo: private collection

Nachum Lev, Unit deputy commander during the eighties. Planned and led Operation Show of Force in Tunisia, April 1988.
Photo: private collection

Moshe (Bogi) Yaalon, the Unit commander 1987–1989.
Photo: private collection

Pinchas Buchris, combatant and officer in the Unit during the seventies and the eighties, deputy commander of Bogi Yaalon, who later became the commander of Intelligence Corps' technological unit and Unit 8200.
Photo: private collection

Ran Shachor, Unit commander 1989–1991, led Operation Lovely Youth, the abduction of Sheikh Obeid in Lebanon, July 1989.
Photo: private collection

Nitzan Alon, Unit commander 1998–2001.
Photo: private collection

Doron Avital, Unit commander 1992–1994.
Photo: private collection

Shachar Argaman, Unit comma
1994–1996.
Photo: private collection

Sayeret Matkal knows, therefore, how to embark on a process of change, difficult and painful as it may be, to admit its faults and learn its lessons. And that's exactly what makes all the difference between banging its head against the wall in vain—and getting fighting-fit for the next round.

Chapter 10

THE SAVOY HOTEL ATTACK— TEL AVIV, MARCH 1975

Giora Zorea is tapped to lead Sayeret Matkal in 1973, a few months before the Yom Kippur War. He and Ehud Barak, his predecessor, come from similar backgrounds: both grew up in the kibbutz movement, from kibbutzim in the same part of the country. Nevertheless, it is hard to imagine two greater opposites, in terms of both appearance and character.

Giora is a tall, broad-shouldered man, who walks in long, gangly strides. Barak is short, round, and looks nothing like the decorated soldier he will one day become. Barak took Sayeret Matkal's intelligence and operational capabilities up a notch in such creative missions as Spring of Youth, boosting the unit's prestige in the eyes of the IDF General Staff and general public, making it a totem of national pride. This was all thanks to his extraordinary planning and operational abilities, his courage, and his originality, but also his fine capacity for public relations, mostly to advance the unit but also a little bit for himself.

Giora steps into Barak's huge shoes in a heartbeat, despite knowing for sure that whoever takes over from Barak will be judged by totally different standards from the pre-Barak era. Nevertheless, Giora's appointment as

Barak's successor is a wise choice by Maj. Gen. Eli Zeira, the IDF intelligence chief. Barak, like Digli before him, pushed the limits of what Sayeret Matkal could do to totally new levels. He would have to be followed by a commander who could reorganize the unit to suit the proportions of the operations that Barak and Digli had spearheaded.

Giora might be an "unpolished diamond," as Barak calls him, but he is also supremely capable in building an organizational infrastructure suitable for a modern military unit. He is also a stickler for detail, which is exactly what the unit needs as it tries to find its bearing again after several years of spectacular operations that left no time for building an organized pyramid. But Giora is also an eminently experienced commander and possesses a captivating charisma, which allows him to build a fine team of young and highly determined commanders, many of whom will rise to command the unit and fill the top ranks of the IDF.

In the spring of 1975, Sayeret Matkal is still licking its wounds from the Yom Kippur War, which only really ended a year earlier with the signing of the separation of forces agreement on May 31, 1974. Since then, the unit's commandos have managed to take part in the conquest of the Syrian side of Mount Hermon, the failed takeover of the school in Ma'alot, and the raid of the apartment in Beit She'an where three terrorists were hiding. Of these three operations, two ended with a military success and one with an abject disaster. But besides a few significant major operations, Sayeret Matkal is beginning to recover some of the confidence it lost in the sands of the Sinai Desert, on the western bank of the Suez Canal, and on the Syrian Golan Heights.

* * *

At 23:15 on March 5, 1975, a squad of eight Fatah terrorists makes landfall on the beach in Tel Aviv. They sailed on a mothership from Beirut and descended onto two rubber dinghies off Israel's shores, but one boat broke down out at sea, and the men continued on one vessel.

These eight terrorists have been sent by Abu Jihad with one mission: to take hostages as chips to secure the release of Palestinian terrorists jailed in Israel. The attack is also intended as revenge for Operation Spring of Youth in April 1973, in which three Fatah commanders were assassinated. This operation, as will become clear later, was supposed to take place two months earlier on the beaches of Nahariya, but the terrorists, who were already sailing from Lebanon, couldn't find the town from the sea and the attack was pushed off. Its target was also changed: instead of Nahariya, the metropolis of Tel Aviv.

The eight terrorists have been instructed to seize a youth center in Tel Aviv and the opera house—and if they fail, then any other populated building in the area. Once they have hostages, their orders are to demand that every Palestinian prisoner jailed in Israel be released and flown to Syria. If Israel refuses, they are to massacre the hostages and commit suicide. And if somehow they are taken captive, they are to tell their interrogators that they came from Egypt—in order to exploit the opportunity to sabotage the nascent Israeli-Egyptian separation agreements talks.

When they reach the beach in Tel Aviv, the terrorists break into a run toward the closest built-up area along the beach, near the corner of the Herbert Samuel promenade and Yona HaNavi Street, opening fire at passing vehicles and chucking grenades. In the chaos, they forget some of their weapons on the dinghies—a fact that will make life slightly easier for the Sayeret Matkal force that will swoop in to intervene.

After crossing Herbert Samuel Street, the terrorists try to break into a cinema, unsuccessfully, and turn south down the promenade, grabbing a few pedestrians on the way as hostages. The terrorists then break east and storm the Savoy Hotel, a three-story building located at 5 Geula Street. They shoot the receptionist immediately, fatally wounding him, release the hostages they picked up on the street for some reason, and start rounding up the guests in a room on the second floor, shouting at them in Arabic and hitting them with the butts of their rifles.

A Golani soldier, at home on furlough, hears gunfire from the hotel and sprints over with his gun. At the door, he runs into the terrorists, some of whom are on their way out in order to seize another target.

In the ensuing gunfight, he is fatally wounded and later dies of his injuries. He is posthumously awarded the IDF Medal of Distinguished Service.

Sayeret Matkal receives an initial report about the incident at 23:45. The duty officer, Alon Shemi, and the operations officer put together a force at lightning speed, and at 00:15, they leave their base and head to Tel Aviv. Another eight officers are sprung into action from their homes and rush straight to the scene of the crime.

The first man at the scene is Nehemiah Tamari, Sayeret Matkal's deputy commander, who is about to take the top job. Nehemiah reached the unit after commanding the Paratroopers' commandos, and given his rich combat experience and the calm that he projects even in the most dangerous missions, there could be no more appropriate first responder.

Even before Giora arrives, Nehemiah conducts an initial sweep of the area and sends men to lookout points from the north and south.

Nehemiah dispatches Amnon, who has swooped in with his squad straight from the unit's training grounds, to the next-door building in order to make sure there are no terrorists there. He can't see any terrorists and loops back to the primary force.

The Savoy Hotel has gone dark since the terrorists took over, with only the lights in the corridors and lobby left on. The squads positioned on the adjacent roofs and in apartments overlooking the hotel to provide cover will serve as snipers, armed with rifles with scopes for daytime and nighttime use and walkie-talkies. If positioned correctly, snipers play a critically important role in any hostage rescue mission. Until the takeover operation begins, the sniper squads are the commander's eyes and ears, observing different sections of the target from various angles and reporting on any developments in real time. The moment the operation begins, they will turn into an active, targeted killing force with a single tap on their Motorola devices, giving them the order.

* * *

The Savoy Hotel is the scene of a massive drama. The lead actress is Kochava Levi, a guest at the hotel who with extraordinary calmness and resourcefulness takes command of contacts between the terrorists and the hostages and helps the Sayeret Matkal force, which has begun to deploy around the hotel in preparation for a raid. First of all, she becomes the go-between in the negotiations with the terrorists and starts liaising with an IDF intelligence officer from Unit 504 who speaks flawless Arabic.

At exactly 01:44, Kochava appears in a window on the second floor and announces in Hebrew that she is a hostage, and there are others. She reports that the terrorists want to talk to the French ambassador in Israel and are demanding a plane within the next ten hours to fly them to Rome. At 03:15, the terrorists are informed, through Kochava, that the French ambassador is on his way to the hotel.

Besides Kochava and her partner, the other hostages, eight in total, are foreign tourists who have come to explore the beauty of the Holy Land and have been thrust into an event that is anything but pretty. The terrorists place chains of explosive devices around the hostages. For her own part, Kochava is physically attached to the commander of the cell and is dragged around with him wherever he goes.

During the negotiations, Kochava manages to communicate critical information about the location and number of the terrorists. The eight terrorists are spread out with six guarding the hostages on the second floor, one on the roof, and one hiding in the lobby downstairs. But Kochava does not only supply the Sayeret Matkal force with up-to-date information; she also assumes the role of "responsible adult," reassuring the young and anxious terrorists and preventing them from making the situation worse by starting to shoot. When Kochava, looking out of the window, realizes that the roofs of all the neighboring buildings are overflowing with IDF soldiers, she implores the terrorists not to dare approach the windows, in order not to expose themselves to sniper fire—thus preventing them from seeing that they are under siege.

* * *

Giora Zorea arrives straight from his home and takes command of the Sayeret Matkal force. Despite the priceless information that Kochava has conveyed, a heavy fog of uncertainty continues to cloud his ability to plan the takeover operation. But he knows that he must plan the raid as quickly as possible, in order not to give the terrorists enough time to prepare and maybe even start attacking the hostages in their possession.

As soon as he arrives, Giora takes a quick tour around the building and consults with Nehemiah, in order to take advantage of his long presence on the ground. Amiram Levin, who was recently discharged from the IDF but never misses an opportunity to participate in Sayeret Matkal operations, also shows up outside and takes a short tour with the hotel's manager. By now, it is clear that there are multiple hostages and that negotiations with the terrorists are beginning on the instructions of the head of Central Command, who is already at the scene. It turns out that the hostages have all been corralled in the northeastern part of the second floor. The IDF checks the possibility of sliding a horizontal ladder across from the roof of the adjacent building to the roof of the hotel, so that one of the squads can break in through a small structure on the roof.

Walking around, Amiram spots a way to sneak into the second floor of the hotel undetected from the north, far from the street, by climbing onto a roof at the back that reaches one of the balconies. He also finds a glass door on the northern side of the building, which the commandos can smash and slip easily into the hotel.

The final plan coming together, therefore, looks like this: Team Amiram Levin will sneak into the second floor through the main staircase as quietly as possible and will advance in silence until they open fire. If they encounter resistance on the first (ground) floor, they will lose the soldiers at the back, who will cleanse the area while the rest of the force proceeds upstairs.

Team Omer Bar-Lev will break in through the glass door that opens out to the street on the ground floor as soon as Amiram Levin's squad gets detected.

Team Nehemiah Tamari will also break in through the main staircase as soon as Amiram Levin's squad is detected.

Team Alon Shemi will reach the roof of the hotel with a ladder, breaking into the building from there. They are ordered to steady the ladder only after Amiram is detected, because they haven't had enough time to practice and there is a fear their cover will be blown early. Giora instructs Alon to scale the roof and sneak in only if he suspects that the other forces have not managed to break into the hotel, and until then to be prepared to cleanse the roof in case there are terrorists there.

Despite these conditions, Giora explains to the squad commanders that they must each know how to complete the mission as if the other squads were not in the building at all.

After years of working together and countless operations, Giora and Amiram can understand each other without exchanging words or even glances. Amiram's presence in the strike force helps to calm Giora as he grapples with the pressure of planning and commanding such a complicated and sensitive mission. For commanders, there is no harder test of leadership than operations in which their soldiers will risk their lives. But operations in which soldiers will not only risk their own lives but also those of many hostages are even more agonizing.

Nehemiah Tamari is also a star addition for such a takeover operation, thanks to his rich combat experience and icy coolness, which seems to blast out of him like a powerful AC unit, chilling the beads of sweat dripping down the foreheads of dozens of young soldiers, for some of whom this is their first, or maybe second, taste of combat.

Because of the conditions at the scene and the time pressure, there is no orderly briefing for all the forces. Giora simply speaks over his walkie-talkie with the commanders, some of whom are already stationed at the exits for the takeover operation. The commandos are all wearing hats over their helmets, so their comrades can spot them in the dark.

* * *

At this point, Col. Uzi Yairi shows up at the scene. Now the assistant head of the IDF Intelligence Directorate's research department, in charge of operations and deterrence, Yairi was the commander of Sayeret Matkal from 1967 to 1969 and then headed the Paratroopers Brigade during the Yom Kippur War. The commanders who are supposed to storm the besieged hotel at any moment and fight for their and the hostages' lives are thrilled to see him. In the past, Uzi was the officers' commander, and his appearance gives the soldiers a fresh injection of morale.

Even the bravest soldiers, when preparing to charge into the unknown, especially in events with civilian hostages, feel like they're carrying 200-pound weights on their shoulders, with blocks of lead tied to their feet. In such crises, the tailwind that commanders give their soldiers is no less important than the type of weapon or quality of ammo in their possession. Yairi is one of the commanders whose mere presence, with his stern gaze and kind eyes, instills his men with boundless confidence and inner calm. Amiram, the most senior officer in the force about to storm the building, consults with him at the last minute about the exact angle of the raid on the hotel. Yairi believes that the best way is to sneak into the hotel from the east or the north. Amiram is taken aback by the new idea but agrees immediately, not because Yairi pulls rank, but because he is persuaded that this is indeed the best way to reach the hotel undetected. In the end, this is also Giora's chosen option.

The snipers positioned around the hotel receive an order to open fire if they hear gunshots or if one of the terrorists sticks his head out of the window and might endanger the forces sneaking into the building.

Meanwhile inside the hotel, Karol Feldman, a wounded and bleeding Dutch tourist, starts screaming in fear and pain. One of the terrorists walks over to him, points his gun at him, and prepares to shoot him point-blank. But not on Kochava's watch. She launches herself at them with incredible courage, stands between Feldman and the terrorist, begs him in Arabic to let her evacuate the injured tourist from the hotel, and promises that she won't run away with him. The terrorist is convinced, and at 04:17 Kochava leads Feldman out of the hotel, a gun poking into her back. She drops him off at the entrance of the hotel and suddenly sees the receptionist, Max Halperin, lying wounded and dying—before he takes another bullet from the terrorist escorting her. Kochava honors her side of the bargain, of course, and returns to the second floor with her personal bodyguard. The tourist's life is saved.

* * *

At 05:16, at first light in Tel Aviv, the last squad commander confirms by tapping his Motorola device that he is ready. Giora orders Amiram to begin.

For his own part, a tense Giora climbs up to a room in the top-floor apartment in an adjacent building that has now been commandeered as a command center and observes Amiram's thin shadow leading his soldiers toward the ground-floor patio. Amiram reports to Giora that he is facing the front door, between the patio and the hotel itself, and that he is considering opening fire of his own accord. Giora asks him to first exhaust all possibilities for quiet action and open fire only if there is no choice. Nehemiah hears the update that gunfire might start at any moment and gives the dozen soldiers in his squad a heads-up.

Udi, leading Amiram's squad, approaches the door, opens it with a knife, and immediately sets the house on fire. Heavy gunfire erupts in his direction, giving the signal for the battle to commence. Giora whispers into his walkie-talkie, asking whether anyone in the sniper squads opened fire before Amiram entered the building. One of them answers that he shot one of the terrorists, the one closest to the roof, after the terrorist took potshots at the force.

The heavy gunfire that erupted earlier from the far end of the corridor catches Udi and his men entering the building with Avishai. They immediately spot one of the terrorists shooting at them and return automatic fire, hitting the terrorist as he tries to escape, injured, to the nearest room. Udi and Avishai run up the stairs in seconds and advance along the second-floor corridor under cover of massive gunfire.

Exactly ten seconds later, an almighty explosion rocks the building, resounding across southwest Tel Aviv. The terrorists set off the bomb that they laid earlier to blow up the hotel. The explosion destroys the southwest corner of the top floor and alerts all the local residents—at least those who were still sleeping—that something out of the ordinary was happening right under their noses.

Just as the reverberations of the explosion begin to subside, Nehemiah reaches the ground floor with his men and asks Udi whether anyone has reached the second floor already. Udi's negative reply sends Nehemiah running up to the second floor, followed by Amiram's squad, all sprinting up the stairs together. Massive gunfire greets the men on their way upstairs and they return fire.

Nehemiah's squad, running up to the second floor at the same time as Udi, Amiram, and their men, finds two dead terrorists outside the room with the hostages, lying on top of each other. They were both killed in the explosion, it seems. In the darkness and dust of the explosion, and in the fog of war, Sayeret Matkal's soldiers start sweeping the rooms and discover in one of them a terrorist lying in a bathtub, shocked, a Kalashnikov lying next to him. When the terrorist hears the soldiers' voices, he grabs his rifle but immediately absorbs two bursts of gunfire from Nehemiah, and the white bathtub is splattered with his red blood.

Meanwhile, Alon Shemi and his squad are waiting with their ladder on the roof of the adjacent building. When the gunfire begins, they immediately steady the ladder between the two roofs and start climbing over to the roof of the hotel. The explosion catches them between heaven and earth, dangling between the buildings. They enter the top floor of the hotel through the little room on the roof and there, in the clouds of dust and smoke belched out by the explosion, they find one of the terrorists. At that exact moment, Alon and his men hear Nehemiah calling them from the second floor and barking orders at his men. Alon identifies himself at the top of his lungs, makes sure that Nehemiah and his men are not in his line of fire, and takes down the terrorist on the roof.

Amnon Peled and his squad, part of Team Nehemiah, enter the hotel as soon as they hear the first gunfire. As they run up to the second floor, which has been cleansed by Udi, the terrorist who was shot and seriously injured regains his senses for a single, fateful moment, spots one of Amnon's men standing next to the room into which the other injured terrorist just leapt, and empties a long and lethal hail of bullets into him. The man is killed.

* * *

Outside the hotel stands Uzi Yairi, a soldier inside and out, wearing full battle gear and holding a gun, listening to the gunfire. The dozens of soldiers waging a ferocious battle in the hotel are his former subordinates, and he feels like they are all his sons. He has to forcibly stop himself from joining the raid, as his conscience urges him but his reason forbids. And then comes the monumental explosion from the hotel, consuming all the rules of the game in one big fireball. Yairi has been a soldier his whole life, and now he can't fight the urge to run into the hotel and physically defend his men. When he is about to break in, he bends down and takes a peek under a doorframe, like the professional soldier he is, but the lone terrorist wounded by Udi, who has already managed to kill Amnon's soldier, spots Yairi, shoots him in the head, and kills one of the finest commanders that Sayeret Matkal and the IDF have ever known.

Amnon shouts at everyone running up behind him not to approach the room from which shots were fired at Yairi.

Ilan, from Team Nehemiah, is just on his way down from the second floor after getting stuck in the long bottleneck of soldiers going upstairs, and he whips out a grenade and chucks it into the room from which the lethal gunfire emerged, ending the life of the last terrorist.

The battle is over.

Omer Bar-Lev's force was supposed to enter through the glass door on the ground floor as soon as Nehemiah's force entered the hotel. But by the time they manage to smash the glass panes and get inside, there is little left for them to do, and they run into Nehemiah and Amiram's teams as they start converging on the exit.

Amiram conducts an organized sweep, floor by floor, in an attempt to find any additional terrorists. And when the hotel is finally declared clean, the men spill out into the street, chastened and downhearted.

* * *

Seven terrorists are killed during the raid on the hotel: one on the roof, four on the second floor next to the room where the hostages are held, one in the bath, and one—the one who killed Uzi Yairi—in a room on the ground floor where he lay in ambush for Sayeret Matkal after taking a bullet from Udi, before eventually being killed by shrapnel from the grenade that Ilan lobbed his way. Another terrorist manages to sneak out of the hotel in the morning and open sporadic fire before he is caught by police officers.

The seven hostages are killed in the bombing, a few seconds after Udi enters the hotel. Max Halperin, the receptionist, is murdered by the terrorists even earlier. Only three of the ten civilians originally in the hotel survive: Kochava Levi and her partner, the liaisons with the Israeli forces, who work out where to hide during the raid; and Karl Feldman, the Dutch tourist, whose fifteen-year-old son is killed in the explosion.

The dead and injured, the terrorists' bodies, and of course Kochava the heroine are picked up and treated by the medical teams swarming the street outside the rubble of the hotel. For the soldiers discharging their weapons and casting off their battle gear in the street, glowing in the morning sunlight, this battle feels like a colossal failure. They lost their comrade from Team Amnon and also Uzi Yairi, their commanders' esteemed commander, and everyone, even the youngest soldiers, knew him well from the annual reunions of Sayeret Matkal veterans and events where they heard stories of the unit's most daring raids.

There is nothing that can be said to make things better or assuage their pain. The death of such a titanic commander as Yairi, in a gunfight right in the heart of Tel Aviv, is one of the hardest emotional blows to recover from, not just for the soldiers who participated in the battle itself but also for everyone else in Sayeret Matkal, in active duty and reserves.

IDF intelligence chief Maj. Gen. Shlomo Gazit, who comes to Sayeret Matkal's postmortem analysis the next day with the whole unit in attendance, tries to assuage their pain, saying that "this mission was an operational success by any criteria, and the unit's performance was elegant." In those words exactly.

He tells the shamefaced soldiers sitting in the auditorium that when the General Staff convened at the Kirya in Tel Aviv at midnight to discuss the attack, a Kalashnikov bullet suddenly flew through the window and landed right next to one of the generals. They sent men straight to the gates of the base to check the guard's gun, to see whether it had accidentally discharged. Only a few minutes later did they realize that the bullet had been fired by one of the terrorists and had made its way unmolested from the beachside hotel all the way to the Kirya deep inside Tel Aviv.

The head of Central Command joins the postmortem and notes that Giora's planning was impeccable, because it was the raid from four different openings, given that the terrorists were not concentrated in a single place but rather scattered around the building, that ultimately led to the elimination of seven of the eight terrorists. Their performance was also excellent, says the general, who wraps up by telling them, "I want to conclude with one word: bravo."

But not even the general's kind words can scrape away even a scintilla of the soldiers' pain and disappointment, having acted with such speed, determination, and courage, almost without a single mistake, only to leave with the nasty, sour taste of failure in their mouths. This relatively small clique of soldiers and officers, some of whom had already taken part in hostage rescue missions time and again, had coolly and calmly decided to risk their lives, without a moment's hesitation or doubt, just to save the lives of complete strangers. But for all their rigorous preparations, outstanding teamwork, and rapid pursuit of the terrorists, and for all their lightning-fast reactions and precise fire, they also needed an ounce or two of good luck. That's what they were missing this time.

Chapter 11

OPERATION THUNDERBOLT— ENTEBBE, JULY 1976

On Sunday, June 27, 1976, an Airbus jetliner takes off from Ben Gurion Airport on an Air France flight to Paris, with a layover in Athens. Shortly after taking off from Athens, the plane is hijacked by four terrorists: three men and a woman. They belong to the international terrorism ring orchestrated by Wadie Haddad, a Palestinian Christian doctor-turned-arch-terrorist. The plane is forced to land in Benghazi, in Libya, for refueling—and then to continue to Entebbe, Uganda.

In Entebbe, the passengers are forcibly disembarked and concentrated in the old airport terminal, guarded by the four hijackers. They will soon be joined by other terrorists and Ugandan soldiers.

The hijackers present a list of demands to free the hostages, including the release of terrorists jailed in Israel, France, and other countries, as well as a ransom. A few days later, the terrorists release some of the passengers—keeping only the Israelis and Jews.

* * *

Naturally, in any airplane hijacking or hostage crisis, Sayeret Matkal is the first to be called to arms, thanks to its rich experience in freeing hostages and its soldiers' intensive training for these scenarios. Sayeret Matkal's commander is Yonatan "Yoni" Netanyahu, who took over from Giora Zorea around a year ago. Yoni is the eldest of three brothers, who all served together in Sayeret Matkal. By the time the Air France plane is hijacked and taken to Entebbe, Benjamin and Iddo have long finished their military service, leaving Yoni as the sole representative of the Netanyahu family in the elite commando unit.

Yonatan was named for two men. The first part of his name comes from his godfather, Lieutenant Colonel. John Henry Patterson, the commander of the Jewish Legion and a close friend of Yoni's parents Tzila and Professor Benzion Netanyahu. The second half of his name comes from Nathan Mileikowsky, his paternal grandfather, a rabbi, educator, and Zionist activist. And Yoni, even when not in active service, bears on his sturdy shoulders the whole of the weighty history symbolized by his name.

Yoni Netanyahu joined Sayeret Matkal as a young and outstanding officer from the Paratroopers at the recommendation of his brother Benjamin ("Bibi"), who served in a squad commanded by Amiram Levin and was certain that this connection would do wonders both for Yoni and for the unit. And so it was. Yoni insisted on beginning almost from scratch, as the commander of a combat squad, "Team Yoni." After that, he was tapped to head the training company, and after that, he became the unit's deputy commander under Giora Zorea. When Zorea came up to the end of his term, Avraham Arnan, who from the lofty heights of IDF Intelligence often meddled with appointments of commanders in the unit that he founded, wrestled with the question with intelligence chief Shlomo Gazit, before eventually tapping Yoni as Zorea's successor.

Arnan, the founder of this dynasty, is infatuated with Yoni, not just as a fighter and a commander but also as a brand—as someone who looks the part. Who looks exactly like the sort of brave and experienced commander that such a daredevil unit deserves, and like the right sort of idealist to instruct the soldiers of a unit with such stratospheric ambitions, and not just operational ones, vital as they may be.

Born to a family of intellectuals from Jerusalem, Yoni ticks all the boxes and adds his own special charm, a real bonus: he exudes an aura of American refinement, the product of his childhood in the United States, which makes quite the stark contrast with the native-born Israelis who commanded the unit before him and will take the reins after him.

Yoni is different, no doubt about that. He has none of the typically Israeli coarseness of other generals, and he is an intellectual and a man of books, but never someone who shows off about it.

Sayeret Matkal commanders are always busy with exhausting, dangerous, and challenging work, planning and executing intelligence operations that demand incredible derring-do, infinite precision, and leadership. But these operations are kept top-secret forever, and frustratingly, the unit's commanders are normally judged by the results of just one or two incidents, whether wartime operations or hostage rescue missions, that randomly fall on their watch. These impulsive hostile events are the diametric opposites of Sayeret Matkal's own intelligence missions, which are meticulously planned down to the number of breaths each soldier takes en route to a target—and one failed response risks trashing an excellent commander's reputation, or making his career.

The entire officer corps is called to arms as soon as news arrives of a hijacked plane, in order to come up with an action plan of some sort to free the hostages in Entebbe, even though at these early stages, nobody's willing to bet even a single Israeli lira that such an operation could ever go ahead or even get a green light.

Sayeret Matkal has just one top commander, Yoni Netanyahu, who's currently in the Sinai Desert, preparing for an extremely challenging intelligence operation, but encircling him, like vultures eyeing carrion, are former Sayeret Matkal commander Ehud Barak and Yoni's eventual successor after his untimely death, Amiram Levin. Colonel Ehud Barak is currently the Intelligence Corps deputy chief of operations, who helps oversee clandestine operations; Levin is the head of IDF Intelligence's special operations branch, at the rank of major; and neither man can let such an event pass him by without getting stuck in, even without participating in the operation itself.

The IDF chief of staff is Motta Gur, who already has two Sayeret Matkal hostage rescue missions under his belt. The first was at Ma'alot, in the deadly hostage crisis in northern Israel immediately after he became Israel's top general, which left him unimpressed with the unit's capabilities. The second came a year later, at the Savoy Hotel, and this time, he liked what he saw. Gur taps Dan Shomron, the head of the Infantry and Paratroopers Corps, to lead the Entebbe operation—if it goes ahead—and it's obvious to both men that the main force that will break into the terminal building where the hostages are held will be Sayeret Matkal. The unit has too many powerful veterans at every rank above it for anyone to even think about tasking another force with the takeover (although the idea briefly pops up—and is dropped five minutes later). It also has a decent track record in such crises, besides the fiasco at Ma'alot.

Barak and Levin, Sayeret Matkal commanders past and future, will obviously recommend Sayeret Matkal for the task, as will Amnon Biran, the unit's former long-serving chief intelligence officer. The unit even has the backing of Prime Minister Yitzhak Rabin, who has become a big fan, and not just because his daughter Dalia served there. Maybe it's because Rabin is such a rigorous perfectionist that he instinctively backs a unit that has "rigor" as its middle name.

At first, Ehud Barak is appointed to oversee the planning, either because of his role in IDF Intelligence or because of his dominant personality. As a former Sayeret Matkal commander, he has already planned and led such awe-inspiring missions as Operation Spring of Youth and the Sabena hostage rescue mission, and he's playing on his home turf. He gets the chief of staff's blessing to start collecting intelligence and planning the takeover of the terminal, and he brings together in his office at the Kirya defense HQ in Tel Aviv a group of officers with enough imagination and creativity to plan a mission that at least on the surface looks totally impossible. Among these officers is Muki Betser, who brings along a few more junior reserves officers, whom he admires for their ability to think out of the box and would trust blindly.

At this early stage, the operational story is totally disconnected from the broader political and diplomatic picture. Prime Minister Yitzhak Rabin and his defense minister, Shimon Peres, are still extremely skeptical about the military option to free the hostages, although Peres is slightly more gung-ho, and government deliberations swing between the relatively simple option of surrendering to the hostage-takers' demands and the proudly patriotic ironclad rule of never, ever giving in to extortion. Even the kidnappers' relatively modest demand this time—the release of just fifty-three terrorists, only forty of whom are jailed in Israel—makes life unbearable for Rabin and Peres.

All sorts of operational ideas are thrown in the air around the drawing boards of the Kirya. Some of them evaporate at once, quickly dispersed by the ceiling fans; others slowly gain sway over the officers.

One of the craziest ideas is for soldiers from Shayetet 13 to parachute onto Lake Victoria and head to Entebbe Airport straight from there. But then someone around the table mentions that the lake might be swarming with crocodiles, which turns out to the true, and nobody would fancy an Israeli commando's chances against a Ugandan croc.

At one point during the brainstorming sessions, Lieutenant Colonel. Ido Ambar from the Israeli Air Force mumbles something about the possibility, however farfetched, of landing Israeli C-130 cargo planes at Entebbe Airport itself, with camouflaged vehicles and heavily-armed soldiers onboard. Muki Betser, who quickly clocks that the officer is onto something, loudly jumps on the bandwagon.

The planes, in Ambar's proposal, will land in pitch darkness, and dozens of Israeli soldiers will leap out and storm the old terminal building, eliminate the kidnappers, and free the hostages.

Easy-peasy. Or so it seems.

Betser's imagination runs wild, and he suggests that the first car to roll out of the belly of the plane should be a black luxury Mercedes, just like those used by Ugandan government and military officials, with its own motorcade of jeeps. The Israeli soldiers, in Betser's plan, will wear camouflaged uniforms exactly like those worn by Ugandan soldiers.

Ehud Barak, an experienced planner of special operations, is immediately convinced that Betser's plan is the only practical option. If the political echelon decides on a mission to free the hostages, therefore, it will have to be based on Betser's ideas. Barak has already flirted with every possible danger at the head of so many commando operations—declassified and top-secret alike—and he loves the idea of Israeli soldiers dressing up as Ugandan troops. Previous commando missions in which Sayeret Matkal's soldiers went undercover, such as the Sabena Flight hostage rescue mission or Operation Spring of Youth, were hugely successful. And Barak, the commander of both missions, believes that costume will add a crucial element of surprise—which is critical for any commando mission, especially in hostage rescue operations.

Barak writes down all the suggestions that have come up in his office, and together with Betser and his comrades, he presents them one by one to Avigdor Ben-Gal, a senior officer in the IDF Operations Division, and then to Major General. Yekutiel Adam, the head of the Operations Division, who passes them on to the chief of staff, Motta Gur.

But taking out the terrorists and freeing the hostages might be the easiest part of this operation. Reaching Entebbe Airport, landing in total darkness, and taking off again with the freed hostages will be far more complicated and problematic. Moreover, the whole audacious plan is clouded by fears that the airport is completely controlled by the Ugandan military. For years Uganda had practically familial relations with the IDF and the State of Israel, but it flipped overnight, thanks to the whims of its mentally unstable dictator Idi Amin, and became a vocal opponent of Israel—and an ardent supporter of its worst enemies.

* * *

The IDF chief of staff summons Baruch Bar-Lev, who headed the Israeli delegation to Uganda for many years and became Idi Amin's personal friend, and asks him to call his friend to try to turn him into an objective mediator between Israel and the terrorists, hoping to avoid a massacre of innocents. The Ugandan tyrant will of course reap a generous dividend of international glorification in exchange for his help. But this attempt fails, and the IDF ploughs ahead with intensive operations for this presumptuous mission, knowing clearly that the hostage-taking terrorists are not its only enemies—so are the dozens of Ugandan soldiers streaming into the airport to guard their new Middle Eastern buddies.

The main problem with using C-130 (or "Hercules") cargo planes is the vast distance between Israel and Uganda—over 2,000 miles—requiring refueling on the way. The IAF's Yellow Bird Squadron only has two planes that can make the journey without refueling, but that will mean taking a relatively small force to save fuel. The problem is finally solved when Israel gets permission from the Kenyan government to refuel in the capital, Nairobi (allowing the operation to proceed with four planes in the end). Maybe the Kenyans don't exactly understand Israel's strange request, or maybe they do and choose to turn a blind eye, but this makes it possible for the planes involved in the mission to return home without worrying about running out of fuel mid-air.

The approval to land for refueling in Nairobi returns some color to the cheeks of the many Israeli planners—from the Air Force, the IDF Operations Division, and Sayeret Matkal—because now they can send a relatively large force of soldiers and vehicles on the planes, which will be able to whisk the strike force from the remote runway at Entebbe Airport to the old terminal, where the hijackers are keeping the hostages.

The resolution of the refueling problem takes a huge worry off their chests, but this fantastical operation remains almost as big a challenge. Flying such a huge force thousands of miles away on heavy and clunky cargo planes, and landing them in secret and in darkness in a quasi-enemy state, when there's a real fear that the Ugandan army won't let them take off again—the mission looks *almost* impossible. But the C-130 squadron, the Air Force HQ, the General Staff, the Defense Ministry, and the Prime Minister's Office must be packed with people for whom the word *"almost"* excites their imagination and sends their heartbeat racing. Now that the Israeli military has a tailor-made operational plan to free the hostages, which stands a relatively solid chance of success, it looks like none of the leaders who must authorize it will dare to call it off because of "logistical" problems.

In reality, the situation is a world away from being as neat as it looks in hindsight, but let's not give away the ending.

* * *

It's Thursday, July 1, and the IDF top brass understands that it is marching in the direction of a hostage rescue mission. And when it becomes clear that there's a real operational chance to "do it," Sayeret Matkal finally sets in motion preparations to seize the terminal in Entebbe. Yoni Netanyahu and his top team are summoned back from the Sinai, briefed on Betser's plans and preparations, and from that moment the whole unit is mobilized solely for the mission in Entebbe.

The senior squad in the unit at the time is led by Amnon Peled, whose men are on leave before the end of their military service and whose thoughts are as far from a takeover operation as Tel Aviv is far from Entebbe. Usually, the squad that leads such an operation is chosen by virtue of its seniority, or length of service. But in hindsight, if Sayeret Matkal's officers had to pick any squad from the unit, there's no doubt the task would have fallen to Amnon Peled's team anyway.

Peled is the kind of guy you'd always want by your side in an operation like this. He's cool-headed and brave, measured and incredibly rigorous, and he knows to squeeze the most out of his soldiers, quietly and peacefully, maintaining impeccable interpersonal relations. He's got the whole package, making him the ideal commander for these missions, with soldiers who would do anything for him. His men have already taken part in one mission to rescue hostages, at the Savoy Hotel in Tel Aviv, losing one of their own number in the attack—Itamar Ben-David.

On the night between Thursday and Friday, between July 1 and 2, Peled and his men are therefore recalled from leave. When he meets his soldiers at the unit, in the early hours of the morning, before he has even had a chance to miss them after they all went home at the end of their long, action-packed years of service, Peled informs them, without beating around the bush, and without a hint of invective or jubilation: "There's an IDF-wide operation to free the hostages, Sayeret Matkal is the tip of the spear, and we're the pointy end." "We," of course, means Amnon Peled's own team. He doesn't need to say another word.

At 09:00, they enter an initial briefing with Omer Bar-Lev's team and many other Sayeret Matkal officers and reservists, as well as several soldiers from Arnon Epstein's team, who are all hoping this will be their lucky day and they'll get to participate in this historic mission. Yoni Netanyahu, who only came back last night from an action-packed week on active duty in the Sinai, takes the stage.

The briefing is fairly abstract, focusing mainly on the number of terrorists ("between eight and fifteen," according to Yoni) and Ugandan soldiers at the airport ("between 200 to 1,000"). By this point, the unit is talking about approaching the old terminal in cars from the drop-off point where the C-130s will stop, and about the exterior perimeter, which will be guarded by a team that will land a few minutes after Sayeret Matkal's forces and will move around in four lightly armored vehicles. The hostages, the soldiers are told in the briefing, are being held in two halls: the first, the closer one from the Israeli forces' perspective, has two doorways; the second, which is further away, has only one. Yoni puts one officer and three soldiers in charge of each opening, for now.

Although Yoni Netanyahu is delivering the briefing, there's a stubborn rumor doing the rounds among the soldiers that Ehud Barak has been given command of Sayeret Matkal's forces for the operation. This rumor is the product of a jumbled chain of command, and it gains a hold over the soldiers during the briefing by Yoni, their esteemed commander over the past year.

It's not a totally ridiculous idea: Barak only relinquished his command of the unit three years earlier, and thanks to his senior role in military intelligence and his practically innate impulse to play a key role in every high-stakes (and maybe highly-publicized) operation, he's definitely trying to maneuver for command of this mission. Only the swift and assertive intervention of the operation's commander, Dan Shomron, helped by IDF operations chief Major General. Yekutiel Adam, who both understand that such a substitution simply won't fly, puts each man back in his place. Major General. Adam decides to send Barak as the head of a small delegation to the Kenyan capital of Nairobi to coordinate the landing and refueling of the Hercules planes, and Yoni keeps the job that he has so richly earned: the commander of Sayeret Matkal's strike force. At the end of the briefing, the soldiers in Sayeret Matkal's force leave to grab their equipment and study the little information that has poured in.

* * *

Dan Shomron and his officers put together the final plan, which will include three forces:

1. A Sayeret Matkal force, commanded by Yoni Netanyahu, which will be the first to reach the target, subdue the terrorists, free the hostages, and take them to the C-130 planes on the runway;
2. A Golani infantry force headed by brigade commander Uri Sagi, which will provide back-up for the main forces and help them to evacuate the hostages;
3. A force from the 35th Paratroopers Brigade, under brigade commander Matan Vilnai, which will seize control of the new terminal, in case it is occupied by a large Ugandan military force.

Uri Sagi picks fifty men, mostly from Golani's special reconnaissance unit, and peppers them with a few outstanding officers from its battalions.

Matan Vilnai is supposed to choose sixty soldiers, and he picks them out with tweezers from Battalion 890, Battalion 202, and the Paratroopers' special reconnaissance unit. Surgically selecting a small proportion of the soldiers, from both Golani and the Paratroopers, is an unenviable task for the commanders of the brigades and Sayeret Matkal. They are all under incredible pressure, certain they'll have to read about their friends in the papers after the operation inevitably makes sensational headlines the next morning.

Meanwhile, at Sayeret Matkal—pandemonium. On the one hand, intensive efforts are underway to secure equipment for this fantastical operation, with the instructions about the gear and uniform worn by the soldiers changing every few minutes. On the other hand, the veteran squads mobilized back to the unit are incredibly skeptical about the feasibility of the whole mission. Even these men, who have already been everywhere in the Middle East and beyond, and have already done the impossible several times over, can't wrap their hyper-imaginative brains around an operation 2,000 miles away, based on just a few hours of prep work. It goes against Sayeret Matkal's basic DNA, which has entered the bloodstream of every soldier who has ever served there.

Nevertheless, as the hours go by, and the cancelation order is nowhere in sight, the heavy shroud of skepticism gives way to an intensive, high-pressure battle over the right to take part in an operation that nobody believes will actually happen. The soldiers pressure their direct commanders, who apply even stronger pressure on the force commanders, and everyone together piles insane pressure on Yoni, who first needs to finish putting together the operational plan and thoroughly study the terrain and all possible hitches and solutions.

It's not just because all the soldiers understandably want a piece of "real" action—the ultimate test for any fighter after years of grueling exercises and drills—but also, and maybe mainly, because Entebbe is their entry pass to the exclusive club of those who've "done it."

Every officer, without exception, keeps knocking at Yoni's door to present scenarios they came up with only a minute earlier and make the urgent case for Yoni to take just one more man, or maybe two, from *his* team—and not that of another, hapless, inexperienced comrade. This is not just a war over the credit for their top soldiers; it's also a war for their own cachet in their commander's eyes.

On Friday, July 2, at 16:00, Sayeret Matkal holds its last review of the soldiers' gear. Muki Betser, who is supposed to be Yoni's deputy in the operation and to command the first squad to breach the terminal, inspects the soldiers and decides to arm it with more explosives, in case the terminal doors are locked. He also orders Amir Ofer from Team Amnon to take a megaphone so that he can bark instructions at the hostages during the break-in. The megaphone will soon prove its use.

During the roll call, a white Mercedes pulls up at Sayeret Matkal's base and immediately receives a place of honor in the planning, replacing one of the jeeps in which the break-in squads will be driven from the plane to the old terminal building. The Mercedes, which is supposed to look like Idi Amin's car, was tracked down at some garage in Jaffa by "Alex" from Mossad, in advanced stages of mechanical death and looking like a piece of scrap on its way to the junkyard. But Danny Dagan, Sayeret Matkal's vehicle officer, together with weapons officer Amitzur Kafri and his right-hand man in special operations Roded Oriyan, have worked on it all night with their men, painted it black, and given it quite a regal appearance ahead of the departure to Entebbe.

Immediately after the inspection of the gear, Sayeret Matkal receives a delivery of striped camouflage uniforms like those worn by Ugandan soldiers, and they are handed out to the men on the first plane, those who will break into the room where the hostages are held, in order to bolster the element of deception and surprise.

* * *

It's Friday night. A midsummer's night descends on Sayeret Matkal's base, and the soldiers preparing to be sprung into action are waiting for IDF Chief of Staff Motta Gur on the runways next to the unit's HQ, in order to conduct their first and last practice run in his presence. The soldiers wait for several hours, going out of their minds with fury. Each of them has dozens of tasks, large and small, to perform before their departure, and they can't understand why they have to waste their precious time sitting around waiting for the chief of staff. They're used to being the leading actors in every spectacle they take part in. But waiting for a general, no matter how high up? That isn't in their job description.

Later, they discover that the chief of staff was flying in one of the C-130 planes, checking for himself whether the pilots could land in total darkness, without navigation equipment, and that's why he reaches Sayeret Matkal's headquarters after such a long delay.

Now, with the high-profile presence of the chief of staff and a rabble of senior officers, the decisive test run begins. Its success will determine whether Gur advises Defense Minister Shimon Peres to approve the mission, Peres adds his signature and sends it to Prime Minister Yitzhak Rabin, and Rabin submits the final recommendation to the whole cabinet. And this entire military and political pyramid, the tallest in the land, is transfixed on a few canvas sheets tied to iron rods, which are standing in for the terminal where the hostages are held.

The schematic drill takes place for the first time without any hitches. The soldiers clear out the "rooms" they have been assigned, marked out rugs on the floor, with efficient professionalism and then the chief of staff asks them to perform another drill, and this time—to make the whole journey from the planes to the target in the real cars they will use. When the men reach the target for the second time, they are surprised to discover an "enemy" force stationed just a few feet away from the rugs, which unleashes a frenzied hail of blanks on them. Sayeret Matkal's soldiers have to leap out of their vehicles before their scheduled spot, return precise fire, eliminate the enemy force, and once again seize control from the terrorists inside the terminal marked out with canvas sheets.

Motta Gur and his officers find the soldiers' execution extremely impressive, and it gives them the confidence they were still lacking to recommend the mission to the political echelon for final approval. But it's the fact that the drill is so easy and simple that freaks the soldiers out and feeds their doubts about the mission's feasibility. There is so little confidence that a few prominent officers even consider taking the matter themselves to the top of the pyramid and asking for the whole operation to be thought through again. They're afraid that the preparations are not serious or thorough enough and could lead to a major disaster.

But the IDF's machinery is turning at full-throttle, crushing all doubts and hesitations, building a packed timetable because of external restraints that have nothing to do with the preparedness of any particular unit, and bringing all hands on deck for a joint effort directed ultimately at just one goal: liberating the hostages, and killing or capturing all the terrorists.

IDF Chief of Staff Motta Gur asks for a few soldiers to be taken off the advance force's vehicles because of overcrowding and excess weight problems. But none of the soldiers who have already elbowed their way into the mission after strenuous internal fighting is willing to give up his spot, at any price. The war over flight tickets to Entebbe moves up a notch, until the chief of staff reluctantly gives in—and the only excess weight removed from the cars and the operation is two Doberman hounds, the tongue-lashing monsters that have been trained for years to identify terrorists in a thick swarm of people, and for which Entebbe was supposed to be the peak of their combat careers. No longer.

Sayeret Matkal's soldiers spend the night between Friday and Saturday checking their weapons and topping up their gear. The chatter among them before take-off on Saturday is that "this mission is either going to be the biggest, most glorious fiasco in the history of the IDF—or its greatest-ever success." Nothing in the middle is conceivable.

* * *

On Friday night, after a vigilant waiting period, Sayeret Matkal finally receives a detailed report from Amiram Levin, who has flown to Paris to scoop up every possible morsel of information from the non-Jewish passengers who were released by the terrorists and flown back to France. The information, accurate as of Thursday morning, when they left Entebbe, includes precise sketches of the old terminal (which perfectly match the blueprints already obtained by the unit's intelligence officer, Avi Weiss), the location of the Israeli hostages (they were all rounded up in the large hall in the old terminal), the number of terrorists guarding the Israelis ("around ten"), and the number of Ugandan soldiers aiding the terrorists and guarding the terminal ("between five and 100"). The report also totally negates the possibility that the transit hall is booby-trapped.

Levin's detailed report, after being studied inside-out by the intelligence officer and passed on to Yoni, succeeds, if only for an instant, to alleviate the horrible feeling that Sayeret Matkal is embarking on a fiendishly complex mission without the basic preparations that it usually takes as a unit that lionizes rigor and absolute perfectionism.

In the early hours of Saturday morning, the Sayeret Matkal force leaves the base in the direction of the military airport at Lod, where the C-130 "Hercules" planes are waiting to take them to Sharm-el-Sheikh in the Sinai and from there, after landing to refuel and be briefed, to Entebbe. The July heat, and the bumpy ride on the heavy and cumbersome aircraft, upsets the soldiers' digestion. The massive tension before the operation seems to also have an effect, and not a good one. Most of them puke their guts out throughout the flight, stumbling out of the plane at Sharm-el-Sheikh pale and sweaty. Who needs the terrorists in Entebbe, or their Ugandan military allies, to defeat this tiny Sayeret Matkal force, which still can't believe that such a perilous operation is actually going ahead?

Only Dr. David Hassin, Sayeret Matkal's in-house medic, scuttles around, cramming anti-nausea pills into the soldiers' mouths and trying to reassure the "tough guys" who in just a few hours will take part in the most heroic mission in the IDF's history—but are currently imploding from a little bit of turbulence and the unbearable heat of the Sinai Desert.

Yoni gathers his men for the absolutely final briefing before they board the planes again and depart for Entebbe. In situations like these, the smell of gunpowder in his nostrils, Yoni is always at the top of his game. During the first stage of the planning and preparations at Sayeret Matkal's HQ, he was busy prepping for another major intelligence mission, leaving the planning for Entebbe to Muki Betser and his men. It was assumed that the chances the operation would go ahead were close to zero, and so the unit's commander was better off focusing on its ongoing intelligence and operational work. But now, in Sharm-el-Sheikh, as the forces wait for the final green-light, which should arrive at any minute from the prime minister, Yoni assumes the moral authority befitting a unit commander leading his men into the most complicated mission that Sayeret Matkal and the whole IDF have ever known.

Yoni Netanyahu's pep talk is the kind of inspirational and trans-formational event that will be remembered for years by everybody present, and also by many others who will hear about it directly from those who were present. Yoni really captures the moment and manages, with succinct and icy coolness, to give his men absolute confidence in their mission and its inevitable success. Countless thoughts and doubts have plagued the hasty preparations for this mission, dampening the soldiers' mood as they board the plane that will whisk them away to Entebbe. And now, at the one and only moment of truth, Yoni chooses his words and body language carefully so that all his men, without exception, can precisely calibrate their combat readiness and their per-sonal readiness for the needs of this operation. Combat soldiers, always and everywhere, draw their confidence from their commanders' words, their body language, their tone, and a whole host of other significant but subtle nuances in the relationship between a commander and his men.

"We know how to execute this and bring the hostages home," Yoni tells his soldiers. "I'm sure you're much better and more skilled than them, and in a one-on-one battle, we'll always beat them."[1]

* * *

---

1   Tal Shalev, "Yoni Netanyahu's Final Briefing," *Walla*, 4 July 2016 [Hebrew].

When the Sayeret Matkal soldiers board the first Hercules plane, piloted by Yehoshua "Shuki" Shani and Avi Einstein, they are completely different from the men who disembarked just a short hour earlier. Someone—Yoni, that is—has flipped the secret switch in their heads to "on" mode, putting them on an instant war-footing. Sixty-five Sayeret Matkal soldiers take off from Sharm-el-Sheikh. Thirty-three fighters, who will breach the terminal at Entebbe, board the first Hercules plane; thirty-two fighters, commanded by Shaul Mofaz, who will guard the break-in force in four armored vehicles, split between the second and third planes. Another airplane, the fourth, is supposed to bring the hostages back to Israel. The soldiers in the break-in force change out of their regular uniforms into "Ugandan" ones (which are just IDF camouflage fatigues from before the Six-Day War) in order to perfect the great deceptive ruse.

At 15:05 on Saturday, when the four Hercules planes take off from Sharm-el-Sheikh, the Israeli government is still sitting on the fence and agonizing over whether to approve the mission. Prime Minister Rabin and Dan Shomron, the overall commander of the forces, have agreed that if the government decides for whatever reason to scupper the mission, the Hercules planes will perform a U-turn in the air and return to Israel.

The departure from Sharm-el-Sheikh is perhaps the hardest take-off that the eight pilots have ever attempted. The planes are crammed full of people and vehicles, far beyond the aircraft's weight limitations, the runway at Sharm-el-Sheikh is quite short, and the oppressive heat places even more pressure on the creaking engines. And when the pilots go full-throttle, their planes keep limping along the runway, showing no signs of being willing to point their noses up and disconnect from the ground. The blue sea quickly advances on the pilots, ready to welcome them. And only in the last few feet do these four metal beasts manage to take off from the runway and slowly inch toward the sky. When they reach cruising altitude, most of the soldiers are enjoying a well-deserved nap. And then a message comes through the comms system, loud and clear, in Yitzhak Rabin's unmistakable cigarette-stained voice: "Approved."

* * *

The flight takes seven and a half hours, and the first Hercules plane lands without difficulties at Entebbe Airport and drops off the Paratroopers force. Its mission is to secure the plane on the runway. Afterwards, another Paratroopers force disembarks to place lights along the length of the runway in order to illuminate it for the incoming planes, just in case someone in the control tower realizes what's going on and pulls the plug on the electricity, including the critical runway edge lights.

Amir Ofer, a soldier in Amnon Peled's squad, who will become one of the heroes of this mission in just a few minutes, a born-and-bred Jerusalemite, cocks his weapon the instant that the wheels make contact with the African asphalt. Another comrade screams at him, "Don't cock your weapon on the plane!" Ofer answers him with uncharacteristic bluntness: "Shut it. This is a real war."

Sayeret Matkal enters this "real war" from the belly of the plane in three vehicles, packed with thirty-three soldiers, on whose personal abilities and readiness for battle the whole operation will depend. Everyone's eyes are glued on them: the hundreds of soldiers who land behind them and peer out from the three other planes into the Ugandan darkness, the many generals huddled in the aerial command and control center in the skies of Africa, the many dozens of IDF planners who have labored day and night over the operation's details, and the whole Israeli nation, sitting at home, completely clueless but worried sick about the dozens of Israelis and Jews held captive at Entebbe, without the faintest clue about the new morning that they're about to wake up to.

The black Mercedes, the piece of scrap from Jaffa that was hastily patched up and repainted to look like Idi Amin's official car, is the first to break onto the runway. It is followed by two jeeps, which are standing in for the Ugandan dictator's security detail, the Israeli soldiers inside dressed in camouflage fatigues, their hearts popping with nerves and fear.

In the Mercedes are ten soldiers: in the front, next to the window, is Yoni Netanyahu, the commander of the Sayeret Matkal force; in the middle sits Muki Betser, the commander of the first break-in squad, and next to him is Amitzur Kafri, the driver. Behind them, sit seven more men. The other soldiers who will break into the transit halls where the hostages are being held are in the two jeeps at the back. Everyone understands that the moment of truth is approaching at the speed at which the three cars race to the terminal.

The vehicles proceed at a moderate speed, their headlights on, as befits the proud Ugandan dictator's motorcade, and when they reach the T-junction of the runways, they turn toward the illuminated terminal building. Everything unfolds exactly to plan, and a sense of cautious confidence takes hold inside the vehicles. But not for long. A few hundred feet after the left turn, Yoni and the soldiers in the Mercedes spot two Ugandan security guards, one on each side of the runway, about 300 feet before the old terminal. The guards, not acting like what you'd expect of Ugandan soldiers who see their supreme leader's motorcade approaching, raise their weapons, ready to shoot the force immediately.

Two lightning-fast, totally contradictory events happen at the same moment inside the Mercedes: Betser, an expert on Ugandan soldiers and their orders, shouts at his men, "Don't shoot!" and at exactly the same fraction of a second, Yoni gives the order to shoot and whips out his handgun, equipped with a silencer, and another combatant in the row behind him does the same. They both open fire, and they both miss the Ugandans.

The men in the first jeep, cruising behind the Mercedes, see the unplanned shooting, take a sharp right to overtake the Mercedes, and rain machine-gun fire on the Ugandan guards, taking them down. But the immaculately planned deception, which was supposed to bring the soldiers right up to the terminal doors quietly and securely, is toast.

In the original plan, the vehicles were supposed to come to a halt between the control tower and the terminal building. But the early shooting, which immediately attracts return fire from the control tower, toward Sayeret Matkal, forces the soldiers to stop around 160 feet before the planned drop-off point and to leap out of the vehicles.

The real test for every soldier or officer in Sayeret Matkal comes now: when they have to improvise because a plan goes haywire.

Sitting in the second jeep, Amir Ofer scrambles to find Amnon Peled, the commander of his squad—but in vain. He assumes that Amnon is already en route to the terminal and breaks into a manic sprint toward the doorway his squad is supposed to blow open. From a distance of about sixty feet, maybe more, he spots the second opening, the farther one, in the windowed wall of the terminal building, and he runs there in a straight, diagonal line.

He spots the rest of the force getting ready, in the order they planned, to run to the side of the terminal and from there to spread along the windowed wall to the two openings. But Amir is convinced that Amnon is already inside, because he has years of experience of his commander's grit and unflinching ambition to strike his targets, and he only has one thing on his mind: to catch up with Amnon and join him. He can't possibly abandon his commander in the most critical battle of their lives.

When Amir runs, as sharp as a razor, he spots from the corner of his eye, on the left, that Muki Betser, the commander of the break-in force, has paused for a millisecond on his way along the terminal's wall, and he hears Yoni urging him to push on. Suddenly, Yoni's voice gets cut off, and Amir sees him collapse on the floor. Somebody shouts, and it's a harrowing and unimaginable cry: "Yoni's been hit."

* * *

Nothing can distract Amir now or confound his senses. When he's fifteen feet from the terminal, the glass windows in the wall of the building explode, right in front of him, and with long hail of gunfire the terrorists try to stop him from running inside. One of the terrorists is lying right by the door, fifteen feet into the transit hall, and Amir raises his trusty AK-47 and empties three lethal bullets through the window. The terrorist's head slumps and the gunfire that greeted Amir stops for a second. When he enters the transit hall, the terrorist at the entrance is still bleeding, and

Amnon Peled is nowhere to be seen. Amir suddenly clocks that he's a lone ranger. Six soldiers were supposed to breach two different openings simultaneously, but now he's alone, staring with astonishment at around 100 people in the hall, including several terrorists—who probably can't believe that Israel has only sent a single soldier to eliminate them.

Amir understands his tricky situation at once, leaps back against a wall, so he can at least shield his back, and sweeps the hall with his eyes to try to identify the other terrorists.

And while Amir is looking for Amnon—jumping out of the car, running to the terminal, and inside the building—Amnon is also looking for Amir. Amnon is intimately familiar with Amir's determination and knows he's not one to get delayed in such dramatic events, when every millisecond can swing the fate of the operation. When he enters the transit hall, short of breath and anxious, mostly for Amir's wellbeing, he spots two terrorists, a man and a woman, one on each side of the doorway he has just entered, their fingers already pulling the triggers of their Kalashnikov rifles, pointed at Amir's back. Amnon is equally quick on his feet, and the two terrorists each get hit by a pair of bullets, returning their souls to their creator without taking Amir with them. Both terrorists, by the way, are Germans who linked up with Wadie Haddad's cell.

Before they died, both terrorists managed to spot the main force advancing along the wall and turned toward it. When Amir entered and shot the lone terrorist lying next to them, they spun around to find the shooter and aimed at him, to settle the score. But neither they nor Amir, firmly in their crosshairs, accounted for the perfectly-timed entry of Amnon, who with four precise bullet saves the life of his soldier.

Even before Amir manages to thank God for saving his skin, and even before he gives his friend and commander a trembling thumbs-up in gratitude, he holds the megaphone on his back to his mouth and shouts in Hebrew and English, "EVERYBODY GET DOWN!" and then hollers to Amnon not to enter the hall, so he won't cross his line of fire.

With Amir's trembling voice still echoing in the transit hall, in come Muki Betser, and his team of four—from exactly the same entrance Amir and Amnon just stepped through. The four men were supposed to enter from the first opening, but for some reason they charged straight past it without noticing it was there. And the second Muki and his squad enter the hall, one of the terrorists springs up from within the crowd and raises his Kalashnikov. Amos Goren, one of the team's members, beats him by a split second and sends him to join his three comrades, those already shot by Amir and Amnon, and thus finishes "cleansing" the hall.

At that exact moment, up pops a hostage, Jean-Jacques Maimoni, thrilled by the killing of the terrorists—and is accidentally shot dead.

The six Israeli soldiers who are just finishing to "cleanse" the main hall where the hostages are held, almost flawlessly completing the main task for which the mission was launched, are anxious about stepping outside and meeting the reality everyone has been trying to repress: the fact that their commander Yoni is injured—and might even be dead.

* * *

As Muki Betser and his squad enter the terminal from the second opening, not the first as originally planned, they are spotted by other team members—who are supposed to enter through the second opening. They know that they're meant to be exactly one doorway along from Muki, so they run by mistake to the third doorway, yet another team's station, which leads to the VIP facility adjacent to the transit hall. And thus, while Amnon and Amir successfully clear out the main hall with Muki Betser and his men, storming the VIP lounge, where the terrorists who are not "on shift" in the main hall are resting.

Giora Zussman, the other team commander, the first to burst into the tiny lounge, spots a small bed on his right, empties a hail of bullets into an imaginary terrorist, and then notices a corridor that did not appear in any of their maps. He enters with another man, who tags along, and discovers that all along it are other VIP rooms. Only in the last room do they detect movement, and two terrorists jump out. He shoots from the hip and hits both of them, causing a grenade held by one of the terrorists to detonate. The explosion in this closed space makes an almighty boom, and only miraculously do he and Giora emerge unscathed.

Dani Arditi and his squad, who were supposed to clear out the VIP lounge, reach it and find the door closed. Arditi hears shooting inside, has no idea that it's coming from Giora Zussman's team and that they got there before them and managed to enter from another entrance, and he's determined to storm inside. He chucks two hand grenades at the door, which refuses to budge, but the shock waves from the explosion injure two of the soldiers, and Arditi tries his luck with another door. When he finally manages to breach the facility, he stumbled upon two dead terrorists and Giora's team, who have just finished clearing the site.

Yiftach Reicher and his men are supposed to clear out the customs hall on the left of the main transit hall where the hostages are, as well as the second floor of the terminal. They kill eleven Ugandan soldiers and complete their mission without a single shot being fired toward them, and after at least sixty Ugandan soldiers in the building manage to flee for their lives. Within ten minutes, the terminal is clear.

While Sayeret Matkal "cleanses" the terminal, two forces under Shaul Mofaz—each commanding two armored vehicles and eight Sayeret Matkal soldiers—burst out into the plaza in front of the terminal and unleash a hail of bullets at the control tower, the source of a trickle of gunfire throughout this whole operation. As the other squads secure the terminal, they hear heavy gunfire in the background and RPG anti-tank rocket launcher explosions, which make the whole airport quake. During the "cleansing" of the terminal building, a no-less-dramatic battle is raging outside: a battle for Yoni Netanyahu's life.

The sequence of events that led to Yoni getting shot begins with the initial strike force getting off the first plane and the incident with the Ugandan soldiers. Yoni understands that this unplanned conflagration might botch the whole mission because of the loss of the painstakingly-planned element of surprise, and in his soft but assertive voice he orders the break-in force to get a move on and reach the terminal doors. Like all of his men, Yoni knows that every wasted second risks turning the operation into a stunning fiasco with dozens of casualties.

And while urging his men to hurry up, Yoni suddenly chokes up and falls down some twenty-five feet from the wall of the terminal, a Kalashnikov bullet in his chest, leaving his team to complete the mission without its commander, without the undisputed leader of the operation.

Dr. David Hassin, the unit's physician, running with the break-in team behind them, reaches the wall of the terminal without noticing that Yoni is down. One of the soldiers calls his attention to the first casualty. Hassin turns back and is shocked to see Yoni sprawled on the floor, motionless and unconscious. He drags Yoni to the wall, which provides them shelter, and sees that he's completely pale because of all the blood he has already lost. The doctor cuts Yoni's shirt open, removes his flak jacket and undershirt, and finds a small entry wound in Yoni's upper back, right under his collarbone, and an exit wound right next to his lumbar spine on the right. He patches Yoni up, lifts him on a stretcher to the jeep with the help of two men, and sends him off to an airplane nearly 1,000 feet away from the terminal. This is the fourth plane, which is supposed to transport the hostages back to Israel.

The medical team on the plane spends a whole hour trying to do the impossible and to bring Yoni back to life and the esteemed commander to his unit. But it's no use. Yoni dies of his wounds after the Hercules plane takes off.

When Amnon Peled and his men finish securing the terminal, and Amnon steps out of the transit hall for a second, he sees Dr. Hassin treating Yoni and understands that the force has been left leaderless. He darts back inside and updates Muki Betser, the most senior officer on the ground, that Yoni is wounded and that he, Muki, must seize command. Dan Shomron, the commander of the overall operation, shows up at the entrance to the terminal and gives the order for the immediate evacuation of all the hostages to the fourth Hercules plane.

Amnon Peled and his soldiers urge the hostages to cram into the vehicles and get evacuated to the planes. Most of the hostages still can't believe that the horror show is over, and they don't understand where these angels swooped in from to free them from the worst nightmare of their lives. They run outside, some of them in their underwear, barefoot and shellshocked. An officer coordinates the evacuation and makes sure all the hostages board the fourth Hercules plane and get whisked away to freedom.

Sayeret Matkal's soldiers board the planes in which they arrived, after making sure several times that no man has been left behind at the airport. The men, who have just successfully completed one of the most complicated and heroic missions the IDF has ever undertaken, are buoyed by a sense of immense relief and supreme satisfaction—but this satisfaction is clouded by the knowledge that "Yoni is seriously injured." Nobody's talking about it out loud yet. Nobody dares to contemplate the nightmare scenario. The soldiers, like their commanders, try to dispel thoughts of the news that will undoubtedly come knocking soon.

And when they fly to Nairobi, where they will refuel on their way back to Israel, they hold the only debriefing that was ever conducted about the battle at Entebbe. Muki Betser calls over the commanders of the forces, one by one, and there, on the bonnet of his jeep, the memory of the battle still fresh in their minds, they try to reconstruct their activities during exactly sixty minutes on the ground in Entebbe.

There, in this first and last debriefing, the first seeds of conflict begin to germinate, which will tarnish the sheen of glory around this mission for decades to come. There, on the bonnet of the jeep, every man has a precise picture in his mind of every action he took, every time he cocked his gun, every fateful delay, and every bullet that hit or missed its target. But the picture described by one man with absolute certainty is the diametric opposite of the one described of the exact same event by his comrade. That's part of human nature. And thus, every man settles on his own personal war movie in his head, which no proven fact can dislodge.

* * *

When Sayeret Matkal's Hercules plane lands in Nairobi, Ehud Barak comes onboard, and they tell the men, in faces pale with anguish: "Yoni was killed." The victors' joy and satisfaction gives way in an instant to a sense of pain. When Rabin authorized the mission, he said explicitly that anything more than twenty fatalities in the operation would be considered a resounding failure that would force him to resign. In reality, the fatalities were four hostages and one soldier: Yoni Netanyahu. But his rank, his seniority, and the fact that he is the unit's commander turn this objective, unparalleled success in the eyes of the men who participated in it into a fiasco, or at least justify a kind of depression from which it will take ages to escape.

Mixed feelings gush through the soldiers' minds on the long flight from Nairobi to Israel. They find it hard to be happy, and hard to be sad. The death of Yoni Netanyahu, the commander of their unit, who had already dodged enemy bullets so many times before, in far more challenging situations than at Entebbe Airport, is like a punch to the gut.

They land at Tel Nof Air Force Base into a hysterical outburst of joy and national pride. The whole of Israel is in a state of total euphoria. The success in Entebbe has made a whole nation, still licking its wounds from the Yom Kippur War, lose its senses in a way that it has never experienced and probably will not experience for many years to come. And only Sayeret Matkal's men, returning to a unit they don't recognize, soon to be commanded by Amiram Levin, can't muster the joy and satisfaction they so richly deserved after such a perfect execution. Statistically, one fatality out of the hundreds of soldiers taking part in an operation is a reasonable operational result, but when that fatality is the commander of the unit, joined at the hip through comradeship and friendship and a history to each and every one of the fighters who took part in the operation—no statistic, good as it may be, can relieve his men's pain.

In hindsight, the operation's success seems almost inevitable. That's what things should look like when everything works almost without hitches, and with tons of proven Israeli initiative and derring-do, both at the planning stage, and in the audacious and visionary stage of government approval, and of course—during the execution itself.

But we have to remember that there are inestimably more fiascos in complicated hostage rescue missions than there are successful ones. It's enough to recall the American operation at Sơn Tây in North Vietnam, in November 1970: the whole U.S. intelligence apparatus labored over the operation for months, and in the end, the Americans got the landing spot wrong and killed dozens of Soviet and Chinese officers in a nearby base, nearly sparking a world war. Or the botched American attempt to free the hostages in Tehran in 1980 (Operation Eagle Claw), in which eight American soldiers were killed in a helicopter collision even before reaching their target.

The IDF, with all its forces, including Sayeret Matkal, proved its exemplary skill at planning and implementation, and there was more than enough glory for everyone who participated to revel in for years to come. And human nature, petty, pedantic human nature, which can't deal with major failures and apparently also major successes, is the only reason for tearing it to shreds. Years of futile arguments, about who shot whom and why, who took the right flank and who took the left, who crouched when he should have stood up, and who broke into a run when he should have lingered for a millisecond. An apocalyptic war broke out, when what was needed most was restraint, and understanding, and an equal sharing of the glory. Because there's enough for everyone.

Chapter 12

THE MISGAV AM MASSACRE– APRIL 1980

I t's April 7, 1980, the last night of Passover, and Uzi Dayan, Sayeret Matkal's commander, is fast asleep at home at Moshav Hayogev. Uzi has been through a long and arduous journey to make it to the commander's chair in the modest office that has already hosted the electrifying presence of such celebrated commanders as Dovik Tamari, Ehud Barak, Yoni Netanyahu, Amiram Levin, Nehemiah Tamari, and others.

None of the royal glory associated with the Dayan family name, thanks to his uncle, Defense Minister Moshe Dayan, could have helped Uzi reach the top job. Only hard work, ambition, extraordinary grit, and yes, probably good genes, the genes of born warriors, inherited through the family genome and imprinted on Uzi's character, have helped him to pull it off. Uzi parachuted into this new role just two months earlier, succeeding Nehemiah Tamari as the commander of Sayeret Matkal, and has not enjoyed a moment of rest since. In March 1980, exactly one month into the job, a naval commando drowns during a joint operation between Shayetet 13 and Sayeret Matkal to cross the Yarmouk River at night. Sayeret Matkal is responsible for the mission, and IDF Chief of

Staff Raful Eitan has been muttering to his generals, "Uzi won't remain Sayeret Matkal's commander under me."

Raful's mutterings were known to evolve sometimes into personal vendettas, which usually end with the painful ejection of the subject of his mutterings. Now it's Uzi Dayan's turn to stand in the crosshairs of the chief of staff's figurative rifle. Not even the fact that they live in neighboring moshavim in the Jezreel Valley will help to save Uzi's skin.

* * *

At 03:00, in the middle of the night, the phone rings at Uzi's house. The duty officer on base passes on an initial report about a terrorist attack in Kibbutz Misgav Am, right at the northernmost tip of Israel, abutting the border with Lebanon. Uzi tries to glean as much information as he can. The situation is still unclear, and they decide to send a helicopter to Sayeret Matkal's base to pick up the standby teams, who are already kitted-out. The chopper will stop off at IAF's AFB Ramat David to pick up the "northerners," including Dayan, en route to Misgav Am.

When Uzi and his men reach Misgav Am, there is nobody to greet them or direct them to the scene of the crime. They stumble across the head of Northern Command, who quickly updates them that terrorists have seized the children's dorms in the kibbutz. (In the collectivist kibbutzim, children used to sleep apart from their families, in a designated "children's house.") On their way there, the terrorists ran into the kibbutz secretary and murdered him. Seven infants are now being held hostage, along with the kibbutznik on guard duty that night.

It soon becomes clear that the terrorists belong to the Arab Liberation Front and are armed with rifles, machine guns, and hand grenades. The same group was responsible for a hostage crisis in Kfar Yuval five years earlier and apparently specializes in breaking into people's homes and kindergartens. In the previous attack, on June 15, 1975, four terrorists broke into a village in the Galilee, entered a home, and held its inhabitants hostage. Two of the hostages were killed, along with one Israeli soldier who came to rescue them and also the terrorists.

The inhabitants of Misgav Am only realize that something dramatic is happening when they hear the first gunshots, the ones that kill the kibbutz secretary. They call in the army, and the first commando force, Sayeret Golani, arrives quickly and deploys around the children's house. The terrorists see the soldiers and open fire. The Golani force retreats and prepares for a lightning raid on the building, seriously fearing that the terrorists are about to start shooting the babies inside.

In the meanwhile, the terrorists grab the kibbutznik guarding the children's home, cuff his hands and legs, and place two babies seized from the bottom floor on a small table. The babies cry their lungs out, but they tire and fall asleep after an hour. The scene falls silent.

At 03:00, the first attempt is made to negotiate with the terrorists, to soften the ground for the Sayeret Golani commando force to storm the building. For their opening gambit, the commandos unleash an insane amount of gunfire at the building, but they are met with return fire. The medic is killed on the spot and the force commander is injured. The attempt to free the hostages fails, and one of the terrorists immediately unloads his rage onto the shackled adult hostage, shooting a single bullet point blank into his foot.

At this point, the terrorists break into a shouting match. Some of them want to start killing the babies, but their commander holds them back. In the morning, the terrorists announce an ultimatum: if Palestinian terrorists jailed in Israel are not released, they will start executing one baby every half-hour.

After Golani's failed rescue attempt, the head of Northern Command, Avigdor "Yanush" Ben-Gal, arrives at the kibbutz with Uri Sagi, the local division commander. The scene of the attack also fills up with soldiers and dogs from the IDF's canine unit, whose covert activities are exposed for the first time in Misgav Am. The dogs are trained to attack the kidnappers in hostage crises and can be incredibly useful to the commandos storming the scene. They are joined at the staging grounds by Golani's commandos under the command of Giora Inbar. Also at the scene are Moshe "Bogie" Ya'alon, Sayeret Matkal's deputy commander, whose leg is in a cast and whose role will therefore be limited to running the command-and-control center, and Amos Ben-Avraham, the fresh commander of its operational company. Both men, Bogie and Amos, will one day be commanders of Sayeret Matkal.

*　*　*

Bracing to command this devilish operation to storm the children's house, Uzi Dayan feels two burdens weighing down on his lean shoulders: one is the chief of staff's barely-disguised desire to get rid of him, come what may; the second is the memory of the Ma'alot hostage crisis six years earlier, when twenty-two children were murdered before Sayeret Matkal could storm the school and kill the terrorists. Bearing such immense responsibility, a commander must obviously keep his cool, put himself in "on" mode, and filter out background noises, but these two events have trickled into Uzi's bloodstream—and their impact on his decisions and conduct, even if he doesn't know it, is immense.

Uzi, a veteran of the battle in Ma'alot, knows well that the window of opportunity between the moment that the terrorists realize that a raid is underway and the first bullet that hits one of them in the head or heart will make all the difference between success and a fiasco. This interval can be a fraction of a second. The slightest delay, because of cold feet or a technical hitch, will mean a death sentence for the hostages.

That's the whole rule book in a nutshell. Uzi walks between the soldiers standing against the windowless wall of the children's house, injecting a healthy dose of courage and grit into their veins. The lives of the babies inside will now depend on the bravery of Uzi and his men. So will Uzi's future in the unit.

Two squads of Sayeret Matkal soldiers are dispatched from the base to Misgav Am: an older squad headed by Ziv, and a younger one under Gal. After Uzi and the force commanders tour the perimeter, they decide on an action plan in collaboration with the head of Northern Command: ten snipers will be positioned at six different points. The snipers will not only storm the building and kill the terrorists, but will also provide real-time intelligence about developments inside. They must provide constant reports to Uzi and to Ya'alon's command-and-control center about what the men they can see through the windows are doing.

The snipers are supposed to open fire in one of three situations: if they hear gunfire inside the building, that is, if the terrorists have started shooting the hostages; if they see at least two terrorists through the windows at the same time and Uzi gives them permission to shoot; or if they are given an order when the planned raid gets underway.

The strike force divides into four, with one backup force: a Sayeret Golani commando force headed by the unit's commander Giora Inbar positions itself north of the building and plans to enter the northeastern room. The second force, under Amos Ben-Avraham, will enter after Giora's team through the entrance to the rocket shelter, move to the middle room in the north, and then proceed to the bathroom. The third force, Ziv's, will shuffle underneath the southern windows of the children's house and enter through the balcony into the southwestern room. And the fourth and final force, commanded by Gal, gets into position on the roof of the building and prepares to storm the eastern room through an opening on the roof.

Uzi briefs all the forces participating in the raid. He spells out the latest intelligence and stresses the importance of reaching the source of the fire as quickly as possible and neutralizing it immediately. The men try to memorize the internal layout of the children's house from the sketches frantically drawn by quivering kibbutzniks just minutes earlier. There isn't a single man in the force, whether he was at Ma'alot himself or only heard horror stories from comrades who participated in that bungled rescue mission, who doesn't have the events of that massacre at the forefront of his mind, imagining graphic images of dead children.

The commander of the sniper force arranges his snipers in position on the second floor of a building south of the children's house, in the middle room of a single-story building south of the children's house, in the eastern room of the same building, on the roof of the kibbutz cafeteria east of the children's house, and at a point northwest of the building. For his own part, the commander of the sniper force takes up position in the westernmost room of a building south of the children's house.

Ziv manages to give his men a short brief of a few minutes, and gets ready at the appointed spot. He is the only one who has managed to see the building from every angle, and he leads the force into action.

Amos Ben-Avraham leads a force of ten men. They wait next to the windowless wall of the building, parallel to the Golani command force.

The long wait of close to two hours, from 08:15 to 10:15, is nerve-wracking for the soldiers. It is practically impossible to remain on high alert and maintain total silence just a few inches away from the terrorists, who are just on the other side of the wall. If only it were possible, they would have stopped their own thumping heartbeats. Their heavy ceramic flak jackets are making it difficult to move and breathe, and the helmets, which Sayeret Matkal soldiers are not used to wearing, add to the stress and discomfort as they wait on high alert to be sent in. This is a competition for life and death—a battle over whose nerves will fray first.

* * *

Yanush, the head of Northern Command, sends in a helicopter to hover right above the children's house in order to distract the terrorists, and the sound of its blades muffles the commando forces' final preparations. When the helicopter leaves, the snipers have still not been able to catch two terrorists simultaneously through the windows of the children's house, and Uzi decides to start counting down. He whispers into his Motorola device, "10, 9, 8, 7, 6, 5, 4, 3—," swallows, "2, 1," and then *boom*, four snipers fire four perfectly synchronized bullets through the windows of the children's house, downing one terrorist and apparently injuring another.

At that exact moment, four squads charge forward.

Ziv sprints toward "his" door on the south side of the children's house, opposite the wide lawn, across of which, 260 feet away, all the generals who have reached the scene watch this action movie unfolding with a few kibbutzniks rapt with worry. He shoots at the two windows where until just a few seconds ago the terrorist leading the negotiations with the Israeli army was standing. When Ziv skirts past the second window, he feels a bullet splicing through his hand. He pins himself to the wall and shouts for his soldiers to run around him and go straight in. The gunfire raining down on Ziv's squad is coming from the other window. No bullets are fired from the half-open door next to it.

Sayeret Matkal's commandos are going to get used to their guns jamming and creating life-threatening scares—a consequence of the IDF's decision to require them to use Uzi submachine guns during hostage rescue missions, because their bullets are slightly less lethal and therefore less likely to accidentally kill the hostages. The soldiers have hardly ever practiced with Uzis (their signature weapon is the AK-47), and besides the discomfort of using an unfamiliar weapon, it jams far too often, with dangerous consequences.

The soldiers in Amos's squad hear the shriek of the sniper bullets and start charging at the door of the rocket shelter. Amos shoots a few bullets at the window of the bathroom, next to the door, and goes to open it. The door is unlocked, but it is blockaded from the inside with tables and chairs. Amos is not exactly the brawniest man in the unit, but he knows to get the most out of his men, who will definitely be enough to send the door and all the furniture on the other side flying, opening up a twenty-inch opening that can easily swallow his ten men whole. He takes a small step back and signals for one soldier to chuck a stun grenade inside, as planned. Two seconds go by, which feel like an eternity and end with an almighty explosion inside the room. Amos mistakenly assumes the explosion was caused by the grenade and storms inside.

Gal also hears Uzi counting back, sees the sniper fire, jumps from the roof with his men eight feet down to the balcony, and breaks into the first room through the broken glass window. The room is completely empty and Gal lurches at the wooden door leading to the second room. Heavy gunfire erupts in his direction through the door and soon starts lashing through the interior wall, shredding small holes, bullets whizzing into the room with the commando force. Someone on the other side has lost his patience.

The Golani commandos are waiting outside, holding axes to smash the window and stun grenades. At exactly 10:15, Giora also hears Uzi's countdown through the headset of the Motorola device glued to his chest and registers the shriek of the sniper fire piercing the air. One Golani commando smashes the window on his right with an axe and immediately lobs a stun grenade into the southeast corner of the room. The soldiers behind him jump inside through the open door, flung open by Amos Ben-Avraham a second earlier, and position themselves on both sides—to find one of the terrorists standing right there.

Giora sees the terrorist immediately and fires half a dozen bullets into his body. His deputy fires three bullets before shouting, "JAM!" and he is replaced by a third soldier. The adult hostage cuffed in the room jumps to his feet and is dragged outside at once. Someone tries to send the dogs in, but they suddenly develop human sensitivities and refuse to enter (perhaps offended that they were not sent in first). In the meanwhile, heavy gunfire rains down from the southern window into the room where the soldiers are standing. They return long bursts of gunfire at the bottom of the window and the incoming fire stops in an instant.

Yoram from Team Ziv darts into the small room, with another comrade running behind him. They can hear gunfire in the next room, and they respond with fire toward what they think is the source of the fire. The ferocious explosion of a grenade, apparently from the same room, grabs their attention for a split second but they get their act together and converge on the doorway of the room opposite, which contained two terrorists until a second or two ago. One of them lies dead under the window, having taken the sniper bullet that gave the signal to begin; the second is next to the doorway, still not moving. Two more bullets, and the two terrorists will remain as still as each other for eternity.

Team Ziv's soldiers take a deep breath and storm the doorway that the men entered a few seconds ago and they see Giora coming toward them from the corridor. Behind him, they see Uzi Dayan poking his head out and hollering, "Stop! Stop!"

In an instant, they see two children lying on mattresses at the far end of the room. They are alive, their eyes open. The men are overcome with indescribable happiness—a split second before their minds roam to the inevitable thought that it was all worth it, just to hold the children alive. They run out, the infants in their arms, hearts bursting with joy.

Seconds earlier, when Uzi Dayan confidently observes that the forces are steaming ahead without a hint of hesitation, he leaps over the fence around the children's house and joins Team Ziv. With the Dayan family's signature determination, he overtakes most of Ziv's squad and reaches the vanguard. He too reaches the terrorist in the middle room and pounds him with one final bullet before joining the others in the corridor and shouting, "Stop! Stop!"

Amos, who has entered at the head of a column through the door he blasted open, takes a left with his back against the wall, shooting at the rim where the ceiling meets the wall. The room responds with silence and Amos shouts over his shoulder that the room is empty, and he continues to the door on his left, leading to another room. He peeks through the doorway into the other room and sees one of the Schnauzers from the canine unit lying dead in the middle of the room, a terrorist sitting to his left, an RPD machine gun between his legs. The terrorist aims his gun at Amos and fires a single bullet, which pierces Amos's left foot. Amos instinctively grabs his injured foot and drops his gun, shouting, "Terrorist on the left!" Amos's squad sprints arounds him, spots the terrorist, and sends a long and absolutely final hail of bullets his way.

They will later discover that there was another terrorist with him—one the soldiers didn't notice when they first moved in.

Amos thanks God for his good fortune and Shahar for his flawless maneuver and orders a squad to go down to the rocket shelter, to check that there's no one else there. Uzi's cries of "Stop! Stop!" reach them too.

Meanwhile, Gal understands that the terrorists are mere inches away from him and his soldiers, behind the wall. He spots a narrow window at eye-level, right of the door, and shoots through it into the other room. Another soldier joins him. Gal's Uzi jams and he quickly moves aside. The soldier replacing him by the window takes a bullet to the arm and is thrown backwards. This dangerously awkward moment ends with the colossal explosion of a hand grenade chucked by the terrorists. Gal lunges into the room and sends two bursts of gunfire at the two terrorists who were just shot a second earlier. They too hear the cries of "Stop! Stop!"

The battle is over. The babies are whisked outside, safe and sound.

* * *

The five terrorists who stormed the children's house are killed in the gunfight, while two men from the combined Sayeret Matkal and Golani are moderately injured and another seven lightly. One Golani commando, Eldad Tsafrir, is killed earlier during the first botched raid. Ziv, an officer and squad commander, will be killed two years later in the First Lebanon War.

The soldiers and senior officers around them breathe a mighty but silent sigh of relief, which ripples across the Galilee. Nobody can even begin to imagine the scale of the disaster if this mission had failed.

The whole difference between success and failure is a split second here, a sharp instinct there, and maybe, just maybe, a truckload of good luck that makes it to the door of the children's home where six infants are sleeping. The fact that the hostages were babies, asleep in their cots, made them too small to be "legitimate" targets—the terrorists were not originally planning to seize the children's home and murder babies—and must have saved their lives.

Defense Minister Ezer Weizman, whose helicopter has landed in the kibbutz in the meanwhile, rounds up all the soldiers to sing their praises. He too deserves some praise now. Not always do politicians of his rank remain at the scene of hostage crises until their safe conclusion.

Dozens of journalists try to huddle within an earshot of the defense minister talking to the troops, but instead they get an earful. "Don't you dare come closer!" shouts Weizman. "These guys can be dangerous."

And Uzi Dayan, who is not only Moshe Dayan's nephew but also a relative of Ezer Weizman's, suppresses a wry smile and just about manages to kick the resentful chief of staff out of his thoughts.

Chapter 13

THE BUS 300 HIJACKING— APRIL 1984

It's April 12, 1984, exactly four years after the attack in Misgav Am. Shay Avital is the commander of Sayeret Matkal, and in three days' time, he is set to be succeeded by Omer Bar-Lev.

Shay Avital was born into Israel's socialist movement, a son of Moshav Arbel, a collectivist community near the Sea of Galilee, a farmer born to farmers, and a man who attaches great importance to working the land as a life philosophy, not just an empty slogan. He is short, really quite diminutive, cast in the same mold as many of Sayeret Matkal's commanders before and after him—a mold created by someone who made sure to inject it with superb mental faculties, at the apparent expense of physical size. He is energetic, hyperactive, quite wordy, and possesses boundless willpower, yet he also comes across as friendly and unassuming, a great believer in his ability to marshal his powers of speech and persuasion against anyone and in any situation.

Shay has slowly but surely climbed the ranks of the IDF, and in nearly every role, it is clear to everyone that he has reached the highest and final station of his military career. Everyone, that is, besides one: Shay himself.

He already declared in the tryouts for Sayeret Matkal, with uncharacteristic modesty, that he would command the unit one day.

His brand of leadership combines tremendous pathos with superb intuitions and sharp instincts. This mixture, peppered with titanic willpower, creates an outstanding and inimitable style of command.

Shay climbs his way to the top with a hammer and a hoe. Some commanders have sailed to this lofty position almost effortlessly, or at least not with any effort that can be seen on their faces. Shay isn't one of them. He listens to people, takes their opinions into account, and is usually convinced that he can make almost anyone do whatever he wants. For this reason, he falls back on a good old appeal to patriotism as a means of persuasion and invokes the legendary commando Meir Har-Zion from the groundbreaking Unit 101 as a beacon of inspiration.

Shay's team loves him and is willing to follow him through fire and water, and his men have often followed him through both fire and water, sometimes both at once. And he is one of the most fearless men around, in both military and civilian life. He held his ground in an astonishing way in the First Lebanon War, for example, when he told Chief of Staff Raful Eitan and the head of Northern Command that he refused to go along with the plan to enter Beirut because it bordered on insanity, and that he did not intend to waste his soldiers' and officers' lives on this act of lunacy. The chief of staff, just as happened two years earlier with Uzi Dayan, hated what he was hearing and even thought of taking revenge on Shay after the hostilities. This didn't happen, in the end.

* * *

Exactly as Shay Avital scrubs and shines the baton that he is about to pass onto his successor, Omer Bar-Lev, bus number 300 glides down its usual route on the Tel Aviv-Ashkelon highway one sunny spring afternoon, carrying dozens of its regular passengers—and four Palestinians from the Gaza Strip, who pay for the bus fare and then hijack it by threatening the driver with a knife, take the passengers hostage, and drive them to Dir al-Balah in the Gaza Strip. There, playing on their home turf to a gallery of adoring crowds, they believe that they will finally be able to pull off what the "inventors of the idea," the terrorists who came from Lebanon in 1978 and perpetrated the Coastal Road massacre, were never able to do: to force Israel to release dozens or even hundreds of jailed terrorists.

One thing is for sure: the four young men from the southern Gaza Strip never imagined the security and political maelstrom into which they were about to thrust the State of Israel and every senior official in its government, prosecution service, and the Shin Bet.

The bus travels south, and the quiet inside cannot disguise the fear that grips the passengers who boarded as free civilians and in the blink of an eye became hostages, extras in a horror movie in which they never intended to star. And only Esther Ben-Hur, her responsibility for human life and resourcefulness enhanced by her visible pregnancy, manages to scare the four inexperienced hijackers by faking nausea and vomiting. They are probably less concerned for her health and her fetus than they are about the commotion at such an early stage of their operation. The terrorists order the driver to stop at the Ashdod Junction and practically kick Esther off the bus. They fail to realize that this decision, giving them a momentary sense of relief, is exactly what will seal their fate.

Esther understands that the bus passengers' fate rests on her shoulders alone, and she stops a truck driver at the junction and asks him to tell the police about the hijacking. Nobody has cell phones—it's 1984—and the driver relays the report over the radio system in his cabin.

Now, at long last, Israel's security behemoth awakens from its slumber, and when the pagers start beeping, generals and commanders at different ranks and units are all kicked into action, united by a single goal: to each reach the target first, come what may.

Benny Lavi is Sayeret Matkal's operations officer. At exactly 20:00, he receives a phone call from an officer in the IDF General Staff operations department with a general alert about a bus hijacking. The alert is immediately conveyed to the five teams on base, two section commanders, the operations officer, and the HQ. The unit also tries to get a hold of senior officers and medics at home, to spring them back to base.

Sayeret Matkal is just starting to scrape away the first signs of rust after four quiet years, after the Misgav Am incident, during which it was not sent to deal with any hostage rescue missions. The reason is quite prosaic: there were simply no such incidents. In the meanwhile, the unit has watched the rise of a fierce competitor, trained for precisely such incidents: the "YAMAM" counterterror unit in the Israel Police.

Nevertheless, in the long pause (by Israeli standards) between terror attacks, Sayeret Matkal has been refining, honing, and practicing its rules of engagement to rapidly respond to hostage crises. All the necessary teams for such events, and all their commanders, happen to be on base that Thursday, April 12—a relatively rare coincidence, which certainly doesn't augur well for the four terrorists on the bus.

Israeli security forces are in hot pursuit of the bus, which is making its way through the Gaza Strip. The bus's wheels are hit in a gunfight, and it comes to a halt at the entrance of the Dir al-Balah refugee camp.

* * *

Shay Avital, who is supposed to hand over command of Sayeret Matkal on Sunday, makes a superhuman pitch, including a first-order appeal to patriotism, for another year on the job. He feels that it is finally time to give full expression to his abilities, and it would be a waste not to take advantage of his accumulated experience. But his efforts fall short, not because he failed in his role—quite the opposite—but because the Intelligence Corps has decided that Sayeret Matkal commanders will serve for exactly two years—and then hand over to the next in line.

In the future, there will be several exceptions to this rule, but for now, the bus overflowing with terrorized Israeli passengers is parked in an open field near Dir al-Balah, between Gaza City and Khan Younis, and Shay's head is exploding with operational and logistical thoughts about how to reach the scene of the crime quickly and save the hostages. He also allows himself to recite a small, intensely personal prayer: that no last-minute hitch will stain his glorious career in Sayeret Matkal.

Omer Bar-Lev, who is still in Jerusalem, is saved from the "forgotten at home" syndrome thanks to someone in operations who takes the initiative and calls him at home. Despite the role lined up for him after the weekend, he is still not on the unit's emergency list, and he might have spent the night at home and beaten himself up over it for years to come if not for the resourcefulness of this one desk officer.

Shay's successor as the commander of Sayeret Matkal is almost his complete opposite: he is tall and thin, blue-eyed, annoyingly introverted, and projects coldness and aloofness. His career in the unit has been a long story of unrequited love: about a girl (the unit) in love with her childhood sweetheart (Omer), who aggressively courts him for years, while he keeps agreeing to one last fling, but this time for real. Omer did not want to be a squad commander and was persuaded against his better judgment to go to officers' school after the Yom Kippur War, and for years he was always on the point of quitting the army after every role but agreed to come back, each time for the last time, when Sayeret Matkal begged him to save the day. Even when he was nominated as the unit's commander, perhaps the most highly-coveted role in the IDF, he was convinced almost against his will to accept the job, and that was only after a mighty persuasion effort.

Omer Bar-Lev is thoroughly rational, analytical, and cold. He is a man who sees the world through reports, realistic analysis, tables, and hard data. Everything else—feelings, emotions, intuitions—is meaningless nonsense. He listens to others, asks questions, always interrogates basic assumptions, blithely slaughters sacred cows, no matter how old they are, without a drop of mercy, and is an expert in breaking consensus. It is this ability that has led him, despite intense opposition and attempts to thwart his rise, to spearhead dramatic changes in every corner of the unit—many of which still remain in force today.

Despite being a difficult and withdrawn man, not exactly an affectionate and highly visible figure, his soldiers are willing to follow him into the most dangerous and challenging operations, even after enduring extremely grueling periods of unbearable tensions with him.

* * *

Sayeret Matkal's commanders and soldiers are stampeding to collect their special personal gear before the helicopters arrive. Among them are the unit's mythological firearms instructor, an extraordinarily coolheaded man, who is therefore destined to play a critical role in the raid; Shay Avital's two deputy commanders; Shahar Argaman, the commander of the operational company and a future commander of the unit, and no fewer than four medics. The squads on base are those headed by Yoram, Gideon, Gilon, Nir, and Ronen.

At 20:30, the general alert becomes an operational order and Sayeret Matkal is told that an incident is unfolding around Khan Younis and Rafah. The squads and their commanders, all kitted up, start advancing on the runways, to wait for the helicopters that will collect them and drop them in a matter of minutes straight onto the heads of the YAMAM police forces deployed around the bus, ready to storm it.

Three helicopters packed with Sayeret Matkal soldiers take off one after the other toward the Gaza Strip and land near Dir al-Balah, and the commandos are whisked away to the scene of the crime. The site is swarming with dozens of soldiers, police officers, Shin Bet agents, and a rabble of functionaries who clearly have no business in such a sensitive and fissile place but might be hoping for little shards of glory to fly their way. If there's any glory going around.

Tovi Shur is leading Doron Kempel's squad through basic training at Sayeret Matkal's training grounds. Both men, Tovi and Doron, drop everything when they hear the news, jump into Doron's BMW, and fly back to base to grab their special gear and maybe even make it to the helicopters in time. Tovi serves as a sniper in terror attacks like this, and he runs straight to his squad's emergency storehouse to find his rifle. It's not there, and he assumes that his squad has taken it for him and flown south with it to Gaza.

It turns out that the helicopters took off long ago, and the two men return to the BMW to test this German-made vehicle's maximum speed. Doron Kempel is still a young officer, but his name and reputation precede him by a country mile. It's clear to everyone that he is the kind of soldier who, if he makes it in time, will play a central role in the operation to seize the bus. No doubt about it. He will always be a member of the team. Of any team. Usually spearheading the whole operation.

The legend of Doron Kempel will make an appearance in countless incidents in many far-flung countries. Tovi, his partner on this road trip, is the younger brother of Avida Shur, who was killed exactly eleven years earlier in Operation Spring of Youth in Beirut, and on this frenzied drive south, he tries his best to suppress the nagging "what if" questions in his mind. When he forced his parents to sign the forms that all bereaved families in Israel must sign for their surviving children to serve in combat roles, they came to meet officers in the unit, who tried to win them over by describing Sayeret Matkal as "one of the safest" combat units in the IDF. But when Doron's BMW whizzes past the gates of the kibbutz where Tovi's family lives, he clutches the passenger seat with all his might, till his fingers are so white that they nearly illuminate the car's interior.

Shay, the unit's commander, takes two officers on an initial tour of the area and they receive a preliminary briefing from the commander of the YAMAM, the police counterterror unit. Then he is summoned for a three-way conversation with Chief of Staff Moshe Levi and Itzik Mordechai, the head of the Infantry and Paratroopers Corps. It is obvious to Shay that Sayeret Matkal will be the unit to storm the bus, even though YAMAM officers are already deployed at the scene, waiting for the signal to move. Sayeret Matkal enjoys a historic reputation for daring raids like this one, and of course it has the recent memory of the successful takeover of the children's dorm in Misgav Am to its credit. But the hall of fame of Sayeret Matkal's successful operations also has a dark stain: the catastrophe in Ma'alot. Nobody says it out loud, but it is very much on the minds of the three officers engaged in a shouting match about which force should lead the storming of the bus. The argument is settled in Sayeret Matkal's favor and Shay starts planning the raid at once.

The intolerable conditions make it impossible to find enough quiet to focus on planning the raid on the bus. The commanders bombard Shay with loud demands, advice, and questions. Omer, the unit's next commander, understands that only the creation of a physical buffer between Shay and his officers will allow him to think clearly and plan the operation quickly and smoothly, and he blocks their access.

Shay devises an initial action plan. The bus is a relatively small cuboid, with only one space, which makes the operational plans much simpler. Unlike in other hostage crises, there is no need to study the blueprints of a complicated building with dozens of rooms.

The idea is to storm the bus from three directions. Ronen's squad, which includes Shahar Argaman, will be the primary intervention force, which will break into the bus through the back door. Yoram's squad will get into position next to a nearby building, opposite the right flank of the bus, while Nir, Aviv, and Gilon's squads will wait behind the bus and storm it through the back window.

The unit's firearms instructor, known for his cool-headedness and expert marksmanship, will approach the windshield of the bus at the start of the operation and shoot the terrorist next to the driver's seat. Running to the front of the bus, he will be joined by squad commander Omer Bar-Lev and three other men, all wearing civilian clothes in a bid to slightly dampen the terrorists' suspicions.

The snipers, who will assume positions around the bus, will shoot and take down the terrorist on the back seat.

Several variations of this plan are presented to Chief of Staff Moshe Levi, and he finally gives this version his approval. He refuses to allow sniper fire, other than for the terrorist in the back row. The entire Sayeret Matkal force is sent to practice on another bus driven here for the purpose of their drills, holding several dry runs of the authorized plan.

Shay insists on storming the bus while it is still dark, and under no circumstances to postpone it till daybreak. Sayeret Matkal always prefers to act under the cover of darkness. Darkness is the unit's best friend, which will always give the commandos a clear edge over the enemy. Over any enemy. Sunlight risks blinding them and usually deprives them of the element of surprise, which is a necessary condition for success. Obviously, circumstances do not always allow for this, but this time Shay puts his foot down: the operation will take place at night.

Sayeret Matkal's commandos take up position in the exact places where YAMAM officers are already lying, replacing them. This brief changing of the guard makes both sides uncomfortable, but with so many innocent lives hanging in the balance, there is little time for sensitivities.

Meanwhile, the rising sun has no intentions of waiting for the IDF to iron out its last-minute doubts, and daybreak is in fifteen minutes' time. Itzik Mordechai, the head of the Infantry and Paratroopers Corps, tries to add another change to the plan, but the chief of staff rules out any further delays and gives the signal to launch the operation.

* * *

The advance force sets out in civilian dress, advancing on the left-hand front window of the bus. Next to the driver's seat, the firearms commander whips his pistol out of its holder in a slow-motion, quiet maneuver straight out of a Western, straightens his arm, locks his elbow into place, and fires four lethal bullets: two at the terrorist's head and two into the center of his chest.

The primary force, with Ronen and Shahar Argaman, appears at the front door with the first gunshot. Shahar goes first, but he can't open the door. The soldiers with him find the button and open the door, and Shahar leaps inside with Doron Kempel and another soldier just behind him. They spot someone hiding between the rows, practically standing on the feet of a couple of passengers. The woman screams that the man is a terrorist, and Doron prepares to thread a bullet through him. The suspect cries in flawless Hebrew, "I'm not a terrorist!" but Doron is unconvinced and steadies his aim. He asks Shay Avital, who has shown up behind him, whether he should kill him, and Shay orders him just to "neutralize" him. Doron thumps him with the butt of his gun, and the terrorist is dragged off the bus.

The first strike force splits and the men take a sharp right, to the window on the left of the bus, where only five minutes earlier they spotted a terrorist through their binoculars. One soldier gives his comrade a leg-up to the window. He can't see the terrorist they spotted standing in the window, but he does spot another terrorist on the other side of the aisle. He empties a hail of five bullets into the terrorist, who slumps over and sprawls on the floor of the bus, between the seats.

At the exact moment as this commando unleashes a burst of gunfire through the window, Omer spots a man leaping toward the back of the bus, to try to shoot him. Without hesitating, Omer shoots him. In hindsight, it turns out that both men shot the same terrorist.

They are not alone. When the sniper eighty feet behind the bus hears the shriek of the first bullets at the front of the bus, he squeezes the trigger of his rifle and sends a bullet through the back window at the exact same terrorist, who according to Sayeret Matkal's intelligence was supposed to detonate the bomb that would blow up the bus with everyone inside.

Straight after this direct hit, the force storms the back of the bus. The men use axes to smash the back window, designed as an emergency escape hatch. The window shatters into a million pieces and two other soldiers climb through it and spot the fallen terrorist, who has just taken a sniper bullet. Another officer, breaking through the back door at the same moment, also sees the terrorist and lunges at him. He immediately unleashes another hail of bullets into the belly of the terrorist, whose condition is still unknown, and for all anyone knows might detonate the bomb with his dying breath.

* * *

Two of the four terrorists are still alive: Majdi Abu Jamaa, the terrorist hit with the butt of Doron Kempel's gun and dragged outside, and his accomplice Subhi Abu Jamaa, who hid behind a row of seats in the middle of the bus this whole time, praying and maybe even thanking his lucky stars. Neither imagines that in just a few minutes, they will both join their friends on the highway to hell, igniting one of the nastiest security scandals in the history of the State of Israel.

One innocent passenger, Irit Portuguez, a nineteen-year-old female soldier from a moshav near Ashkelon, is killed during the rescue operation, most likely from friendly fire. Irit, who according to witnesses acted with exemplary resourcefulness during that long and terrible night, calmly and devotedly caring for the shellshocked passengers, apparently gave her life trying to shield the passengers who suddenly became her wards.

Another three passengers are injured and evacuated immediately. Sayeret Matkal completes the operation without any casualties.

The sapper who boards the bus as soon as the gunfire stops finds a circuit board and a single, rusty grenade. After evacuating the passengers, the soldiers also find a suitcase with two RPG grenades, connected to an improvised circuit with a pipe full of explosives. All this is wired up to a six-volt battery, and the chances that it could have blown up are close to nil.

And thus, despite the cramped conditions on the bus and the enormous firepower unleashed by Sayeret Matkal's commandos, the hostage crisis ends with only one casualty from Israeli fire (Irit Portuguez), two dead terrorists, and two terrorists hauled off the bus. The pair are handed over alive to the Shin Bet. Alex Levac, a news photographer, manages to snap the two terrorists standing on their feet, being led by two Shin Bet agents away from the bus. This image, published on the front page of the *Hadashot* newspaper the next day, will be the trigger for a scandal known as the "Bus 300 affair," which will continue to haunt the Israeli political system for years to come.

The two terrorists are killed later by the Shin Bet's operations chief, on the instructions of Avraham Shalom, the agency's director.

And when Moshe Arens, the defense minister, suddenly shows up, his face gripped with worry, he grabs Tovi Shur and asks him: "How did it end?" Tovi tells Arens what happened and a small smile spreads across the minister's face. "I knew we could count on the YAMAM," he says, plainly confused and oblivious about what just went on.

Chapter 14

OPERATION LOVELY YOUTH— THE ABDUCTION OF SHEIKH OBEID IN LEBANON, JULY 1989

I f you had told Ran Shahor that one day he would command Sayeret Matkal and show up in the village of Jebchit in southern Lebanon for a rendezvous with its Shi'ite leader, Sheikh Abdel Karim Obeid, he would have burst into laughter and had you committed to an asylum for the insane. But the reality in the Middle East often calls for unusual encounters between figures without even an inch of common ground.

Ran Shahor enlists into Sayeret Matkal in 1976. He is cast in the mold of Amiram Levin, short and stocky, and although these features are not as pronounced as in Levin's case, this compact image leaves no room for doubt: their Creator poured tons of grit into their thickset frame.

Ran's outward appearance is only part of the story. He brings with him to Sayeret Matkal boundless ambition, an ambition concealed behind his moderate and even gentle exterior and of course his cool-headedness, a prerequisite for getting anywhere in this unit. He is not a "princeling," a soldier who struts into the unit naturally exuding an intoxicating aura of leadership, like Ehud Barak, but the kind of guy who blazes his own path through superhuman efforts. In order to stand out in Sayeret Matkal, it almost goes without saying, you have to triumph over a whole column of comrades, all hand-picked with military precision and all brimming with motivation and an insatiable hunger to always be the first. At everything. Ran stands out in his team from the get-go, and nobody doubts that he will go to officers' school and return to the unit as a team commander. When he graduates, he is given a team of truly giant men from the cohort of 1977, and he's the "little boy herding them," to borrow an image from the Prophet Isaiah, forging a high-caliber team of disciplined, strong, and mission-driven soldiers. As a bonus that mustn't be downplayed, they are also all good friends with each other, including their commander Ran.

After completing his service with his team, Ran returns to ploughing fields on his kibbutz, and it looks like he and Sayeret Matkal have broken up for good. But Omer Bar-Lev, Sayeret Matkal's commander from 1984, can't imagine giving up on an officer like Ran and urges him to come back. Not even the most assertive soldiers and officers in Sayeret Matkal are capable of saying no when asked to return to serve their unit and their homeland—in that order—and Ran doesn't hesitate for a heartbeat before saying yes.

He slowly climbs the snaking path to the commander's office, at no point setting himself any targets beyond his present position, and after completing his term as Bar-Lev's deputy, Ran ditches Sayeret Matkal once again in favor of a law degree. This time, he's convinced that his active service is over, and from now on he can comfortably sail into civilian life on the gentle currents of nostalgia.

But Sayeret Matkal and the IDF Intelligence Directorate have other ideas, and in 1989, toward the end of Moshe "Bogie" Ya'alon's term as the unit's commander, the shortlist contains just two candidates with the skills to take over the top job: Nahum Lev and Ran Shahor.

When the final decision is made, it raises eyebrows in Sayeret Matkal and the IDF Intelligence Directorate. Not because anyone thinks that Ran is unsuitable—far from it,—but because Nahum has the rockstar quality that should be enough to catapult him into the commander's post. But the eyebrows raised in astonishment slot firmly back down when Ran assumes command and leads the unit into several operations that remain etched in its history books. One of the biggest ones is Operation Lovely Youth: the abduction of Sheikh Abdel Karim Obeid from Lebanon.

* * *

In early 1989, Sheikh Obeid appears in a televised BBC report about rising Shi'ite forces in several Arab and other Muslim countries. He was recently appointed the sheikh of the village of Jebchit in southern Lebanon after completing his studies at Qom University in Iran, where his extremism seems to have taken root. In a soft and quiet voice, gracefully flirting with the cameras, Obeid eloquently explains to the interviewer that the Jews must be swiftly slaughtered to clear the path for Muslims, and especially Shi'ites, to Jerusalem, or for him—Al-Quds.

It has been seven years since the start of the First Lebanon War, and since reaching the outskirts of Beirut, the Israeli army has retreated to a narrow "Security Belt" on Lebanese soil, creating a buffer along the Israeli-Lebanese border that becomes the scene of regular clashes between the IDF and the South Lebanon Army (SLA) on one side and a flurry of terrorist organizations, chiefly the Shi'ite groups that later morph into Hezbollah, on the other side. The sheikh's village lies even beyond this Security Belt, in an area beyond Israel's military control.

Eyal Ragonis, Sayeret Matkal's scarily talented chief intelligence officer, can't take this lying down, and he takes the cassette with the recording of the interview, thunderstruck, to the senior officers in the unit to show them the rising star in the Shi'ite leadership in southern Lebanon. Ragonis is not a venerable historian fighting for the Jewish people's good name, but a razor-sharp intelligence officer thinking only about his unit's next operations.

In October 1986, during a routine night-time foray of Israeli Air Force planes over the skies of southern Lebanon, one of the F-4 Phantom jets suffers a technical hitch and its two crew members are forced to abandon the aircraft. The pilot is picked up soon after by a rescue helicopter dispatched to the region, but the Israeli military fails to rescue the navigator, who parachutes into the same wooded, inaccessible area. The navigator, Ron Arad, is discovered and caught by members of Amal, a Lebanese Shi'ite group, and they keep him hostage for over two years. The negotiations with them, under the auspices of the Red Cross, fail, partly because the Israeli government and public are still haunted by the memory of the Jibril Agreement, in which over 1,100 Palestinian terrorists in Israeli jails were released to Lebanon in exchange for just three IDF soldiers. The negotiations hit a brick wall, and in late 1988, two years after Ron Arad ejects from his plane, he disappears without a trace, and nothing is known about his fate.

The IDF Intelligence Directorate's special operations branch and Production Department are feverishly searching for valuable and kidnappable Lebanese figures who can be used as bargaining chips for meaningful information about Ron Arad and, if luck is on their side, even for Ron Arad himself. Ideally, Israel would want someone of the caliber of Subhi al-Tufayli, Hezbollah's secretary-general, or his deputy Abbas al-Musawi, but they are deeply embedded in Beirut, and the chance of yanking them out alive from their heavily guarded hideouts is close to zero. But nobody less fulsome than these two gentlemen will be able to be used as bargaining chips, even against their own terror organizations.

After the sheikh's BBC interview, and after Israel fails to find more suitable potential captives, Sheikh Obeid jumps to the top of the list as a valuable target who might just make Ron Arad's captors' care but isn't too high-ranking to make his abduction impossible. And thus, by a single, fatefully coincidental TV interview, this soft-spoken sheikh jumps to the top of Israel's "most wanted" list as part of its unprecedented efforts to bring Ron Arad back home.

But all this is just in theory. The reality is something else entirely. The sheikh lives not too far from the border with Israel, but his home is right in the middle of the village, on the main road, inside a warren of tightly packed houses, as dense as a casbah.

Sayeret Matkal has never abducted anyone living in the heart of a sleeping village. Abductions, by the way, are much harder and fiddlier than assassinations. And if that's not enough, the sheikh's apartment is on the second floor of a four-story building owned by his extended family. From the outset, it is clear that flooding the village of Jebchit with a large Israeli force without getting discovered, with dogs barking in the streets and stone fences crumbling underfoot, is practically impossible. And even if they can reach the sheikh's house in silence and pull him out of his bed alive, how the hell are they supposed to pull out of the village without triggering a mini-war, or a genuine war, on their return?

Sayeret Matkal is given this mission in February 1989, when Moshe Ya'alon is still the commander but has started handing over to Ran Shahor. At this stage, everything is still very theoretical and there is no concrete decision yet to abduct the sheikh. The two commanders, the incoming and outgoing ones, decide that there is no point planning or training for this mission in the meanwhile because of the low likelihood that it will ever get approved, but they do decide to gather thorough, targeted intelligence, down to the color of the duvets that the sheikh sleeps with, as the chief intelligence officer Eyal Ragonis loves doing, and as Sayeret Matkal's high command loves having him do.

But operations like this one have a preordained dynamic: the more intelligence is gathered, and the more the picture of operational possibilities comes into focus, the impossible slowly becomes possible, and the coterie of officers involved in the planning cast aside their doubts and become vocal, even ardent, supporters. Over the years, Ron Arad's disappearance has become a genuine national trauma, and Sayeret Matkal cannot remain indifferent to a practical possibility of making even a slight contribution to finding him. Sheikh Obeid's case file does not spend long on the shelf, therefore, before the unit puts itself on a war footing.

During the preparations, in April 1989, Moshe Ya'alon salutes his officers and soldiers for the last time, sheds a single tear of sorrow, and hands over the baton to Ran Shahor. Sheikh Obeid, who by now is all that Ragonis and his intelligence officers dream about, is not privy to this information and keeps going about his life as if it made no difference whether Ya'alon would come knocking on his door in the middle of the night or Shahor would be his unannounced guest.

And as the detailed intelligence dossiers updated and presented almost every morning to Ran show, Sayeret Matkal will need to prepare a massive force with impeccable military skills—one capable of walking in total silence from Israeli territory to Sheikh Obeid's home, throwing him over the back of one of the soldiers (not an easy matter at all, given his weight), and returning to Israel in air force helicopters.

And like in many of Sayeret Matkal's combat operations, Ran's plan is based on entering the sheikh's apartment from at least two openings at the exact same moment in order to maximize the element of surprise, and also as essential back-up in case it proves impossible for whatever reason to storm the home from one of the entrances.

As the unit's commander, Ran intends to join the force in person and function as a kind of forward command post, because in combat missions with so many participants, like this one, most decisions have to be made in the field, and any decision, such as whether to open fire, can easily turn a minor mistake into the opening shot of an all-out war.

* * *

Ran picks Amos Ben-Avraham as the commander of this mission. Amos grew up in a kibbutz near Ran's and enlisted in November 1973, straight after the end of the Yom Kippur War, into Omer Bar-Lev's team. Despite Omer being short and narrow-shouldered, nobody could miss his unique soldiering talent from the moment he first donned his olive-green uniform and red leather boots. Nobody could guess, of course, that this skinny and energetic young man would rise all the way to the top of Sayeret Matkal, but even in his training course, it was hard to ignore the sheer energy that he exuded, like a volcano spewing boiling lava. Nobody had to wait for Amos to reach the end, or even the middle, of his training with Bar-Lev's team to know that he would go to officers' school and return to Sayeret Matkal as a team commander. He proved everyone's predictions true and even surpassed them, triumphing over everyone, even himself, to become the commander of the cohort enlisted in November 1975. As a team commander, he led one of the most elaborate operations that Sayeret Matkal had ever pulled off and participated in other missions that bolstered the confidence that the unit's commanders, Nehemiah Tamari and Amiram Levin, had in him practically to the point of adulation.

Beforehand, as a soldier in the training division, Amos participated in the hostage rescue mission at the Savoy Hotel, and as a young officer he also managed to take part in Operation Thunderbolt in Entebbe. After this action-packed period, in which he commanded his team, he was released from the army and returned to his kibbutz. But even before he could unpack his heavy kitbag, he was called back to Sayeret Matkal, to command its operational company. Nobody can say no to a job like that, and Sayeret Matkal's young officers can't say no to anything, and Amos returned to the unit with the same fervor, courage, and signature precision and rigor. But none of these exemplary qualities were enough to stop the single bullet fired by the terrorist from the children's house in Misgav Am. Amos ran headfirst into the scene as a squad commander and was wounded in his left hand and forced to terminate his military service for the second time. Maybe it was this injury that helped him to rethink his future, or maybe it was an old childhood dream. Either way, Amos started a medicine degree and bid his last farewell to the unit. But not quite. Omer Bar-Lev, and later Boggy Ya'alon, kept urging him to come back and lead important, high-stakes missions, and Amos, like many before and after him, couldn't say no.

And when Ran Shahor took over from Boggy Ya'alon, he immediately copied this technique and called on Amos to command the mission to abduct Sheikh Obeid. In later years, Amos would drop his dreams of becoming a doctor, become the commander of the 932 Battalion of the Nahal infantry brigade, and return to Sayeret Matkal in 1991 in order to take over from Ran Shahor as the unit's commander.

* * *

The mission that Amos is given, as the commander of the force, is to bring back Sheikh Abdel Karim Obeid healthy and whole from his home in the village of Jebchit, with minimal harm to his family, and if possible, to bring any other "most wanted" figures found in the sheikh's apartment.

Amos and Ran decide to assign a forty-man force from Sayeret Matkal, a massive delegation by any comparison to the unit's previous operations (in Entebbe, for example, the force that stormed the airport comprised just thirty-three men). The force is supposed to march for over seven miles from the departure point, near the Beaufort Castle military outpost in the South Lebanon Security Belt, to the sheikh's house. The route is not particularly hard to hike but is swarming on all sides with enemies just a stone's throw away. But getting to the village is the easy part of this operation. The hard part will be slipping through the village, slalom-style, making mighty efforts not to get detected or make a sound that might wake up a single villager, who will then wake up his wife, who will wake up her parents, who will wake up their neighbors and so on, until the whole village spills out into the streets with hunting rifles.

Sayeret Matkal has pulled off similar missions before, but never with such a massive force or challenging environment. These previous missions are a massive stockpile of knowledge and experience for Amos and his men in planning this operation. Without them, the unit would undoubtedly need much longer to plan, and the quality of the execution would probably also be much poorer. Experience and tradition, when meticulously documented, guarded like precious gems, and handed down the generations, are the most important and powerful tools that the unit has to offer—and they can be the difference between success and disaster.

* * *

Forty Sayeret Matkal commandos set out, thirteen of them officers, including unit commander Ran Shahor, two future Sayeret Matkal commanders (Nitzan Alon and Amos Ben-Avraham), and some of the unit's finest officers. The lion's share of the force is supposed to enter the sheikh's home while the rear secures the perimeter and creates a sterile buffer during the raid on the apartment.

Nitzan Alon is a product of the elite clique of kibbutzim and moshavim that have become regular feeders of high-caliber fighters to Sayeret Matkal. He joins Sayeret Matkal in 1984—exactly when IDF Chief of Staff Moshe Levi decides to put an end to the embarrassing lack of order and discipline in the IDF, and this effort is supposed to be spearheaded by the special operations units, leading by personal example. His strategy is to actively "hunt" soldiers in these elite units, court martial them for disciplinary breaches, and kick them out of their units as a public warning to the rest of the army. One Sayeret Matkal solider is caught and expelled immediately. The second soldier, caught with his red beret in his pocket instead of on his shoulder, is Nitzan Alon, the stand-out star of Team Michael. Omer Bar-Lev, the unit's commander, realizes that this might be a serious blow to its unit's morale and operational capabilities, but his hands are tied and Nitzan is booted from Sayeret Matkal and transferred to Maglan, another elite reconnaissance unit.

A few months later, Team Michael is supposed to send someone to officers' school. Omer Bar-Lev remembers Nitzan Alon and has a revolutionary, practically subversive idea: to send Nitzan to officers' school, even though he is no longer in the unit. Right around then, Maglan is also planning on sending Nitzan to officers' school. Bar-Lev consults Michael, who throws the idea out of the window. Then he asks Doron Avital, the commander of the unit's training company. Doron, who outranks Michael, thinks that it's an interesting proposal. Bar-Lev decides to meet up with Nitzan and to try to persuade him to commit to signing on for two years' extra service and perhaps thereby atone for his terrible crime.

Nitzan is thrilled by this idea, and only one obstacle remains: how can they skirt around the chief of staff's decision and smuggle someone banished for a disciplinary infraction back into the unit and even send him to officers' school? Amnon Lipkin-Shahak is the head of the IDF Intelligence Corps, making him responsible for Sayeret Matkal, and Bar-Lev knows that he is open-minded and really understands the unit's needs.

And indeed, Lipkin-Shahak grants Bar-Lev's request, and Nitzan Alon soon returns to Sayeret Matkal as an officer. He stands out immediately as a taciturn commander, mature for his age, with fine interpersonal relations with his men and the other officers. Moshe "Bogie" Ya'alon, Sayeret Matkal's new commander, picks up on Nitzan's special qualities and tasks him with leading an innovative shift in the unit's operations, which comes on full display in the mission to abduct Sheikh Obeid.

After finishing his command of his team, Nitzan goes to study engineering at the Technion, but just like his predecessors, he is called back again and again to command some exceptionally fiddly missions that demand extraordinary cool-headedness, leadership, and grit—the hallmarks of anyone truly fated to rise to the top of Sayeret Matkal. For two of these missions, he is awarded the Chief of the General Staff's Citation with another five of his soldiers.

In 1998, Nitzan Alon faces no competition to be appointed the commander of Sayeret Matkal. Despite his lofty status, he remains almost suspiciously modest, a quality that does not stop him from displaying his military and intellectual prowess, including a refined emotional intelligence that is extremely rare at these ranks of the army. Besides these virtues, he is also an exceptionally nice guy, wise, sophisticated, and extraordinarily attentive to his officers and soldiers. After a string of senior roles, including as head of the Intelligence Corps' operations and commander of the Judea and Samaria Division, he joins the IDF General Staff as the head of Central Command and then as the head of the Operations Directorate. Only the semi-political human shredder of the IDF could have prevented an officer and a gentleman like Nitzan from commanding the Intelligence Directorate—and the whole IDF.[1]

* * *

---

1 In 2018, Major General. Nitzan Alon was one of the candidates to replace Lt. Gen. Gadi Eizenkot as the IDF's chief of staff.

But that's still to come, and we're still on the night of July 28, 1989. The arrival to the village is scheduled for 00:30 because according to Ragonis's intelligence, this is usually when activity in the village subsides and quiet grips the houses and streets. It's obvious from the get-go that it will take a very long time, two hours or more, for the force to move through the village all the way to the sheikh's house. Each of the forty men will have to take each step with utmost caution, maintaining total silence. A single foot in the wrong place could cause trouble for the whole force, the whole unit, the whole IDF, and indeed the whole region. And the responsibility for this silence, necessary for not just the success of the mission but also the lives of the forty soldiers, rests on the slender shoulders of Amos Ben-Avraham, the mission commander, who has already commanded missions in other countries in the Middle East, which he entered without a passport and left without a border control stamp. Neither he nor his commanders have any interest in tarnishing this spotless record.

And thus, for two hours straight, forty Israeli soldiers tiptoe through Jebchit carrying minimum equipment and weight—completely unlike regular operations, when every soldier must transfer his whole bodyweight from his back leg to his front leg—making a superhuman effort not to be heard or even make the slightest rustle.

At exactly 02:00, just like in the advance plans, the soldiers cram into the sheikh's yard for another forty minutes' preparation for the raid itself. The perimeter security force spreads out around the house and into the street, to alert the team in case any local insomniacs—or worse, the sheikh's security guards—approach the scene. The rest of the soldiers, who will break into the house, divide into two forces. The larger force takes up position opposite the building's front door; the second, smaller force quickly scales the balcony at the back, ready to smash into the sheikh's bedroom, where, the soldiers already know, he is fast asleep. They use a folding ladder to reach the balcony, propping it against the wall below. Nitzan, who climbs up first, clears the balcony of metal buckets and other clutter so that they won't make a noise before the raid on the sheikh's bedroom.

The primary force, which is meant to storm the front door, must first get past the lock on the front door of the apartment block. One commando, a veteran lock-breaker, opens it quietly and easily. Fifteen soldiers quickly seize control of the building and cruise upstairs to the second floor, to the sheikh's front door. But the first contact with the sheikh is supposed to be made by Nitzan's force, the balcony team, because it is much closer to the sheikh's bedroom. Nitzan reports that he's ready with a quick tap on the keys of his Motorola device, sending the primary force to surgically dismantle the front door at the same time. The force commander also sends two soldiers to skirt the rest of the men in the stairwell and block the floors above the sheikh's apartment.

When the men attach a pneumatic gizmo to the door to force it open, something in the machinery accidentally drops and makes a totally unexpected clatter. "*Min hada?*" shouts someone from the other side of the door. *Who's there?* "*Ihna, iftahu!*" replies one of the soldiers in his broken Arabic: *It's us.* And even before he completes his sentence, someone opens the door wide and fifteen commandos storm inside.

Just a second before this, Nitzan and his men, crouching on the balcony, realize that the door to the sheikh's bedroom can be opened with a gentle touch of the hand, without making a sound. During the tense wait on the balcony, they hear an infant crying from the children's room, next to the bedroom where the sheikh and his wife are sleeping. The infant's senses are much sharper than his parents' and guards, and he jumps out of bed and toddles, crying, to the master bedroom. His mother, the sheikh's wife, wakes up and takes him back to his bed. For an instant, the sheikh is alone in his bed and in his room. That's exactly the moment that Nitzan and his men have been waiting for, and they barge inside.

The commandos wake the sheikh up, shouting, and he retreats into his bed, pulling his blanket up to conceal his modesty. He mumbles some strange, incoherent syllables and is so confused and horrified that he can't even scream. They lunge at him while the others keep shouting in Arabic for him to lie on the ground, on his front. Another soldier steps out of the sheikh's bedroom into the corridor to welcome the primary force entering from the front door. Now the sheikh, all 290 pounds of him, as heavy as the force's two commanders together, recovers from his initial shock and starts resisting the attempts to pin him down. "Let me die!" he hollers at the top of his breath. Nitzan whacks him in the face as the others try to cuff his hands behind his back. And when these efforts to pin the massive and cumbersome sheikh down fail, he is injected with a sedative. At exactly that point, Amos Ben-Avraham and some of his men step into the room. Facing this overwhelming commando force, the sheikh surrenders, his body finally going limp, and his hands are finally cuffed.

An exceptionally strong soldier, his shoulders five feet wide, almost wider than he is tall, hoists the sheikh on his back and goes downstairs into the street. Because of the soldier's modest height, the sheikh's head almost bumps on the road on one side of the commando, his legs nearly scraping the road on the other.

*　*　*

The primary force, which has burst into the apartment, subdues the two guards in the living room. They are cuffed immediately, almost without resistance. One squad from the force pins the sheikh's wife down and leaves her in the room, which the men boisterously call the "women's gallery." The sheikh's children, wrapped in blankets, are all in their bedroom, completely detached from the dramatic events around them.

The takeover of the apartment, including the entry of the main force through the front door and Nitzan Alon's men through the balcony, takes exactly three minutes. The next three minutes are devoted to deliberations in the command center about whether to bring back to Israel the two guards in the living room, one of whom, uncoincidentally, is the sheikh's brother, or to leave them in the apartment. "Yes," announces Danny Arditi from the control room. "Bring them in."

The sheikh himself, still struggling to understand why he has been singled out for this honor, half unconscious but completely cuffed, is pulled into the street on the shoulders of one of the soldiers. The plan is for just one soldier to carry this ponderous, big-boned sheikh as far as a staging post where he can be moved onto a stretcher, his weight shared by the shoulders of four men. Any other way of hauling him from his home to this point would take ages and imperil the force.

At this point, the village of Jebchit begins to wake up to a trickle of gunfire from Kalashnikov rifles, scouring the darkness for moving targets. The gunfire intensifies, and every villager with a Kalashnikov under his bed, of whom there are many, seems to delight in the opportunity for night-time shooting practice through his window. And this hail of bullets is set to the sound of the sheikh's wife crying her lungs out, shouting *"Allahu Akbar! Allahu Akbar!* in a rousing crescendo, standing in the window overlooking the street and announcing to the whole world that her husband was just snatched from his bed.

Meanwhile, in the apartment block itself, the neighbors start pouring into the stairwell to check what all the hullabaloo is about. Two commandos try to calm the situation, but to no avail, until finally one of them fires a bullet, maybe two, at the wall in front of him. The noise and dust send the neighbors scarpering back to their homes in a heartbeat.

In the street and the yard, there are now five different security squads. In Amos Ben-Avraham's ironclad plan, he correctly assumed that as soon as they subdued the sheikh, the center of the action, and needless to say the problems, would move onto the street. Which is exactly what happens. And in order to brace themselves for these potentially explosive developments that might thwart the whole operation, Amos puts an experienced senior commander in charge of the street and gives him the exclusive authority to decide in which direction the force should evacuate—through the street, or perhaps the building's backyard.

* * *

The force pulls itself together in the street for its retreat, doing a headcount while running, the squads giving each other cover. They'll need to get out of the villages as quickly as possible, to somewhere they can stop and the medic can give the sheikh a check-up before he is hoisted onto a stretcher and he and his two friends are carried in a less haphazard manner to the landing site, where a helicopter will pick them up.

Before the landing pad, true to Sayeret Matkal's traditions, the force has a steep climb, and the three captives occasionally drop from their stretchers and plummet onto the ground. One of the officers, the first to reach the clearing, prepares the trapezoid-shaped markings that will show the Sikorsky CH-53 Sea Stallion helicopter where to land. The villagers and the Lebanese forces stampeding in the direction of the incident do not give up easily and open heavy but not particularly discriminate fire, including with rocket-propelled grenades, in the direction that they assume the force is heading. The commander responsible for the zone outside the abductee's apartment switches to the helicopter squadron's frequency, calls in a fleet of attack helicopters, and directs them to the sources of the gunfire, so that the Sikorsky CH-53 Sea Stallion helicopter in the air can land at the improvised helipad and pick up the commando force.

At 04:09, exactly two hours and nine minutes after the force reaches the sheikh's apartment, the chopper takes off with all forty commandos onboard plus three honored Lebanese guests: Sheikh Obeid and his two bodyguards. At 04:40, the helicopter lands on an airstrip near Kibbutz Ein Shemer. The Sheikh and his bodyguards are handed over to the soldiers from Unit 504 awaiting them at the helipad, who whisk them away immediately for interrogation.

Disappointingly, the sheikh's abduction makes zero contribution to solving the mystery of Ron Arad, and he is released some fifteen years later, in January 2004, along with Mustafa Dirani—who is also abducted from his home by Sayeret Matkal, as we shall see in the next chapter—and another 400 Palestinian terrorists, in exchange for the release of the bodies of three IDF soldiers abducted from Mount Dov and a civilian hostage.

And as so often in Sayeret Matkal's operations, even when the mission itself looks practically impossible in the planning and feasibility stages, and when doubts come close to thwarting the mission, for better or worse, that's when outstanding intelligence, meticulous planning, and grueling and rigorous training contribute to a totally smooth, almost banal, operation free of hitches, mistakes, or individual acts of heroism. Just an operation that unfolds exactly as it looks on the drawing board.

Chapter 15

OPERATION VEERING STING—
THE ABDUCTION OF MUSTAFA
DIRANI, 1994

D oron Avital, Sayeret Matkal's new commander in 1992, is a unique character, totally unlike any of the commanders before or after him. There is something quite gentle about him, and elegant, and upbeat, and it is almost impossible to tell, either from his outward appearance or even from his character, that he is the commander of the IDF's most elite intelligence and commando unit. His eyes are kind and his gaze permanently pensive, and his expression reveals none of the rage-suffused grit or sheer hardness typical of the unit's other commanders.

How can this charming and brilliant man be the daring commander of Sayeret Matkal? How can his winning smile and dry humor help him command the audacious operation to kidnap Mustafa Dirani?

Mustafa Dirani was a prominent activist in Amal, a Lebanese Shi'ite movement that will spawn Hezbollah in a few years' time. It is a reaction to the First Lebanon War, until which the Shi'ites were a small, poor, and politically marginal force in Lebanon. Dirani rose to power after capturing Ron Arad, an Israeli navigator who ejects over Lebanon; it was he who handled the negotiations with the Red Cross over Arad's release, and it was he who apparently sold Arad to the Iranians in the late 1980s.

Doron Avital grew up in a youth village near Bustan HaGalil, north of Acre, where his mother is a school principal and his father also works. He is the eldest of six children; the others grew up to be a doctor, an educator, an opera singer, and artists. When he was in fifth grade, his family moved to Jerusalem and Doron studied at a prestigious high school near the Hebrew University. As a talented and ambitious high school graduate, he wanted to serve in Sayeret Matkal but was not even invited to tryouts because of a heart murmur. Yet in the end, the unit that didn't want him as a soldier ended up getting him as its commander. Doron looked around for a high-caliber place to give expression to his talents and enrolled in the Israeli Naval Academy. But the sea was too rough for him, and he switched over to the Paratroopers. On the recommendation of Amnon Lipkin-Shahak, the commander of the Paratroopers Brigade, he joined the May 1977 cohort of the 202nd Battalion, where he started to shine.

When the First Lebanon War erupts in 1982, Doron is the commander of an auxiliary company. His battalion is dropped around the Awali river and starts advancing on the outskirts of Beirut on foot. According to some of his soldiers, Doron leads his company perfectly, with confidence, wisdom, and uncompromising care for his men's lives—not least because he objects to having them wear heavy flak jackets that do more to slow them down and jeopardize their fighting power than protect them. There, on the dusty dirt tracks and deep, dry river valleys of Lebanon, Doron seems to acquire the confidence and experience that will lead him to the coveted post of commander of Sayeret Matkal.

The path that Doron blazes in Lebanon with his dusty red paratroopers' boots propels him into a promising military career and lends him a permanent aura. Outstanding paratroopers tend to catch the eyes of Sayeret Matkal's headhunters, and they start courting him. He briefly considers it, then decides to study mathematics and computer science at Tel Aviv University instead. The rest of his life will continue on this axis between academia and the military, taking him not only to the top of Sayeret Matkal but also earning him a doctorate from Columbia University.

Around now, in late 1984, Sayeret Matkal under Omer Bar-Lev's command is experiencing one of the greatest crises in its history. Bar-Lev is up to his neck trying to rehabilitate the unit after a series of operational mishaps, and he desperately needs fresh blood. Having acquired his fair share of star talent before, he manages to persuade Doron to take a break from his studies and join Sayeret Matkal as the head of its training company. The unit's courtship of Doron develops into a romance, which immediately becomes a marriage between two lovers who know how to squeeze the best out of each other. He takes part in several operations and becomes an operations commander under Moshe Ya'alon, studying for a master's degree on the side.

In 1989, when he finishes his studies, Doron is appointed the deputy commander of Sayeret Matkal under Ran Shahor. In 1991, Amos Ben-Avraham takes over from Ran Shahor as the unit's commander but calls it quits after a year and a half—without Chief of Staff Ehud Barak even trying to persuade him to reconsider—after two soldiers die of heatstroke during a navigational exercise in the desert. Doron Avital is immediately appointed his successor at the helm of Sayeret Matkal.

"Sayeret Matkal's commanders are flying too close to the sun," Amnon Lipkin-Shahak once said. And during his command, Doron Avital definitely feels himself getting burned when five of his men are killed in a training exercise simulating an assassination of Saddam Hussein, a drill that will go down in infamy as the "Tze'elim Bet disaster." Barak, who just a year earlier accepted Amos Ben-Avraham's resignation, keeps Doron in his job, and Doron manages to rehabilitate the unit after another fiasco and profound crisis of morale.

* * *

It is Sayeret Matkal that successfully abducts Sheikh Obeid in July 1989 in a bid for information about Ron Arad's whereabouts, and maybe even to use the sheikh as a bargaining chip against Amal, the Lebanese organization that initially held the captive navigator. But after a long interrogation, it becomes clear that Sheikh Obeid has no relevant information about Ron Arad's fate, and Israel will therefore need to find an even higher-ranking Lebanese figure, or ideally an Iranian one, so that the other side will take seriously the chips in Israel's hands.

In 1991–1992, Israeli intelligence officers throw around many names of potential abductees, including Iranian officials in Lebanon, but the big worry is that abducting Iranian nationals would open the gates of hell, as happened on March 17, 1992, one month after the assassination of Hezbollah secretary-general Abbas al-Musawi, when the Iranians blew up the Israeli embassy in Argentina.

Mustafa Dirani's name comes up quickly during the search for a Lebanese heavyweight to kidnap. He used to be high up in the Amal Movement, a Shi'ite political party, before quitting it and founding the "Believing Resistance" organization, which collaborated with Hezbollah. It was Dirani's group that abducted Ron Arad when he ejected from his plane in 1986, detaining him for two years, and finally selling him in 1988, most probably to the Iranians. Dirani is therefore a top candidate for abduction because of his personal involvement in the kidnapping and detention of Ron Arad, and because of his ability—or so Israeli military intelligence believes—to supply fresh information about the MIA's fate. He'll also be a high-value bargaining chip for a future prisoner exchange, of course.

But Dirani lives in a large apartment block in the suburbs of Beirut, and there's no chance that anyone in the Israeli government or military top brass will approve sending Sayeret Matkal there. The days in which its commandos could throw on a costume and saunter as they pleased through the streets of Beirut, like in Operation Spring of Youth, are long gone and will probably never return.

In any case, Yitzhak Rabin is currently Israel's prime minister and defense minister, Ehud Barak is the IDF chief of staff, and Uri Sagi is the military intelligence chief, and in order to get these three men to give such a kidnapping operation a green light, Sayeret Matkal will have to find extremely creative solutions. And such a solution suddenly pops into the minds of the unit's intelligence officer and his men when fresh intelligence lands at Sayeret Matkal's doorstep.

It turns out that every summer, Dirani and his family visit their holiday home in their ancestral village of Kasar Naba on the edge of the Beqaa Valley. Bingo! Now there's solid intelligence and a feasible operation on the cards, and all that's left to do is to "copy/paste" the successful abduction of Sheikh Obeid from the village of Jebchit just five years earlier.

Well, not quite. Kasar Naba is deep inside Lebanon, a vast distance from the Israeli border, not at all like a quick foray to abduct Sheikh Obeid. Such distance will require helicopter and vehicle access, complicating the whole mission. But in late 1993, Israel begins to realize that it's going to have to take much bigger risks if it wants to nab a bigger prize.

* * *

Sayeret Matkal, under Doron Avital, decides to start training for the operation nearly a year before its execution because of a series of false starts. It already has a baseline for operational plans from previous abductions, especially from the Sheikh Obeid mission, and flawlessly detailed operational files, and all that remains is to add the necessary changes for the new operation and of course to build a new all-star team from the soldiers and officers currently in active service.

Shahar Argaman has already been picked as the next commander of Sayeret Matkal, taking over from Doron Avital, and there's no chance that he will miss an operation like this. Doron himself, as usual in missions like this, will take command at the front, leading his men into battle. Doron decides to tap his deputy Ronen Shapira as the commander of the operation itself. Lior Lotan, the commander of the unit's counterterror division, will command one of the forces. Herzi Halevi, a new recruit from the Paratroopers and head of the unit's training company, will command another of the forces.

* * *

The Shi'ite village of Kasar Naba, where Dirani spends his summers, as Israeli intelligence has found out, sits on the western edge of the Beqaa Valley, on the slopes of the mountains that soar upward to the middle of Lebanon, some fifty miles from the Israeli border. The whole area is under the complete control of Hezbollah and the Syrian military, with the protection of Iran's Revolutionary Guards. Not exactly somewhere you'd go on holiday with your family—unless you're Mustafa Dirani. The relatively large distance from the border requires Israel's military planners to include an Israeli Air Force squadron of Sikorsky CH-53 Sea Stallion helicopters in the initial plans, as well as jeeps adapted for clandestine night-time operations, to take the commandos from the improvised heli-pad near the village to the outskirts of the village itself. Sayeret Matkal's relationship with this helicopter squadron is something of a romance that has blossomed over the years as its pilots display ever-greater combat capabilities, allowing Sayeret Matkal's operational planners to start taking greater and greater risks.

And just like in the operation to abduct Sheikh Obeid, the task of reaching Dirani's house in the middle of the village without getting caught, despite entering with such a large force and so much gear, will be fiendishly difficult. But this time, Ronen and his men have a huge psychological and operational advantage. Sayeret Matkal has proven beyond doubt that it can send a huge force into a sleeping Lebanese village without getting detected and reach a specific house without waking anyone up or turning a quiet operation into an all-out war. Obviously, success in one village is no guarantee of success in another, so much further from the Israeli border and five years later, but the priceless knowledge that this is a real possibility inspires confidence in the whole unit. And it's this knowledge that might just make the top dogs—intelligence chief Uri Sagi, Chief of Staff Barak, and Prime Minister Rabin—authorize a mission that looks totally fantastical.

Meanwhile, the clock keeps ticking quickly and loudly since the abduction of Ron Arad, and Sayeret Matkal, which has carried out its fair share of overt and covert missions in a bid to find the MIA or at least information about him, can't stand idly by. It intends to keep doing everything it can, putting its own men in harm's way, to obtain more information and even a human jackpot for a future prisoner exchange.

Sayeret Matkal takes around ten weeks for this round of preparations and drills, stealing into different kinds of villages across Israel, orienteering exercises on foot and by car, practicing how to take over a building, cooperation with the Air Force, target shooting practices, smashing locks, rehearsing escapes, studying the local geography and the Dirani house in detail, deploying special war materiel, practicing off-road driving, breaking into buildings, intensive physical workouts to prepare for hiking in the mountainous terrain of the Beqaa Valley, scaling fences, and identifying the target—Mustafa Dirani.

At a later stage, they start practicing on an exact scale model of Dirani's house built at Sayeret Matkal's base and planted in a model of the village around it. The unit's intelligence officers prepare flash cards for the commandos, with the names and pictures of Dirani's family, so that they can immediately identify anyone they come across inside. At the same time, the Israeli Air Force launches frequent sorties into Lebanon in order to take aerial photos and spot any changes in or around the house that might impact the operation. Sayeret Matkal also conducts dozens of drills of things that might go wrong and how to respond, based on the rich intelligence gathered and analyzed ahead of this operation.

Doron Avital, the unit's commander, keeps drilling a motto into his soldiers' and officers' minds: "Restraint and alertness to danger." He is concerned about what might happen in Dirani's house when his men run into the family, including his wife and children, and he keeps repeating his mantra until his men print stickers with it and slap them on the officers' cars: "Restraint and alertness to danger."

The operation is postponed several times when intelligence officers in the unit, the Intelligence Corps, and Mossad can't guarantee that Dirani will indeed be sleeping in his summer house that night, before finally setting a date when there are several indications that Dirani will be sleeping in Kasar Naba: Friday, May 21, 1994.

* * *

Twenty-eight Sayeret Matkal commandos take off in two helicopters from the Israeli Air Force's squadron, land at the Mahanayim airfield near Rosh Pinna in northern Israel, and await Prime Minister Rabin's final approval. The prime minister has already given his final approval, but true to tradition, he starts drowning under a new and especially bothersome wave of doubts. On the evening of the operation he summons to his home in Tel Aviv his military secretary (and former deputy Sayeret Matkal commander) Danny Yatom, military intelligence chief Uri Sagi, and of course Chief of Staff Ehud Barak.

They are all about to engage in one of the tedious deliberations that are a fact of life for anyone who works with Rabin, in which he keeps repeating the same operational questions, going down to the resolution of a squad commander, or even finer detail: "And what if the front door doesn't open? And if it opens but in the meanwhile everyone's woken up?" And thus, with Rabin's signature precision and infinite patience, supreme responsibility for the soldiers' lives weighing down on his shoulders, he keeps interrogating every minor operational detail.

Uri Sagi, responsible for both Sayeret Matkal and the operation, loses his patience and drops the niceties befitting such a tight forum meeting in the prime minister's house. There isn't a single question that hasn't been asked, or a single possible hitch that hasn't been explored dozens of times, and now it's evening already, the soldiers are in the helicopters, the engines are running, and rotors are spinning—and only Rabin, with his slow voice and monotonous questions, seems to be dragging the whole authorization process back to square one.

Even expert "Rabinologists" like Ehud Barak and Danny Yatom, who have known the prime minister for decades, are slightly surprised but they feel compelled to play along with his protracted doubts and even suggest delaying the mission by a day or two.

Finally, Rabin pulls himself together, mumbles something that sounds like a go-ahead, and the sighs of relief heaved by everyone around the table can be heard as far as Mahanayim.

The helicopters take off into the night, their lights completely switched off, and only the sound of the rotors, spinning at a constant but annoying pace, might give away the two massive predators zeroing-in on their prey. The helicopters travel with close protection from two other attack helicopters flying alongside them and much wider air cover from Israeli fighter jets. This whole fleet takes to the air to protect the heavy and cumbersome Sikorsky CH-53 Sea Stallion helicopters, the jeeps stowed in their cargo, and the soldiers sitting inside on high alert.

The planes land in silence, into the darkness cloaking Mount Sannine, above Kasar Naba. Due to lack of space on the mountaintop for the two helicopters to land together, the second helicopter can only land after the first one takes off again.

Overnight, the Israelis discover that the attack helicopters escorting the main force were spotted by a Syrian lookout, putting the anti-aircraft batteries in the Beqaa Valley on high alert. Lebanese army forces around Zahlé hear the helicopters and dispatch a vehicle patrol, but by intercepting their communications, the Israelis discover that the Lebanese haven't detected the exact landing point, only the rough area.

* * *

When the force lands on Mount Sannine, Ronen Shapira is the first to jump out of the helicopter. He has all the information in his head, but studying the lay of the land in a briefing room is one thing; experiencing it is something else. The terrain will always be different from what you learn and memorize before heading out. Ronen looks around him, sees how the moonlight is starting to cover the whole landscape in a soft glow, and decides—contrary to the original plan—to take the longer route, better concealed from the houses in the village. When the men reach the cliff from which they must descend into the Beqaa Valley, Ronen stops the convoy. The moon has not yet climbed to the middle of the sky, and the valley is partially still cloaked in darkness. They wait for the moon to start setting. In any other circumstances, it might even be romantic. "*Yalla*, come on, let's do this," Doron whispers to Ronen, and the force start moving again.

The journey takes longer than planned because of the sharp slopes, which look much steeper on the ground than in the aerial photographs they pored over on the base. The vehicles stop exactly at the planned location, and the commandos hop off, embarking on the last and hardest stretch: walking to and inside the village, making almighty efforts not to get caught and set off a commotion even before reaching Dirani's house.

The force marches along terraces packed with grapevines, and the officer leading the column is forced to cut several of the fences separating the agricultural plots with a cloth-wrapped cutter, to muffle the sound of slicing through wire. When the soldiers reach the village, it turns out that the lights are on in nearly all the houses, despite the late hour, which obviously slows down their advance and forces them to be extra-careful. The slightest clumsy step, sending stones tumbling down the hill, will immediately jeopardize the whole force. Luckily, there are almost no dogs in the village, so the force is spared one of the biggest dangers of any night-time operation: barking dogs waking up the villagers.

Dirani is celebrating his forty-sixth summer tonight, and nobody in the force wants to ruin the surprise party that they have been working on for months. When the commandos approach the target's house, they find all the lights on and three cars parked outside: surprise developments that will make it extremely hard to steal into the house undetected.

Lior Lotan's squad, in charge of the front balcony, takes the right flank and advances on the northern wall of the house. Dirani himself lives on the first floor, and in order to reach the balcony, the force needs a ladder. Lior directs Itamar and Amnon as they steady a sixteen-foot ladder, but they are still missing another four inches to be able to prop it against the edge of the concrete balustrade along the balcony.

Lior guides them in a whisper, until they manage to steady the ladder. He climbs up it first, followed by the rest of his squad. When they land in total silence on the balcony, they notice that the door on the balcony, leading to what was supposed to be the guards' room, is wide open. *What a relief,* the four intruders think.

Lior whips out his night-vision goggles, peeks in through the open door, and sees two children sleeping on mattresses on the floor. He gives his men a quick briefing in a whisper, explaining for the last but certainly not the first time the plan for entering the house, and then he steps inside for another, more thorough sweep. This time, he spots another child—three in total.

The soldiers and their commanders wait in growing suspense for the beginning of the countdown, after which Ronen Shapira will whisper, "GO!" From that point on, there will be no more doubts, thoughts, or preparations. They will have to flip a switch, put themselves on autopilot, and mechanically execute the chain of maneuvers that they have practiced so many times, culminating with Dirani landing in an Israeli jail cell.

Lior decides to close in on the target even before Ronen's "Go!", and he sneaks with his cell into the guards' room. These extra few feet will help the whole operation, no doubt about it, but they also give Lior a slight advantage in his own race against Ron's squad—a competition that nobody dares mention, to be the first to reach the coveted target.

Inside the "guards' room," Lior spots a man sleeping on a bed pushed against the wall of the balcony. He passes through the room and tiptoes like a ballerina until he is two feet away from Dirani's bedroom. He's got to get there first. The others are not far behind them, still inside the guards' room.

The second squad, comprising Emmanuel Moreno and another two men, is still waiting on the back balcony, from which it will compete with Ronen's squad after the "Go!" order for the glimmer of glory awaiting whoever can reach Dirani's bedroom first. But this isn't a fair fight, because Lior has silently snuck closer and closer during the countdown, until he is practically within kicking range of the bedroom door.

* * *

"GO!" hears Lior in his earpiece, and he sends his right leg smashing through Dirani's door, with all the force of Ronaldo. Lior raises his gun, its barrel still empty of bullets, and points it straight at the middle of Dirani's torso. The man sits up in bed, his face contorted in surprise, his left hand outstretched immediately to grab his silver 9mm Smith and Wesson pistol on the bedside cabinet. His wife, lying next to him, sits up in a heartbeat and covers her face with her hands, as if trying to catch the bullet that will soon fly out of Lior's gun. Lior hollers, "*antabah, jaysh!*"— "Lie down, army!"—launches himself at the double bed, whacks Dirani over the head with his silencer, grabs him by the hair, and topples him to the ground as Dirani still fumbles around for his handgun. He knows the game is over. He must have realized this the first second he saw this "Rambo," armed from head to toe, looming over him in the doorway, but his natural fighting spirit will not allow him to surrender without a fight.

And exactly then, Emmanuel Moreno and the rest of his squad, which has had to settle for second place in the race for Dirani's bedroom, storms in and pulls apart this game of Twister, this tangled mess of legs and arms as Dirani and his wife tussle with Lior on the floor. Suddenly out pops Dirani's ten-year-old daughter, sleeping with her parents in their bed, and she is taken to the children's room.

* * *

The third squad reaches the front door, covered in grates much thicker than expected, and when they try to activate a special piston for blowing doors open, there's a technical hitch. Herzi Halevi checks the roller shutters by the side of the door and works out that the men can easily enter through them.

Everyone climbs upstairs in silence and stands in front of the apartment door, short of breath, waiting for Ronen to give the order. When they hear "Go!" they cruise inside—a column of eight more men floods the apartment, with two squads already inside. Some of them run toward Dirani's room but see the pile-up of soldiers and turn to the kids' room. Others try to smash the living room door with an axe, following the original plan, but to no avail—and finally, they realize that they can enter through the door at the end of the corridor.

* * *

Moreno takes Dirani to an empty room for quick questioning, in the hope of gauging some preliminary information about Ron Arad's fate. The intensive interrogation, in the seven minutes allocated for it, goes nowhere. Dirani is still a closed book. It's going to take time and superhuman efforts by Israel's best interrogators before he opens his mouth, and even then, it's safe to assume, he will hardly spill the beans.

Lior takes the living room with another soldier, and together they quickly grab dozens of documents and video cassettes. In the bedroom, in one of the drawers in the cabinet next to Dirani's bed, they find more documents and three handguns.

When Lior first stormed into the bedroom alone, his men cuffed Subhi—Dirani's brother and bodyguard—who was sleeping in the guards' room. Now, Ronen decides to untie Subhi and leave him behind.

One of the soldiers throws Dirani over his strong, broad shoulders, after the man was cuffed and his eyes covered, and the force launches a "mother goose" procedure: each squad commander checks that all his men are with him and reports back to Ronen. The whole force heads for the guard post manned by Shahar Argaman, the incoming commander, before embarking on a strenuous hike up to vehicles waiting to take everyone back to the helicopters' landing site. On the way, Lior spots four people at the bottom of the adjacent road and he warns them to enter their homes immediately and close their windows. They do as he says.

But meanwhile, the retreating force comes under sporadic gunfire from the apartment next door, which belongs to another of Dirani's brothers (not Subhi). The rhythmic gunshots provide a musical accompaniment for Dirani's sister-in-law and father, who are shouting out of the window and venting their rage in unliterary Arabic. And then a single bullet hits Shahar Argaman in the leg, as if to prove that his climb to the commander's post will cost him dearly. Shahar applies a tourniquet to himself and pushes ahead with his men, as if nothing happened.

And while dozens of bullets keep whizzing from the next-door apartment and neighboring homes in the rough direction of the Israeli force, two red dots suddenly appear on Dirani's brother's and father's foreheads: laser markers, pointing out the exact spots that might soon be hit by sniper bullets. But no bullets will come flying this time, because that might give away the force's location, and also because the restraint dictated by Ronen and Doron Avital has a moral force and important operational purpose. Dirani's brother and father understand the meaning of the red dots flickering in the middle of their foreheads, and they immediately hold their fire.

Dirani, his hands cuffed and eyes covered, is loaded onto a stretcher, and all the equipment for the hike and the break-in is packed up and divided between the commandos before their retreat. The route that Ronen picks for the withdrawal is different from the arrival, to get as far away as possible from the houses and possible enemy forces. And indeed, the Lebanese Army back-up reaches the village around five minutes after the force scarpers from Dirani's holiday home.

The uphill hike to the two getaway cars waiting for them above the village is extremely grueling, until at a certain point Ronen decides to offload some of their cargo, the ladders and other heavy equipment, so that they can pick up their pace. Despite two easy navigational mistakes, the cars manage to coordinate perfectly with the helicopters, which have been held up at the entrance to the landing pad. The soldiers are counted, and some seem to be missing, but after a recount the number of soldiers who set out for the mission balances out with the number returning (plus one—Mr. Dirani), and the choppers take off back to Israel, firmly protected by a tight envelope of attack helicopters and a wider perimeter of fighter jets.

The helicopters land at the Israeli Air Force's technical school in Haifa and belch out twenty-eight commandos, thrilled with their flawless operational success but increasingly concerned that Dirani won't deliver the goods for which this whole mission was planned and executed.

Dirani is immediately whisked away to a facility run by Unit 504, which interrogates captives. His interrogation does absolutely nothing to push forward the long-running battle to bring Ron Arad home, and Dirani is eventually returned to Lebanon in 2004, in the same prisoner exchange with Hezbollah in which his colleague Sheikh Obeid is sent home.

In 2004, Israel and Hezbollah conduct a prisoner exchange: Mustafa Dirani, Sheikh Obeid, and several other Lebanese are swapped for the bodies of three IDF soldiers killed in a Hezbollah ambush on Mount Dov in the Golan Heights four years earlier as well as an Israeli civilian who was considered important enough to be repatriated at this cost despite the dubious circumstances in which he was abducted.

Dirani's capture fails to shed a drop of light on Ron Arad's fate, and from an intelligence perspective, the mission hardly contributes anything. The operational success helps to reinforce Israel's image as a state that will go to the ends of the earth to bring back its sons and daughters, but in Ron Arad's case, it is no use. His fate is still unknown.

Chapter 16

THE ATTEMPTED RESCUE OF NACHSHON WACHSMAN—BIR NABALA, OCTOBER 1994

Nachshon Wachsman and Nir Poraz, two fine young Israeli men who have never met, come within a pistol's range, or a submachine gun's range, of each other when Nir and his men try to rescue Nachshon from his kidnappers. And only in their painful death, mere seconds apart, with only one stubborn door between them, do their names become intertwined in the Israeli public consciousness. Two talented young men who would have certainly gone far, had they lived, but who tragically make a name for themselves in their deaths, are forced to discover what it truly means to be Israeli, in all its complexity.

Nachshon Wachsman, born in 1975 to a religious Jewish family in Jerusalem, enlists into the Golani infantry brigade and dreams of being a doctor. On Sunday October 9, 1994, he stands at a junction near the town of Yehud to hitch a ride to a friend who lives in nearby Ramle. This ride, which seals his fate, arrives within minutes. An Israeli vehicle, bearing an innocuous Israeli license plate and four Hamas terrorists, disguised as religious Jewish youth, pulls up next him at 17:30. The kippahs on the passengers' heads put Nachshon at ease and he steps into the car without a worry, but then immediately one of them seizes his gun, cuffs him, and places a black bag over his head.

Yitzhak Rabin is the prime minister and defense minister; Ehud Barak is the IDF chief of staff; Uri Sagi is the head of the military Intelligence Corps; Gideon Ezra is the commander of the Jerusalem, Judea, and Samaria precinct in the Shin Bet; and Shaul Mofaz is the head of the Judea and Samaria Division. And the next day, October 10, this heavy-hitting team of generals watches a video broadcast from Gaza, in which a Hamas militant addresses Rabin with his organization's conditions for releasing the kidnapped soldier.

The next day, October 11, the Prime Minister's Office is given a recording from the Gaza Strip in which a keffiyeh-clad Hamas militant holds up Nachshon's ID card and then Nachshon himself looks into the camera and reads out his kidnappers' demands: the immediate release of all Hamas prisoners and another two Lebanese prisoners, the real jackpot—Mustafa Dirani and Sheikh Abdel Karim Obeid. The pair were abducted by Sayeret Matkal from Lebanon in two operations, a few years apart, and are both behind bars in Israel. If they are not released by 21:00 on Friday, October 14, Hamas threatens, Nachshon will be executed.

The Hamas militant speaks in a Gazan accent, the video itself comes from Gaza, and from the announcements in Gaza's mosques that day, Nachshon seems to be held in the Gaza Strip. But this is a sophisticated deceit by Hamas, which is trying to make it look like Nachshon was smuggled to Gaza while in fact he is dozens of miles away, in an abandoned house in the village of Bir Nabala in the West Bank, north of Jerusalem. The Oslo I Accord has just been signed, and most of the Gaza Strip—besides the limited areas of Jewish settlement, mainly Gush Katif—has come under the control of the autonomous Palestinian Authority, and the IDF no longer ventures in. But the situation in the West Bank is different, and the IDF still exercises total control. Moreover, Hamas is waging a fierce campaign of opposition to the Palestinian Authority in the Gaza Strip.

It seems quite logical, therefore, that the kidnapped soldier is being held in a place where the IDF will struggle to maneuver.

* * *

The IDF Central Command's intelligence department starts trying to crack the mystery of Nachshon's whereabouts. The IDF has already mobilized forces toward the Gaza Strip, but a golden tip-off from the Shin Bet points to the possibility, and not a slim one, that Nachshon might be in the West Bank. And if that's the case, then Hamas is trying to lead Israel astray in order to eliminate the possibility that the IDF might locate the safe house where Nachshon is being held and try to free him by force, as in similar cases in the past.

With this clue in hand, Central Command's chief intelligence officer meets Gideon Ezra from the Shin Bet and together they decide to search all the car rental companies in the Jerusalem area for a vehicle with an Israeli license plate rented on October 9 and paid for in cash, because no terrorists planning to kidnap a soldier would pay for a car with a credit card under his own name.

It's a real shot in the dark, but this zany idea is part and parcel of intelligence work, especially in situations like this one, when nobody has any other operational ideas. Indeed, on Thursday, October 13, a day and a half before the terrorists' ultimatum expires, it turns out that a Palestinian living in the West Bank did indeed hire a car from a rental firm in Jerusalem on Sunday morning and returned it on Monday afternoon. He paid in cash, and from the mileage, the car could definitely have been driven to Gaza and back. The faces of the Shin Bet and Intelligence Directorate's officers, who have been searching for a needle in a haystack for several days now, immediately turn white.

But then they see the signature scrawled on the rental form, and a red light starts flashing in their heads. The Palestinian who rented the car, a man by the name of Jihad Yanmur, turns out to be the brother of a Hamas member arrested in the West Bank just a few months before the kidnapping. A police force is dispatched immediately to his home and brings him in for interrogation. The young man is not yet a signed-up Hamas militant, just a helper, so his ability to withstand interrogation is hardly commendable, and that night he completely collapses and is willing to tell his interrogators whatever they want to hear. He lays out the whole story in intricate detail, including Hamas's attempt at deception, and reveals that Nachshon and the cell of kidnappers are in an abandoned house on the outskirts of Bir Nabala. He also identifies another man, who brings the terrorists daily food deliveries. Bingo.

Now Prime Minister Rabin and Chief of Staff Barak have all the tools and information they need in order to decide what to do. They don't hesitate for even a minute before deciding to prepare an operation to free Nachshon from the place where he is being held captive. The army knows where it is and knows exactly how to get there.

The mission that Rabin and Barak decide on, without even convening the security cabinet, is entrusted to IDF Central Command, which in turn calls up Sayeret Matkal and the YAMAM, true to tradition. In the perpetual tug-of-war between these two elite units over their participation in hostage rescue missions, Sayeret Matkal always has an obvious advantage, albeit not always for professional operational reasons: the decision-makers are almost always veterans of the unit. In this case, Ehud Barak, a former Sayeret Matkal commander, is the chief of staff himself, and Shaul Mofaz, a former deputy commander, heads the Judea and Samaria Division and is about to be tapped to manage this event. It's the perfect "air cover" for Sayeret Matkal to get a slice of the action.

At this point, IDF Central Command decides not to send massive forces into the area, in order not to make local Palestinians suspicious that something is afoot. Sayeret Matkal commander Shahar Argaman and the deputy commander of the YAMAM are called in for a quick briefing at Central Command. The YAMAM's commander, David Tzur, happens to be in the United States. Clearly, the absence of this experienced officer does not help to sway the deliberations in the YAMAM's favor.

At the same time, the Central Command intelligence department starts hoarding every morsel of information it can find about the apartment where Nachshon is being held, about the Hamas operatives holding him, and about possible access routes to storm the site.

* * *

Shahar Argaman enlists in the IDF in 1977 but drops out of its fighter pilots' course after nine months because of an irregular heartbeat and switches over to Sayeret Matkal. This introduction leads to a highly successful marriage, and Shahar is eventually given command of the unit, but not before proving time and again that he's made of the right stuff and that at the end of a long and arduous path up the ranks of the unit, only one job awaits him: that of Sayeret Matkal's commander.

When Shahar joins Sayeret Matkal, and in the long slog after that, he doesn't look like a commander in waiting. He is skinny, short, and rarely speaks, only when he doesn't have a choice.

Shahar, by nature and upbringing, must always choose the most challenging option. He welcomes the incoming cohort of August 1980, whom he will command for over three years. Immediately thereafter, Shahar receives command over the operations company, in many respects the most interesting and challenging job in the unit, maybe even more so than the commander's. That's where he clearly projects the special qualities that will lead him all the way to the top of the pyramid. He seems to have the same focused determination possessed only by Sayeret Matkal commanders-in-waiting. He also has an ability and urge to get down to the tiniest details, to see every tree in the wood but also the wood itself—from above, from the side, and through the roots.

And besides all this, Shahar is also utterly fearless, brave not only as a commander leading his men into dangerous missions, but also as one storming straight into the line of fire. A rare breed indeed.

Courage is often a badge of honor for relatively shallow people, who can't wrap their heads around all the terrifying scenarios that might unfold in a dangerous event. Not in Shahar's case. He is highly intelligent, extremely attentive to other people's opinions, and makes decisions by carefully selecting the best advice that he is given. He is also a good communicator, but his natural introversion often trumps his presentation skills, and when he has to speak in front of an audience as part of his job, he always reads from a piece of paper.

* * *

Three days before the eventual operation, on Tuesday, Sayeret Matkal is whisked to the Southern Command, because the IDF's official assessment is still that the Nachshon Wachsman is being held in the Gaza Strip. Shahar dispatches his standby teams from around Gaza to Camp Ofer, a military base north of Jerusalem, because it is clear that Nachshon is somewhere nearby and they need to get ready. At 14:30 on Friday, October 14, the unit sets up its command center at Camp Ofer, and Shahar's cluster of soldiers sits down to start planning the raid. At 16:00, they have to present a plan to Major General. Mofaz, who is in charge of this whole event. As a former deputy commander of Sayeret Matkal, Mofaz is intimately familiar with its officers' jargon, mannerisms, and ways of thinking. He has immense respect for the young men who are about to pitch him a plan, and the feeling is mutual: perhaps a necessary condition for the success of an operation like this. Necessary—but insufficient.

The working assumption is that the mission must be executed at night, because there's no way to guarantee that commandos can reach the target in secret in broad daylight. Besides, the terrorists' ultimatum is about to expire in five and a half hours, and Sayeret Matkal needs as much time as possible to prepare for the operation.

The leaders involved in this mission are in total agreement that there must be no negotiations with the kidnappers: the raid on the apartment must be a complete surprise. Since there will be no contact with the kidnappers, there is no way to buy time and delay the ultimatum. The operation will have to be before 21:00 on Friday. The chances of saving Nachshon's life will therefore depend on whether the kidnappers can be caught off guard. It's a solid, indisputable working assumption.

In cases like this, because of the time pressure, there's no way to build the best plan, only the best given the circumstances, or as it's called in the IDF's military jargon: to enter "hasty battle mode." The YAMAM is also supposed to pitch its own plan to Mofaz, immediately after Sayeret Matkal presents its own, but all the top officers from Central Command, Sayeret Matkal, and the YAMAM know that the privilege of executing this mission will fall once more to the commandos from Sayeret Matkal.

And until the show begins, the intelligence officers in Sayeret Matkal and Central Command conduct intensive reconnaissance to find every snippet of information that might help the soldiers. First, they prepare a sketch of the house based on information from the interrogation of the Palestinian who rented the car and was arrested by the police. Second, soon after, they receive aerial photographs that help them to understand the building's exterior, the location of the windows, and possible ways of reaching the second-floor balcony without a ladder.

The accomplice who delivers them food, who has also been arrested, confirms that Nachshon is being guarded by three terrorists holed up in an apartment on the second floor. The kidnapped soldier is cuffed in the bedroom under the constant watch of one of the terrorists. The two others walk around the apartment and occasionally sit down to watch TV in the living room. The shutters are all closed, and the windows are also covered in blankets, to stop any light escaping. When he brought them food, the accomplice used to ring the intercom at the entrance to the yard, and after they confirmed his identity, he passed through two locked doors, one to enter the stairwell, and another to enter the apartment on the second floor.

In hindsight, minor gaps in the IDF's knowledge about the structure of the building turn out to be critical to the mission's success. Based on the latest sketches and aerial photographs, the door on the roof is supposed to lead the soldiers straight into the apartment. In reality, it turns out that this doorway leads to the staircase, which leads to the front door of the apartment, such that both entrances—one on the ground floor, the other through the roof—lead to exactly the same locked door on the second floor. Moreover, in the blueprints prepared with the accomplice's help, the front door is somewhere different from reality. Similarly, according to the blueprints, there are three windows at the back of the building, with the middle one belonging to the bedroom. In fact, this window is attached to the bathroom, which doesn't even appear in the sketches studied by the commando force.

Shahar understands that the little time he has left until the operation requires every level of the planning to proceed in tandem, and he decides to send in two forces: a primary force and a back-up force. The primary force will be commanded by his deputy Yuval Rachmilevitch; the back-up force, by Herzi Halevi, the commander of the unit's training division.

Herzi is the kind of guy who has radiated star potential as a soldier from the day he joined the army, and not just because of his chiseled good looks. Sayeret Matkal has always been good at spotting star talent, even in regular infantry brigades and especially the Paratroopers, having them transferred over, giving them its backing and, in a relatively short time, making them feel at home and even like potential future commanders. The unit has a knack for flexible thinking and has never insisted on reserving the top job for officers who grew up within its ranks. Everyone benefits from this tradition: Sayeret Matkal enjoys a wider pool of talented officers, the officers themselves enjoy the move from the Paratroopers to Sayeret Matkal, and even the Paratroopers can take pride in their ability to produce stars. But the biggest beneficiary is of course the IDF, which thanks to this unusually liberal approach can enjoy the excellent fruits of cooperation between its units. Moreover, these military "stars," from the Paratroopers and Sayeret Matkal, have learned to cooperate, often bringing their strong personal chemistry all the way up to the General Staff.

The primary force, under Yuval's command, is supposed to sneak under cover of darkness all the way to the building and break in, while the second force, under Herzi's command, will arrive by car exactly one minute after the green light is given, jump out of the vehicles, and provide back-up in case the primary force runs into trouble.

Shahar tasks Yuval with coordinating the operational planning for the team that will steal into the building. Yuval plans to seize the building using three subsidiary forces, manned by the team's most veteran squads.

"Team Balcony," commanded by Michael, will comprise Nir Poraz's team and another team; "Team Roof" will be commanded by Nitzan Alon and contain another team; and "Team Front Door," commanded by Lior Lotan, will contain a third team. Most of them have already worked together on the abduction of Mustafa Dirani five months earlier.

Shahar's big idea is to create organic squads of soldiers who have already seen action together and know each other inside out, down to the minor caprices and nuances that no outsider could possibly understand. The personal chemistry and full synchronicity between the soldiers, acquired over countless joint drills, are unimaginably important for the success of such a dangerous mission, in which every millisecond and millimeter will be fateful, for better or for worse.

* * *

Sayeret Matkal is still weighing up several subterfuge options, but they are all thrown out of the window for various reasons, and the plan returns to square one: reaching the building's three openings as quietly as possible and storming it in tandem, exploiting the element of surprise.

The idea is to reach the bedroom, where Nachshon is being held, as quickly as possible—whichever force gets there first—and to eliminate the terrorists in the living room and other rooms on the way.

At around 16:30, Sayeret Matkal pitches its plan to the division commander. Mofaz emphasizes that even if they run into trouble before entering the building, they must storm inside and finish the job. After the half-hour presentation, and after the YAMAM presents its own plan, Mofaz announces that Sayeret Matkal will perform the raid on the safe house.

For the raid, it is agreed that one of the unit's officers will run the operation from the control center. Yuval Rachmilevitch will join Nitzan's team; Shahar Argaman will join Michael's. In such a sensitive and dangerous operation, it doesn't even cross the unit commanders' minds to run the show from the rear, in the command center, and it's only natural for them to join the strike force, with all the danger. Shahar reasons that Michael's squad, which will enter through the balcony, has the strongest chances of running into the terrorists, because it only has one door to breach. And since the result of this shoot-out probably rides on this squad, Shahar has to be wherever he will have the biggest impact.

The plan that Mofaz approves is presented to Prime Minister and Defense Minister Yitzhak Rabin, and he approves it without comment.

* * *

At 18:00, the Shin Bet's lookouts spot a car approaching the building. Mofaz and the Shin Bet decide to let it pass. It's another accomplice, who is also delivering food. When he leaves the house and steps back into his vehicle, he is allowed to drive for a few hundred yards and is then arrested and taken to interrogation. It turns out that Nachshon is alive and whole and is eating together with his captors.

Sayeret Matkal's commandos start arming themselves and getting ready for the raid. The force commanders have direct access to the intelligence streaming in from multiple sources to the unit's intelligence officer, and they pass it onto their men.

Each of the three team commanders briefs his men separately. In Shahar's briefing, he presents the picture in very general terms, just so each force knows what the others are doing. There is no time for anything more. The doomsday clock is ticking away at lightning speed. There are only three hours left until its clock hands hit 21:00: the time when the terrorists have threatened to carry out their terrible ultimatum.

* * *

At 18:30, the three squads in the primary force squeeze into military trucks, which after a short while takes them to the drop-off point, from which they will continue on foot, a few hundred yards from the building. At 19:00, the commandos on the trucks hit the ground and start marching in total silence toward the house. Meanwhile the second force, Herzi Halevi's team, waits in two vehicles at the exit point adjacent to Camp Ofer, waiting for the green light to send them all guns blazing all the way to the yard of the building.

Yuval Rachmilevitch's team manages to sneak up on the house without getting discovered, and the squads spread out near the three openings, exactly according to the plan devised just a few hours earlier. The apartment where Nachshon is being held is pitch-black, and not a squeak can be heard.

The best option at this point is for Michael Kafri's "Team Balcony" to break into the apartment through the bedroom window, landing straight into the room where the intelligence says Nachshon is being held. But on the ground, it turns out that the window is covered in steel shutters, which will be hard to breach. Michael recommends in a whisper not to try breaking in through this route. It also turns out that a whole new window, which nobody knew existed, has popped up out of nowhere. Suddenly there are four windows, instead of the three in the sketch based on the accomplice's interrogation. *Good luck guessing which is the bedroom window*, thinks Michael to himself.

Shahar accepts Michael's recommendation and goes back to the original plan—to break in through the balcony door.

The three squads reach the three steel doors covering the three openings in tandem: the front door, the balcony, and the roof, which they scale with a ladder. They prepare their noisy gear, which should send the doors flying off their hinges.

The explosive charges work by charging and then discharging a capacitor, so there may be a minor delay of a couple of seconds between one explosion and the next. Michael's bomb explodes first, then Nitzan's, and finally Lior Lotan's.

Michael's door (on the balcony) and Lior's (on the ground floor) are easily breached, blowing open enormous holes that swiftly swallow the commandos. Nitzan's door, the one on the roof, stubbornly refuses to budge even after the explosion.

But this explosive frenzy, pumping adrenaline into their bloodstream, is just a preview for the horror show that awaits the commandos as they storm one room, maybe two, in pitch darkness, coming under heavy fire from just a few feet away. You'd have to be made of steel, much stronger than the doors just blown to smithereens, to storm into a room without flinching, into a hailstorm of bullets sprayed with such rigor and efficiency from a sea of rifles and machine guns.

Team Michael, led by Nir Poraz, breaks into the kitchen through the balcony, breaks out in a sprint to the living room, and in five seconds flat reaches the door of the bedroom, where Nachshon is being held. This rapid arrival is supposed to be the key to eliminating the terrorists before they can harm the kidnapped soldier. But the terrorists understand exactly what the strike force wants to do, despite the dizzying speed of events, and so two of them lock themselves in the bedroom and a third hides in a toy room, right across from the bedroom. The apartment is totally dark, with only the commandos' headlamps lighting the way—but also exposing them to the terrorists.

Nir Poraz, an officer with nearly three years' experience in Sayeret Matkal, is the first to reach the bedroom door and is immediately hit by gunfire from the third terrorist, the one hiding across the corridor, whom Nir and his men failed to spot. Itai is also wounded, and just as the two officers are hit, the bedroom door is slammed shut. In the next few seconds, most of Michael's commandos are shot by the same terrorist.

Just as Team Michael breaks in through the balcony, Lior Lotan and his men storm through the front door on the ground floor and run up to the second floor. That's where they are surprised to run into another door, which is not just opposite the front door, as they were briefed, but right at the beginning of the residential floor, across from the living room. Meanwhile, Nitzan manages to breach the door on the roof and flies down at the head of a column of men, joining Lior Lotan's force, which has just come face to face with its door: the bedroom door.

* * *

Shahar, Sayeret Matkal's commander, enters the apartment through the balcony, straight after Team Michael. When he reaches the living room, he takes a bullet to his right arm, which splices straight through his flesh without hitting the bone, and another bullet that sends his helmet flying off his head and blows it to pieces but fortunately doesn't hit him. He spots Nir Poraz lying in front of the bedroom door.

Along the wall, between the entrance to the kitchen and the entrance of the bedroom, are scattered other injured men. Eight in total, all from Team Michael. The soldiers who have not yet been hit are shooting at the front door. They're convinced that the terrorists taking potshots at them are hiding in a cupboard over there—and don't realize that they are shooting at Lior's soldiers, who are furiously spraying bullets at the door that suddenly materialized out of nowhere, to smash it down. Team Michael's gunfire injures two other soldiers from Lior's force. Shahar immediately realizes the mistake and stops the gunfire. He instructs one of his men to evacuate Nir Poraz, sprawled at the entrance of the bedroom, and the other wounded men along the wall.

For a moment, there is no more gunfire in the apartment—besides the gunshots coming from inside the bedroom. Shahar reaches the bedroom door, but the terrorists have barricaded it from the inside with furniture, and it won't budge even when he kicks it with all his might. He wants to rapidly organize a team to storm the room but most of Michael's men are down, and there's nobody left to join him going in.

Meanwhile, Lior orders a soldier to shoot the stubborn front door roof with a shotgun, but the door refuses to budge. His men prepare a special IED for blowing locks and orders everyone to step back, to avoid getting injured from the explosion. The door opens immediately and Lior and his men storm into the living room. Lior's deputy charges at the toy room and eliminates the lone terrorist hiding there, who just caused most of the casualties on the Israeli side.

* * *

From now, Lior Lotan leads the effort to storm the bedroom. Lone bullets are still whizzing through the door, from the inside. Shahar orders one of his men to shout out in Arabic to the two surviving terrorists and offer them a chance to surrender. They reply in Hebrew that they would rather die.

At this point, just three or four minutes into the raid, Shahar believes that there's only a slim chance that Nachshon is still alive. Lior attaches another electric-powered IED to the door's cylinder, and as he does so, another hail of bullets splices through the door, and Lior takes a hit to his left shoulder. Lior's force takes cover behind the corner. The IED is activated electronically from the kitchen. The explosion pushes the bedroom door slightly inward, creating a slender crack between the door and the frame. The gunfire continues from the inside but begins to thin out.

Lior whips out a hand grenade, yanks out the safety, and tries to squeeze it through the gap between the door and the lintel. The gap is too narrow, but Lior widens it with an almighty push from his injured shoulder, making it exactly as wide as the grenade that is chucked in and blows up the door and the barricade of furniture from the inside. Lior storms inside with two other men, into a haze of smoke and dust.

* * *

In the middle of the room, on a broken bed, lies Nachshon Wachsman, and behind him a terrorist who seems to be dead. Another terrorist, this one injured, is lying by the doorway. He lifts his hand and fires four bullets from his handgun at the doorway, at a range of under two feet. Two of the commandos shoot him and thus finish the job of eliminating the three terrorists.

By now, it's clear that Nachshon is no longer alive. It looks like he was murdered as soon as the terrorists heard the first explosion around the perimeter, even before the commandos stormed the apartment. A single bullet to his head and six to his chest ended his life in an instant. This is also when Captain Nir Poraz, who stormed headfirst into the bedroom where Nachshon Wachsman was held, is declared dead.

Sayeret Matkal suffers eleven casualties in the raid, which lasts under five minutes, from the moment of the detonations at the doorways. The terrorist killed in the toy room used an IDF-issued M-16 rifle; his two comrades in the bedroom used an IDF-issued Galil rifle, Uzi, and a handgun.

* * *

In a deathly sad press conference, Yitzhak Rabin sits in the middle of a table with Barak to his left, against the backdrop of a brown brick wall, and the prime minister breaks the news about the operation to the nation. As always, he takes full responsibility. "As prime minister and defense minister, I take responsibility for the decision to launch the operation tonight against the terrorists who took Nachshon Wachsman hostage," he says. His nobility will obviously not bring the two dead young men back to life, but it might just succeed in assuaging the intense public grief.

Given the limited time to gather intelligence, plan, and train, this operation was executed in the best way possible and with ferocious determination, without a hint of hesitation at any point, a real tour-de-force of courage and creativity—but which ended in disaster, leaving the Wachsman and Poraz families mourning a tremendous loss, and Sayeret Matkal and the IDF frustrated and pained for many years to come. Nir Poraz and Lior Lotan are awarded the Chief of General Staff's citation for their role in the operation, but it turns out that heroism and bravery are not always guarantees of success.

That night, Prime Minister Rabin visits the Poraz family home. Nir Poraz, an outstanding Sayeret Matkal officer, was the son of Maoz Poraz, an air force pilot killed when his plane was downed over Egypt in the Yom Kippur War. Two members of this family of five are killed in the line of duty, in units where daily danger is par for the course. Five years before his death, in July 1968, Maoz Poraz was a civilian pilot on an El Al flight hijacked to Algeria and was injured trying to resist the hijackers. Only by miracle, because one of the hijackers' guns jams, did Maoz live to prove in word and deed that there could be no surrender to terrorism.

In floods of tears, Nir's older sister Tamar asks Rabin why Nir, whose father fell in combat and whose family has already paid the ultimate price, had to take part in this operation. Shahar Argaman, the unit's injured commander, asks to answer Tamar in his stead. "The moment Nir joined the unit, definitely when he became a team commander, that necessarily put him on the frontlines of danger," Shahar whispers, his voice trembling. "Just in the last year, he took part in two highly dangerous operations. In the high-pressure preparations to free Nachshon Wachsman, there was no room for making considerations like that, unless Nir himself had raised the issue."

But no answer, however professional, can heal the pain of a young woman who has lost her father in battle and is now grieving her brother.

The next day, Rabin visits Sayeret Matkal's base in order to cheer the soldiers up at this grueling time. He speaks about the unique challenge of freeing a single hostage and reminds the men that even in successful hostage rescue missions, like Entebbe, hostages were killed. No one in the unit takes much comfort from this, but everyone knows that even in the next kidnapping, if God forbid another one happens, the battle among the commandos over the "best spot" in the middle will be almost as fierce as the battle itself.

The same day, when the chief of staff launches an inquiry, Barak notes that while the objective of freeing Nachshon Wachsman was not achieved, two other important goals *were* achieved. The terrorist cell that killed two IDF soldiers was eliminated, and Israel and the IDF sent a resounding message to terrorist organizations and the whole world: the State of Israel does not surrender to terror.

EPILOGUE

This book, *Sayeret Matkal*, only tells the story of the publicized missions in which Israel's legendary commando unit has participated since its creation in the late 1950s. Obviously for national security and censorship reasons, it is still impossible, even decades later, to talk about many of the unit's frequent covert missions, its commandos' bread and butter.

Since 1994, the year of the last mission described in this book, Sayeret Matkal has not been deployed for any hostage crises, abductions, or open raids of the sort described herein. The world has changed, the enemy has changed, and so have the unit's objectives and capabilities.

Moreover, the Israeli police and military have decided that operations such as hostage rescue missions will be transferred to the responsibility of the Israel Police and its own special counterterror unit, YAMAM. This police unit has amassed considerable experience in events involving civilians, especially in places adjacent to the Palestinian Authority's autonomous areas, and it has become a top-tier professional outfit. Meanwhile, the IDF and the security establishment have a keen interest in having Sayeret Matkal focus solely on clandestine reconnaissance operations, which are exactly what it has done with success over the past three decades.

* * *

Now that the bullets have stopped flying, the dust has settled, and the smell of gunfire has dissipated into the wind, we are left only with memories of our fallen comrades, memories that undergo almost necessary metamorphosis over time to keep us emotionally balanced.

The bad memories are forcibly suppressed to the bottom of our subconscious, and the good memories slowly climb up to the front of our minds, to a place where we can easily whip them out when needed. The years that have passed since the events described in this book have certainly suppressed many of the failures and enhanced many of the successes in our personal and collective memories. The passage of time has worn down the roughness of these operations, smoothed over the difficult preparations and operations, and flattened many of the details and nuances into a smooth, black highway of foggy memory.

Here and there, there are still disagreements about the operations, usually in cases when someone tried to grab too much of the glory too forcefully. Sayeret Matkal's veterans leave the unit with an instinct for secrecy, one that has usually served to block arguments that might have otherwise developed after international reports of the "sensational" operations that this book has been devoted to describing.

Operation Thunderbolt, in Entebbe, for example, attracted huge amounts of international attention, and obviously the death of Yoni Netanyahu, the unit's commander, also added to its legendary status. But later on, there arose arguments that instead of fading over the years only intensified, ignited new disputes, pulled friends apart, and stoked anger.

Fortunately, and perhaps thanks to more than good fortune, the large majority of the "sensational" operations described in this book ended in operational successes, and success has a habit of papering over disagreements and leaving a legacy of camaraderie, even satisfaction.

As people who were familiar with most of these operations over the years—as participants, from brothers in arms, and even from the media—and having researched them all in detail, we too were surprised to discover the length of the list of operations planned and pulled off with such perfect poise. This might sound like a boast, and even confirmation of the superhuman image that some of the unit's veterans, mostly politicians, have managed to cultivate for it, but this is also true to the facts, as emerge from the long series of investigations that we conducted.

It is impossible not to end with a special thanks to everyone in Sayeret Matkal, not just for their cooperation in our research, but mostly for what they did for our people and the State of Israel over so many years with such determination and professionalism. We feel fortunate to have belonged to such an outstanding group of people.

Avner Shur and Aviram Halevi.

—Tel Aviv, 2021

ACKNOWLEDGMENTS

Thank you to the many people who read the chapters about themselves, opened our eyes to new facts, and gave us the assistance we needed to describe these events with razor-sharp accuracy. Thank you from the bottom of our hearts to Doron Avital, Shahar Argaman, Pinchas Buchris, Amnon Biran, Omri Bar On, Avinoam Brug, Omer Bar-Lev, Hanan Gilutz, Amos Danieli, Nimrod Vizhensky, Yohanan, Moshe Ya'alon, Amir Ofer, Avi Feder, Tzali Perlstein, Yuval Rachmilevitch, Yiftach Reicher, Tovi Shur, Ran Shahor, Udi Salvi, Dovik Tamari, and the current administration of Sayeret Matkal.

A special thanks to the people at Yedioth Books, which published the original Hebrew version of this book, and chiefly to Dovi Eichenwald for the invitation to write this book and his generosity of spirit, and to the ever-talented Eyal Dadush. A big thanks to the editor of the Hebrew edition of this book, Yoav Koren, for his dedication, knowledge, and professionalism, and to everyone else at the publishing house who contributed to its publication: Renana Sofer, Kuti Teper, Hen Abukarat, and Pini Hemo. We are also grateful to our wives, Martha Reinfeld-Shur and Dana Elazar-Halevi, for mobilizing themselves for this mission and for supporting it in every way possible.